FEATURES OF THE ESCHATOLOGY OF IV EZRA

HARVARD SEMITIC MUSEUM
HARVARD SEMITIC STUDIES
Frank Moore Cross, editor

FEATURES OF THE ESCHATOLOGY OF IV EZRA

by
Michael Edward Stone

Scholars Press
Atlanta, Georgia

FEATURES OF THE ESCHATOLOGY OF IV EZRA

by
Michael Edward Stone

Library of Congress Cataloging in Publication Data

Stone, Michael E., 1938-
  Features of the eschatology of IV Ezra / by Michael Edward Stone.
    p. cm. -- (Harvard Semitic studies ; 35)
  Originally presented as the author's thesis (Harvard, 1965)
  Bibliography: p.
  Includes index.
  ISBN 1-55540-365-4 (alk. paper)
  1. Eschatology--Biblical teaching. 2. Bible. O.T. Apocrypha.
Esdras, 2nd--Criticism, interpretation, etc. I. Title.
II. Series: Harvard Semitic studies ; no. 35.
BS1715.6.E75S76 1989
229'.106--dc20   89-10273
                                                  CIP

Printed in the United States of America
on acid-free paper

FEATURES OF THE ESCHATOLOGY OF IV EZRA

A thesis presented by

by

Michael Edward Stone

to

The Department of Near Eastern Languages and Literatures

in partial fulfillment of the requirements

for the degree of

Doctor of Philosophy

in the subject of

Near Eastern Languages and Literatures

Harvard University
Cambridge, Massachusetts
April 1965

PREFACE

The importance of the period of which IV Ezra is a product is widely recognized by students of both Judaism and Christianity. The Apocryphal and Pseudepigraphical books have preserved by far the largest body of material relevant to this time. Yet they have been largely neglected by scholars in recent decades. The application to these documents of the continually advancing methodology and expanding horizons of Biblical Scholarship can thus reasonably be expected to produce important new insights into a crucial formative period of both Judaism and Christianity. It is to one small step in this significant venture that this thesis is dedicated.

More people than can be named have had a direct or indirect part in this thesis. In particular the author must express his gratitude to Professor Frank Moore Cross Jr. who has been much more than an advisor, he has been a teacher. The imprint of his exciting insights is to be found on every page. It was the late Professor Y. Gutman of the Hebrew University who first directed my attention to IV Ezra and who encouraged my interest in this area in every way.

My wife has helped not only in the physical preparation of the manuscript but her great patience and devoted encouragement during its conception and execution have made it possible. To my parents I am indebted above all for a home in which I learned of the values of the mind and of the human spirit. My teachers at all stages of my education have contributed more than I can say to this endeavour.

It is not for you to finish the work nor are you at liberty to to desist from it. (Avot 2:21)

SECOND PREFACE

The above lines were written before the submission of this thesis in 1965. The reader deserves some explanation of its publication in 1989.

After the approval of the thesis, I was offered the challenge of writing a commentary on IV Ezra for a new series, then being established, to be called *Hermeneia*. I accepted the the offer and, since I was not satisfied with the internal organization of the thesis, decided to put off its reworking and publication until the completion of the larger work, the Commentary. In youthful enthusiasm I resolved that, before writing the Commentary, I should edit the Armenian text. That and other things took my attention for some years. The *opera praeparativa* at an end, in 1977 I began working on the commentary itself. I did not foresee then that the task of writing would not be completed until the Fall of 1988.

Once the Commentary was finished, I devoted careful thought to the question of the future of the Thesis. It was clearly not appropriate that I rewrite it after 23 years. Yet, a substantial part of it had not been included in the Commentary. Moreover, the publications on IV Ezra since 1965 have been quite plenteous. In view of these two factors, I have decided to publish it as submitted in 1965. I am conscious of its defects, particularly in organization and structure. Yet it seems to contain enough of interest to scholars in the field, even from a merely historical perspective, to warrant its seeing the light of day.

The publication is made from the copy of the thesis deposited in Widener Library. This was desirable, if only because thus the numerous references made to that pagination in the Commentary can be verified. I have added only three items. The Table of Contents, originally rather brief, has been replaced with a more detailed one. An index listing primary sources cited in the book has been added. Further, a list of the Errata which turned up during the intervening years was prepared. To incorporate the last two of these three

changes, the Forematter was retyped.

Jerusalem
February, 1989.

TABLE OF CONTENTS

ERRATA

p. 39 line 13, "6:28" should be "7:28)

p. 66 line 23, "new heart" should be "our heart"

p. 73 line 6, "13:36" should be "13:37"

p. 105 line 12, "18:11" should be "18:6"

p. 116 last line "41:1" should be "40:1"

p. 117 line 1 "41:3" should be "40:3"

p. 187 line 15 "14:48f." should be "4:48f."

p. 194 line 12 "44:8" should be "44:9"

p. 209 line 17 "123" should be "125"

p. 270 note 392 line 4 "statute" should be "stature"

p. 274 note 431 "14:16" should be "14:17"

p. 275 note 437 "14:16" should be "14:17"

Throughout "Gildermeister" should be "Gildemeister"

Chapter I

CRITICAL AND RELATED PROBLEMS

Before considering the eschatology of IV Ezra, a number
of critical problems which have arisen in the course of previous scholarly examination of the book must be discussed.
This is especially true where these problems bear on the
treatment of the eschatology.[1]

I

Dating

A. External Criteria

External criteria for dating the book are sparse. The
post quem non date is fixed by a quotation in the writings of
Clement of Alexandria, in the latter part of the second century C.E.[2] There are some passages in the Epistle of Barnabas
which are supposed to reflect the influence of IV Ezra, but
most scholars do not consider the relation to be sufficiently
close to prove more than dependence on common traditions.[3]
No Qumran MSS or fragments of IV Ezra have been discovered,
nor have documents showing Ezra traditions of the sort
reflected in IV Ezra been forthcoming. While this does not
enable one to posit a post 68-70 C.E. date, for there is no
reason to guarantee the occurrence of all extant literature
at Qumran, it is interesting. Thus all that can be said on

the basis of external criteria is that the book was in
existence and had been translated into Greek by the time of
Clement of Alexandria.

B. Internal Criteria

For the more precise dating of the book, then, scholarship is dependent on internal evidence. The primary factor
limiting the range of dates is that the overwhelming weight
of scholarly opinion maintains that the book, at least in the
form of its final or most crucial redaction, presupposes the
destruction of the Second Temple and the Roman decimation of
Judaea in 68-70 C.E.[4] It is clear that a destruction of the
Temple is referred to in IV Ezra. Those who would maintain
that the book was written before 68-70 say that it is part of
the pseudepigraphic garb of the author, writing as Ezra the
Scribe in the period following the destruction of the First
Temple.[5] The destruction, however, is one of the central
concepts which arouse the author's thought and prompt his
questioning, and the beautiful lament over Jerusalem in
10:21-24 is a good example of this.[6]

1) The Superscription

The superscription of the book gives the date of writing
as thirty years after the destruction of the Temple by
Nebuchadnezzar (3:1 cf. 3:29). The question has been raised
whether this is a "type" date, that is whether the author
living thirty years after the destruction of the Second Temple
described his pseudepigraphical self as living thirty years

after the destruction of the First Temple.

The views concerning 3:1 fall into three main categories: there are those who would see it as referring to the date of the author, in the year 100 C.E.,[7] those who take it as an indication of the general period of composition, but not of the precise year, thus giving a date of 95-100 C.E.,[8] and finally there are those who regard it as part of the pseudepigraphic garb of the author with no special significance for the date of the book.[9] The views of the first type may speak of the writing of the whole book or only of a specific part of it. They are generally associated with the Kabisch-de Faye-Box source hypothesis on the one hand,[10] or with the interpretation of the Eagle vision (11-12) as referring to the time of Trajan on the other.[11]

The second view is supported by authors who think that the Eagle vision was written in the time of Domitian (c.96 C.E.). The thirty years is then seen as a reflection of Ezekiel 1:1, which latter point is sometimes maintained by authors of the third persuasion as well, although they generally date the book, or at least parts of it to periods other than the last decade of the first century.[12]

It 'seems clear from this review that 3:1,29 have been used as supplementary criteria to support one theory or another derived from other parts of the book. Moreover, the interpretation given is determined by the view taken in certain other matters such as the source-critical question and

the interpretation of the Eagle vision. It is of significance,
however, that the date indicated by these verses does coincide
in general with the period indicated by the two major interpretations of the Eagle Vision which will be discussed below.
Since, in any case, IV Ezra is post 70 as has been stated
above, the indication afforded by this date further strengthens
theories dating the book within the last years of the first
century C.E. For the purposes of the study to be undertaken
here, this is sufficient.

2) The Signs of the End

The various signs of the end which occur in the lists of
the Messianic woes have also been used as dating criteria.
Certain of these in particular have intrigued scholars, and
while they will be dealt with below in their more general
context, this use for dating should be discussed here.

The most widely employed of these passages is 5:6, the
prophecy of the unexpected ruler who will arise in the time
of woes. He is identified with some historical monarch, most
frequently with Herod[13] or Octavian.[14] This view often does
not ignore the relation of this figure to the complex of the
woes, but maintains that it has also a specific historical
reference.

This, however, is denied by other scholars[15] while many
agree that this figure plays a part in the formation of the
anti-christ type.[16] Keulers, who sees it thus, suggests that
it draws on the idea of Nero redivivus who will return to be

the fearful king of the end.[17] Baldensperger pointed out
that from the time of Daniel, the place of the evil king in
the pattern of the woes was assured.[18] The relation of this
figure to the anti-christ complex, especially in its political
aspect, is also well established.[19]

All this indicates that the "unexpected king" is one of
the traditional elements of the terrible events which are to
precede the eschaton. 9:1 states that certain of these events
are past, but the pattern was firmly established and the
"unexpected king" is clearly part of it. Contemporary events
could be, and from time to time clearly were interpreted as
falling into the scheme; some of its elements could be glossed
over to help this interpretation, others could be emphasized.[20]
The very lack of detail in this passage, a brief reference
to an evidently well-known tradition, makes it an inadequate
basis for dating as it is a further clear indication that the
author had no particular ruler in mind.

The general conclusion here reached bears also on the
attempt to identify the terrible splits in the earth mentioned
in 5:8 with the eruption of Mt. Vesuvius in 79 C.E.[21] or with
the earthquake of 31 B.C.E. mentioned by Josephus.[22] This
splitting of the earth is clearly part of the complex of
events which earlier surrounds epiphanies and later became
an integral part of the description of the "birth pangs of
the Messiah" and other supernatural events and localities.[23]
Likewise, to take the conflict of the nations in 13:31 to

reflect the troubled period between Caesar and Octavian as
Hilgenfeld does,[24] and other similar uses of the signs in
attempts to date the book are based on inadequate evidence,
especially in light of the traditional nature of the scheme
of the eschatological events which informs all of these
descriptions.

3) Esau and Jacob

Another text used by some authorities for purposes of
dating is 6:7-10. The detailed exegesis of this passage is
given below, for the moment it is enough to note that it says
that Esau is the end of this world, that Jacob is the
beginning of the world to come and that none other will
intervene between them. For dating purposes various identifications of Jacob and Esau have been made.

Hilgenfeld and Volkmar both identified Esau with the
Idumaean house of Herod, Volkmar suggesting that Herod
Agrippa the Younger is referred to here.[25] In any case, as
Schürer pointed out, this is of little help in dating for it
brings the date down to the end of the first century which
period is indicated on the basis of other, surer evidence.[26]
Kabisch, followed by Box, says that Esau symbolises this
corruptible age and Jacob the incorruptible age to come.[27]
Most scholars accept the identification of Esau as the Roman
world empire and Jacob as the Jewish world domination which
is to follow it.[28] The implication of these views for the
understanding of the eschatology will be discussed below.

Of immediate importance is that neither the Herodian nor the
Roman identification are of material help in pinning down the
precise date of the book.

4) The Eagle Vision

The main internal reference used for dating the book,
then, is the Eagle vision.[29] This vision of a monstrous
eagle which symbolizes the last Danielic empire[30] has been
the center of great controversy which has concentrated around
the problem of the identification of the kings symbolised by
the limbs of the eagle. In addition certain exegetical problems arise between the vision (Ch. 11) and its interpretation
(Ch. 12). In this section only the main lines of scholarly
discussion will be mentioned. In 1900 Schürer made an
excellent analysis of all previous writing on this matter and
his major conclusions are accepted here[31] for it will become
clear that since that date no innovation has been made in
the exegesis of the chapters.

The central point in any analysis is the identification
of the three heads. The end is generally conceded to come
during the time of the third head (11:1,4 etc.) so this may
be presumed to represent the time of the author. Three main
identifications have been suggested for these heads, resulting
in three major dates either for the book as a whole or at
least for the document containing the Eagle vision. The first
is that proposed by Laurence, Lücke (2 ed.), van der Vlis and
Hilgenfeld who all see the heads of Pompey, Sulla and Caesar,

thus dating the book, with some variations, in the last third
of the last century B.C.E.[32] Schürer has marshalled convincingly the main arguments against this view from within the
chapter to which may be added the observation that the clear
origin of IV Ezra in the period subsequent to the destruction
of the Second Temple precludes this date.

The other extreme to this view is that which would date
the book in 218 C.E. This interpretation of Chapters 11-12
was first proposed by Gudschmit in 1860. He maintained, however, that the Eagle vision was a later interpolation into a
book written in the last decades B.C.E.[33] The same terminal
date was also reached by Le Hir.[34] These two treatments
differ to some extent in their identifications[35] and these
variations and omissions highlight the fact that the crucial
point in this theory is the fixing of the heads oɩ Septimus
Severus, Geta, and Caracalla. The second wing which ruled
more than twice as long as any other is Augustus (11:13,16 f.,
12:15). The identifications in between these two extremes
then vary.

There are a number of serious objections to this view.
First, the book was used by Clement in the last part of the
second century and so it must have been written before that
time. Second, although there are some unevennesses, the
vision as a whole fits in its place and cannot be removed
without destroying the general structure of the book,[36] while
the unity of the text witnessed by the versions weighs against

any major tampering with it at this late date. Third, 12:18,21
state that after the first two little wings rule, shortly
before the middle of the kingdom, there will be an interregnum
which will be a time of distresses and confusions. This does
not fit the time of Titus and Nerva who are, according to
this theory, the first two little wings. Fourth, the identifications ignore the positions of Galba, Otho and Vitellius.
Fifth, the position of Commodus is problematic.[37]

The third major theory identifies the heads with Vespasian,
Titus and Domitian. Since the second wing is Augustus, there
are more wings and little wings than there are known kings
and usurpers (18 or 20 in all). This difficulty is solved in
various ways by different scholars. The wings and the little
wings, or else just the wings may be taken in pairs, each
pair signifying one ruler.[38] This nicely reduces the number
of rulers to a reasonable figure. But, as Box points out,
11:24-28 preclude the possibility of taking the little wings
in pairs. It should be noted further that 12:14-16 state
specifically that the twelve wings are twelve kings (cf.
11:12-14) and 12:20 is equally explicit about the little
wings. Thus it seems that the theory of pairs is inadequate
as an explanation.

Those who suggest that twenty rulers are indicated are
fairly unanimous on the identification of the twelve wings.
They are Caesar, Augustus, Tiberius, Caligula, Claudius, Nero,
Galba, Otho, Vitellius and the three usurpers Vindex, Nymphidius

and Piso.[40] This theory encounters difficulties, however, in
the identification of the little wings and they have been
interpreted in two main ways, either as non-Roman rulers[41] or
as lesser generals and pretenders.[42]

The heads seem indeed to be the Flavians, for the details
given in the text admirably suit the contemporary rumours
about and knowledge of the Flavians.[43] Furthermore, it has
been seen above that the arguments for taking the wings in
pairs are inconclusive. Thus there are too many wings and it
must be admitted that no simple solution to this problem has
been found. We are forced, therefore, to accept some theory
such as that of Schürer and Gunkel and to ascribe to the
author more detailed knowledge of this period than is available today.

C. New Evidence on Dating

In the course of the current investigation certain new
pieces of information came to light which bear on the date of
the book. The detailed exposition of this evidence is given
in Chapter 2 below, but the results are summarised here as
they bear on the dating.

An examination of the Hebrew word עולם shows a shift
from a meaning "most distant time" used only in adverbial
phrases to "age," "time" and finally "world" used as an
independent noun.[44] The earliest dated occurrence of עולם as
"world" is a Palmyrene bi-lingual inscription of 134 C.E. It
is not present in the Dead Sea Scrolls with this meaning

which is, however, common in IV Ezra. This indicates a usage
after Qumran but before fully developed Rabbinic Hebrew in
which the meaning "world" is predominant, which in turn
supports a date at the end of the first century C.E.

An examination of the expression "last time" in IV Ezra
shows that it most probably reflects the term קץ אחרון of the
Dead Sea Scrolls. This expression is less frequent in the
Scrolls than אחרית הימים while in IV Ezra it is found more
often.[45] Since the expression קץ אחרון is new in the Scrolls
and it is not found in Mishnaic Hebrew,[46] this may serve as
an additional indication of the position of IV Ezra at the
end of the first century C.E.

II

An Approach to Apocalyptic Thought

The question of the definition of the mode of thought of
the author of IV Ezra has been intimately connected in the
history of scholarly writing with debate about certain issues
in the literary criticism of the book. It is of crucial
importance to the study here being undertaken to clarify the
terms in which the thought of the apocalyptic is to be
described, indeed to be conceived of. The profound influence
of assumptions about the way of thought of the apocalypticist
on the literary analysis of the book has not always been perceived or made evident by scholars. Naturally, the question
of the literary structure of the book, for example the view

taken by literary critics of its so-called "mosaic" structure
(de Faye), has bearing on the investigation of the modes of
thought in a very simple fashion. If the book is, as the
Kabisch-de Faye-Box hypothesis would maintain, a patchwork
of five independent sources, touched up and added to by an
editor or redactor, then instead of one mode of thought or
even one general conceptual framework, as many as six separate
ones could be involved.

But the connection between the analysis of the literary
structure of the book and the thought of the author lies
deeper than this. It lies in the assumptions made by the
literary critics about what constitutes evidence that two
passages cannot be from one pen. The basic instrument used
by the literary critics for distinguishing different sources
is the logical principle of contradiction. It is clear that
this is a most important instrument in the hands of any
scholar, but exception may be taken to its application to
certain sorts of material. It is relevant, for example, to
questions of language. If passage A is written in Hebrew of
the eighth century B.C.E. and passage B in the Hebrew of the
first century C.E. then, barring precise forgery, they are
not from the same pen. Further, within the limits of human
variability, this sort of reasoning can be convincing in
terms of literary style. It is a matter of regrettable
historical fact that most apocalyptic works have not survived
in their original language and thus questions of style and

language can be seen, at the best, as through a glass darkly. At this level, however, no objection should be raised to the application of this criterion.

The reason that the question of literary unity strikes at the heart of the problem of the analysis of the modes of thought is that, as scholarship developed, the basis for drawing the distinctions between hypothetical source documents became largely one of contradictions so-called between the substance of their theological and eschatological statements. These two problems, literary unity and source consistency are so intimately connected that it is difficult to deal with them separately. The first literary-critical study of IV Ezra was that of Kabisch who published the results of his analysis in 1889.[47] He was attacked two years later by Gunkel, partly on the basis of his logical presuppositions.[48] One of his major points[49] is that Kabisch tries to divide up the thought of the book by establishing false oppositions between slightly misinterpreted passages. Gunkel works this out in a number of cases in what is, at this level, a very telling criticism of Kabisch.[50]

It is clear that the basis for any theory or study must be proper scholarly treatment of the texts. Beyond this, however, Gunkel discusses the categories used by Kabisch to characterize the thought of the sources and points out some key words: Hellenism--Judaism, supernaturalism--naturalism, this worldliness--otherworldliness, cosmopolitanism--

particularism. He evidently does not consider these adequate
categories, but makes   no new suggestions in this area.
He also points out the anomaly present in the concept of a
redactor who was subtle enough to change whole passages yet
stupid enough to leave those blatant contradictions and
inconsistencies perceived by Kabisch.[51]

In the area of consistency Gunkel offers one major
suggestion. This is a product of his psychological approach
to the author.[52] The author's deep and complex nature, he
maintains, involves him in thought which is not always consistent. He introduces the proviso that contradictions must
be such that the sensitive critic can feel their impossibility
before the criterion of consistency can be applied.

Gunkel's suggestions in other matters are most fruitful.
He emphasizes the author's use of oral traditions rather
than source documents[53] especially in the area of eschatology.[54]
He suggests, for example, that the political emphasis of the
last visions is probably not the view of the apocalypticist
for the first three visions show his interest in transcendent,
individual elements.[55] It is rather the result of his using
traditional materials which had this emphasis. The author,
Gunkel thinks, may even have modified these source traditions.[56]

These suggestions show the way which must be taken.
Gunkel has removed the basis for drawing distinctions from
the level of the bald application of a criterion of logical
consistency to the statements of the book to the subtler

level of tradition complexes. At the same time he rightly
draws attention to the psychological state of the author as
an important element conditioning his thought. In spite of
these advances, the basic question raised here is not
answered explicitly by Gunkel. To use the example quoted
above, if the author was interested in transcendental,
individualist elements, why should he devote any space at
all to political elements?

The basic positions of Gunkel and Kabisch have been
maintained and become even more extreme since their time.
The next major source critical treatment was that of Box[57]
and this was discussed from what is basically a modified
Gunkel position by J. Keulers in 1922. Drawing on Gunkel's
division of Ezra's religious problems into "man" and "Israel"
he develops his suggestion that the two eschatologies, the
"universal" and the "national" are respectively answers to
these problems. He sees this duality as the main source of
contradictions of substance within the book.[58] This, of
course, is to beg the question, for if these two eschatologies
are distinct and exclusive of one another, how could they be
included in one work? Keulers maintains that contradictions
exist, but they are not a basis for doubting literary unity
for it is patently absurd, Keulers says, to expect the author
to be a modern logician[59] although he did try to harmonize
the eschatologies showing, this view maintains, that he felt
some need for logical consistency.[60]

Keulers then undertakes a refutation of Box' view.[61] In this argument he engages Box at his own level. That is to say, he is interested to disprove Box' source division, based as it is mainly on supposed contradictions between theological and eschatological statements,[62] by maintaining that most of these distinctions do not exist or are not as great as Box thought or above all, that they are explicable on the basis of the particular formulation of the "two eschatology" theory which he proposes.[63] He himself recognizes, as Gunkel before him, that the materials contained in Box' A,M, and E^2 sources[64] differ from the rest of the book. He says that the views of these sources were different from the author's own but he left them in the book.[65]

The nature of Keulers' argument not only indicates his dependence on Gunkel, whose ideas permeate his book, but also the fact that he has moved no farther than Gunkel in the attempt to find a satisfactory way of handling the materials presented by IV Ezra. In fact, his views represent in some respects a retrogression from the position attained by Gunkel. To describe a phenomenon is not to explain it, and the two eschatology theory, as will become clear below is not even an adequate description of the materials present in the book. It certainly is not an explanation of the rationale which could combine these admittedly divers materials in one composition, and this is the more so because Keulers admits that the author has a concern for consistency.

It is to this problem that we must now turn our attention.
It is clear from the past treatments that the central problem
arises from the heterogeneity of views and the overriding
literary unity.[66] The basis of our analysis is the literary
unity of the book. Even disregarding arguments based on
theories here sub judice, the considerations brought forward
by scholars of the history of tradition school are adequate
to demonstrate its overall literary unity.[67] It is substantially the work of one author living at the end of the
first century C.E.

The major problem which seems to arise from Gunkel's
psychological approach, explaining repetitions and contradictions at least partly on the basis of the author's emotional
and spiritual turmoil, is that other books of the same
period and literary genre, notably Ap. Bar.,[68] have been
subjected to the same literary critical fragmentation. Does
one thus have to posit a similar psychological state for the
author of each book which exhibits these phenomena?

Nevertheless, the recent form critical advance has
strengthened the general approach of the history of tradition
school: emphasis on complexes of oral materials, the need to
establish the Sitz im Leben, the social or cultic context of
the piece being considered and so forth.

Of great importance is the discovery of the Qumran
community with its "apocalyptic" way of life. As Cross says:

> There can be no question here of isolated apocalypticists
> composing spontaneous works reflecting merely private or
> individual idiosyncracies of doctrine or calendar. These
> works are molded by a common tradition, forged within the
> life of a continuing community with more or less
> separatist tendencies.[69]

Yet it should be borne in mind that IV Ezra exhibits no common
peculiarities with the Qumran materials and that even for
Josephus the Essene community was unique in its tight
organizational pattern.[70]

For these reasons it seems that the _Sitz im Leben_
suggested by the Essene materials certainly cannot be transferred _in toto_ to non-Essene books. IV Ezra is later than
70 C.E. in date and is thus presumably Pharisaic. It may
well be the product of a man steeped in one aspect of
Pharisaic tradition, an aspect which continued in Rabbinic
Judaism as the later Jewish apocalypses indicate.[71] It is
not known, however, whether it is the product of a community
in the sense that the Qumran materials are.

A further problem in the form critical analysis is the
fact that this period is one of complete breakdown of the
old _Gattungen_ of pre-exilic times. Not only had the materials
been freed from their _Sitze im Leben_, they had also lost
independence as literary or religious traditions. Fundamental
changes took place in Judaism in the period following
Nehemiah and Ezra. On the one hand, there developed what was
virtually a new culture centered around the Torah.[72] On the
other, the growth and development of the "proto-apocalyptic"

whose origins may be seen in Ezekiel, II Isaiah, the Isaianic
apocalypse, Deutero-Zechariah etc., must be placed in this
period.

Thus it is virtually impossible to throw light on matters
in IV Ezra by the use of older forms and we do not know what
institutions the group from which he stems possessed. Behind
him lay a tradition of 250 years or more of apocalyptic
writing but the immediate antecedents of his work are not
known, how this tradition was borne or his relation to
it. Thus it is almost impossible to differentiate materials
out of IV Ezra on the basis of form critical criteria, for
there is inadequate information available. Although the
place of traditional materials and even of traditional
literary Gattungen in the book is great, it seems unlikely
that the different origins of various complexes of contradictory ideas can serve to explain how and why they are in
the book, for they were probably not carried as cohesive
wholes by different social institutions. In fact the confusion between those different complexes of ideas discerned
by past scholarly analysis weighs strongly against such a
possibility.

Thus, although the criterion of consistency can be
applied to the results of form critical analysis, it does
not seem as if this will serve as a means to the solution
of the problems raised by the presence of logically mutually
exclusive or contradictory statements in the book. Various

elements of particular descriptions may be due to the traditional nature of the materials, but once it is admitted that
the author has enough sense of consistency between propositions to touch up materials which do not suit him[73] or to
produce syntheses of traditions which are disparate in
origin[74] the question of the nature of his thought arises
once more.

In short it can be said that the source-critics have
tried to make sense of the book on the basis of the assumption that the propositions asserted expressly or impliedly
by one author are coherent with one another as to their content. Where such coherence does not appear on the face of
asserted or implied propositions then they cannot be from
the pen of the same author. On the basis of this argument
the sources are distinguished. On the other hand, the
search for implied propositions which may serve as links in
the author's chain of deduction has of course been one of the
causes of the setting up of those general categories which
Gunkel rejects.

Gunkel, by introducing considerations such as the
author's psychological state and the force of tradition,
takes the important step of being prepared to draw on other
elements besides articulated or implied propositions to give
coherence to the statements of the author. He does not make
this point explicitly himself, but it is clearly part of his
approach to the book. Nevertheless, he does not carry the

implications of this to their conclusion, for he does accept, to some extent at least, the necessity for logical consistency as to content between the statements of the author.

The first step in the analysis being suggested here is the clear recognition that the search for such consistency is inappropriate. This is in no sense to deny the need for or the role of logic in the activity of the scholar or critic. It means a willingness to seek elements beyond the meaning of the propositions of the author which "make sense of" and give coherence to his thought. The way to this search was opened by Gunkel and will be pursued in the coming sections.

A. A suggested Description of the Mode of Thought

It is a matter of common knowledge that modes of thought have existed which do not employ the criterion of consistency as described above, which operate in unconsciousness of such a criterion. This is true for example of mythopoeic thought.[75] It has been pointed out that the Egyptians present side by side mutually exclusive descriptions of the same phenomenon without affecting the unity of that phenomenon in that mode of thought.[76] In spite of this, a sense of order and of systematisation was present in Egyptian thought, based on structure rather than on "integrated and sequential systematisation."[77]

Although there is a revival of some mythical elements in the apocalyptic, it falls far short of a revival of mythical thought in Israel, for . . . "the main impulse of apocalyptic is the Old Testament understanding of the history of salvation."[78] Conversely, the historicisation of Israelite religion did not result in the growth of formal logic or of a search for consistency between statements.

Rabbinic thought was called "organic thinking" by Kadushin.[79] In his interesting analysis he points out that modern authorities have been unable to formulate systems of Rabbinic theology, mainly because they have applied to it organizing categories other than those basic to Rabbinic thinking itself. He suggests that there are four different fundamental Rabbinic concepts which are constitutive of all other theological concepts. Different particular views are then different emphases but are functions of the same basic concepts and coherence is not logical or schematic but organic.[80] This mode of thought is harmonious because "in every part, in every concept there is always implicit the whole, all concepts at once."[81] In his analysis of Agadic thought Heinemann emphasizes two main aspects, the systematic and the organic.[82] His discussion of the concreteness of this way of thought is reminiscent of that of Frankfort on the concrete nature of the mythopoeic mode.[83]

Both these analyses show that there are modes of thought which are non-logical in the sense in which this term was described above. Further, Jewish thought, at least in one of its main manifestations was non-logical in the period immediately succeeding that of IV Ezra. It does not seem, however, that Kadushin's concept of "organic thinking" is directly relevant to the apocalyptic in general or to IV Ezra in particular, for he sees Rabbinic thought as the product of group life over generations, as a way of thought largely unconscious of its basic presuppositions.

W.F. Albright, adapting the pattern proposed by Lucien Lévy-Bruhl, distinguishes three stages of ancient thought, the pre-logical or protological typical of mythical thought, empirico-logical covering the logic born of experience by which most ordinary human activity is carried out, and the formal logic which started with the Greeks.[84] These distinctions are helpful in general and what Albright calls "empirico-logical" certainly typified the thought of much ancient natural science. IV Ezra, however, does not seem to fall clearly within the realm of the "empirico-logical" mode, while it is, without doubt, beyond that of formal logic. Thus the direct relevance of Albright's broad classification is not clear. Nevertheless, as was true of other descriptions of "non-logical" thought, so too these categories again emphasize the well-attested existence of modes of thought not dependent for their coherence on logical consistency between their statements.

It seems best, then, to treat the apocalyptic as non-logical in that it employs other organizing principles than logical consistency between the meanings of its statements.

This assumption is given a greater probability in view of the
fact that such modes of thought have existed and indeed they
are major modes in the ancient world. Past scholarship's
difficulties in analysis of the book have been pointed out
above and they indicate the inadequacy of the hypothesis
that the author did employ canons of logical consistency as
between his statements.

This problem cannot be solved by making the author partly
logical. The crux arises in those passages such as 7:26-44
and 12:34 where scholars maintain that an attempt has been
made to integrate the varying concepts of the eschaton found
independently elsewhere in the book. It will become evident
below that adequate explanations of these phenomena can be
found without resorting to this explanation which is fatal to
any attempt to move beyond the stage reached by the literary-
critics. The tight literary structure of the book was
referred to above.[85] The formulation of the questions and
answers also shows deliberate literary artifice as do many
other aspects of the book. The author is highly conscious
of form and structure and this tendency extends beyond the
literary form to the thought. When he describes the total
eschatological process, he does so as a coherent and consecutive structure of events. He is not interested in consistency, however, and feels no need to utilize this same
pattern in all statements about given aspects of these same
events, often in contexts not concerned with their description.

Here the chronologically integrated scheme is not employed
for the center of interest lies elsewhere.

Thus two elements of those which must be described are
evident, structure and the lack of propositional consistency.
These are important for understanding the thought and an
examination of the book in terms of them is most fruitful.
The isolation of these two characteristics, however, does
not suffice. They are features of the author's mental process
and as such are most significant, but they should be supple-
mented by two further observations. The first is that
although many of the questions asked by Ezra of the angel
are given fairly abstract formulations, again and again the
answers are concrete. They are images or small visions,
mĕšālîm from which the angel does not always extract the
abstract answer.[86] This is a further indication that the
discussion is not being carried on under the control of the
rules of consistency between statements.

The second point is that the questions asked in the
first part of the book receive their answers in the final
analysis in eschatological revelations. This is an important
indication that in spite of the deceptive, orderly formulations, the author is not really thinking in "logical" terms,
not interested in reaching an answer to his questions by
means of reasoned, propositional argument. This once again
indicates the non-logical and systematising nature of his
thought, and further it emphasizes the fact that there is

some organizing principle according to which his answers are
adequate responses to his questions.

It could be suggested that apocalyptic expectation and
urgency are the unifying themes or forces which are moving
the author and which supply him with coherence. He is wait-
ing eagerly for the end. This is without doubt one of the
author's main interests; again and again he asks about the
end, the manner and nature of its coming and so forth.[87] Yet
all the material in the book cannot, it seems to us, be
accounted for on the basis of this view alone. There is
information and there are interests in other apocalyptic
books which are even less explicable on the basis of
eschatology alone. In II Enoch, for example, the interest
in cosmology[88] cannot be explained on the basis of eschatological urgency any more than the "Angelic Liturgy" or the
calendrical materials from Qumran.

Scholem has emphasized not only the continuity of the
mystic tradition in Judaism from pre-Christian times, but
also the elements common to this tradition and certain
apocalyptic books.[89] IV Ezra seems to be strikingly out of
tune with these general interests when in 4:5,7 it appears
to deny precisely the possibility of the knowledge of מעשה
מרכבה, of cosmology, one of the main interests of Jewish
mystic speculation and one which it shares with the apocalyptic.
Indeed, no heavenly journeys or visions of the Throne of
Glory or the like are found in IV Ezra, while they do occur

commonly in other apocalyptic works as well in the mystic tradition. Further IV Ezra emphasizes the limitations of human knowledge (4:2,11, 5:38 etc.).

Nevertheless, Ezra's interest in the area of special knowledge is most developed. Despite his protest that he means "not to ask about ways above but of those things which we daily experience" (4:23) he does in fact enquire most eagerly about all sorts of eschatological matters: the time of the end (4:33,44, 5:50, 6:7 etc.), the signs of the end (4:51, 6:11), by whom creation will be visited (5:56), the fate of the soul after death (7:75ff.) and many other such matters certainly lying beyond the realm of daily experience. Further, 14:26,46 refer to the secret tradition of eschatological knowledge as does 3:14 which talks of the revelation of secret knowledge to Abraham. The revelation to Moses is also referred to in this fashion (14:6f.). One of the meanings of "wisdom" in the book is the attainment of special knowledge revealed only to Ezra and those like him. Thus the revelation of eschatological things is made to Ezra alone (7:44, 8:61f.), and the Most High has made known many secrets to him (10:38). In 12:9 Ezra clearly recognizes the special nature of the knowledge revealed to him in the Eagle vision and this is emphasized by the angel (12:36, cf. 13:14). The apocalyptic books are characterized in 14:47 as containing "the fount of wisdom and the stream of knowledge."

Thus, in spite of a specific rejection of certain areas

of special knowledge which marks IV Ezra off from many other
apocalyptic works, it is clear that a concept of special
knowledge of a more or less esoteric nature is at work in
the book. The author sees his information as coming from a
heavenly source and identifies it with the tradition of secret
knowledge which he traces back at least to Abraham. Although
he speaks of the limitations of human knowledge and the
repudiation of certain areas of thought is so pointed as
perhaps to be a matter of polemic, nonetheless his understanding of his own writing is based on the theory that there
has been revealed to him information not available to ordinary
mortals. It is at this point that those areas of esoteric
knowledge involved in heavenly mechanics, geography, and
demography which are common to most apocalyptic books and
to the mystic tradition found their foothold. This element
of secret or special knowledge is another of the constitutive
elements of the apocalyptic.

One more theme must be mentioned, a theme which is
prominent in IV Ezra but which falls more in the area of
major concerns of the author than in that of the constitutive
elements of his thought and this is theodicy. Ezra's point
of departure in much of his speculation is a joint problem,
Israel and man, which is in fact a different aspect of the
problem of theodicy.[90] Below the development of some of the
thought sequences of the book will be examined in some detail
and the nature of the movement from theodicy to eschatology

will be evident. It is not our purpose here, however, to
analyze the problem of theodicy. A sensitive analysis of
the general movements of thought on these themes was made
by Gunkel[91] and to investigate them further would lead beyond
the scope of our present project.

The thought of IV Ezra may then be characterized as non-
logical but systematic. This denies the author any concern
with logical consistency between statements. It admits,
indeed it is based on, the obvious fact that his thought
makes sense within his premises but asserts that coherence
must be sought in elements beyond consistency of the substance
of his asserted or implied propositions. Such elements are
the movement towards systematisation, the apocalyptic moment
and the ideology of special knowledge, especially of the
eschaton. Thus revealed eschatological solutions to religious
problems are adequate and convincing to him although the
solution may be given in quite different terms to those in
which the question was asked. This means that all occurrences
of a given idea do not draw on a preconceived plan or scheme
and are not necessarily consistent with one another as to
content. The author is living in an intellectual world of
many different views and traditions: many factors determine
his use of a particular formulation of a general notion in a
given context.

B. A Suggested Methodology for Study of this Thought

The general purpose of the examination undertaken in

this thesis is to investigate some of the author's basic concepts. The first stages of this examination must be those of critical scholarship of any ancient document, starting with text criticism. The problems of the text of IV Ezra are severe but the attempt to ascertain the best text must be undertaken and for this, naturally, the normal methodology of textual criticism is employed. Once a text has been established the literary critical examination of the book must be undertaken. The methods and results of the literary critical school of scholarship were attacked above. Here, however, the term literary criticism is being used in the broader sense of the assessment and evaluation of the book as a literary document. Problems of style, literary unity and the like must be considered.[91a]

The next stage in the examination of a given concept or passage must be the exegesis of the relevant verse or verses. The words, especially key terms and their implications must be considered, the use of other sources if any determined, and so on. In view of the features of this mode of thought isolated above, it is important first to determine the purpose of the passage from the context. Most important in the treatment of a given idea is to clarify its relationship to the central movement of the passage in which it occurs. Is it being used by the way or is it the main subject under discussion? What is its relationship to the line of thought expressed in the passage? Answers to these questions will enable us to know how it is to be treated in relation to other occurrences of the same or similar concepts elsewhere in the book. Given a mode of thought which is not interested in consistency and given a divers complex of traditions on which the author is drawing, it is not reasonable to expect him to reproduce a general concept in a consistent form each time he refers to it. It is far more likely that the choice of which particular form of a tradition is to be used at a given point will be determined by the context, the subject under discussion and the association of themes and ideas. There will also doubtlessly be other elements determining this choice which cannot be recovered.

It is in the study of the ideas of the author that the approach through context, purpose and association proves most fruitful. In eschatology, for example, there appear certain general terms, the end, two ages and the like, but within these general rubrics many different ideas are used and the choice between them depends on these three factors. Only by reference to them can one hope to be able to describe the different complexes of thought which occur in the book. This in turn is enlightening as to the ideas presented on a given subject which can only be ascertained by this careful investigative method. If the author's views on a given complex of ideas can be evaluated his relationship to the material on which he is drawing can be better understood.

In assessing his use of other sources, as indeed of

comparative passages within the book itself, similar considerations apply. A distinction should be drawn between the
use of parallels to illuminate specific traditions referred
to in IV Ezra and their use to understand how IV Ezra employs
these traditions. For example, in IV Ezra 6:49-52 are preserved detailed traditions about Behemoth and Leviathan.
These occur in a passage relating God's wondrous acts of
creation and mention is made of the fact that they will be
devoured "by whom you will and when." In Ap. Bar. 29:4 these
two beasts are again mentioned and it is stated explicitly
that they are to be devoured at the end by the righteous.
This is clearly a case of a specific tradition preserved in
two separate sources where the information is complementary.

The additional question of whether this means that IV
Ezra has a materialist view of the world to come, or the
like cannot, however, be decided on the basis of this passage.
It can be decided only by a total assessment of all that IV
Ezra has to say about the world to come. Indeed, in view of
the fact that this material is introduced only once, in a
creation context, and that it is mentioned nowhere in connection with the world to come, it is probable that it has little
if any importance in his eschatological view.

Be this as it may, the qualitative differences between
these two questions are important. The one is the use of
two texts to illuminate a specific tradition. The other is
an analysis and evaluation of IV Ezra's use of that tradition.

This latter can also be aided by comparison with other books, but only after appropriate analysis.

Thus in the analysis of the thought of apocalyptic books excessive harmonization and excessive fragmentation should be avoided. The method used should be determined by the realities of apocalyptic thought as characterized above. This implies, above all, a recognition of the importance of contextual and associational features as explanatory of particular formulations in specific instances. By this means the imposition of categories of a type unsuited to this mode of thought is avoided. Yet a sensitive analysis will enable us to achieve answers to questions which have concerned past scholarship.

III

Textual Criticism

A. The Georgian Version

The purpose of this section on textual criticism is not to attempt to give a full exposition of all text-critical matters connected with IV Ezra, but rather to discuss certain recent theories bearing on the text. The situation of the text and versions was admirably set forth by Violet in the introduction to his first volume and was brought up to date in 1924 in the introduction to his translation volume.[92] There is no point in reproducing here the information which he has assembled.

Since his time, however, the Georgian text of IV Exra
has become available to scholars in a publication and Latin
translation by Robert P. Blake.[93] The two manuscripts which
he published preserve the text of about two thirds of the
book. He established that the Georgian and the Ethiopic go
back to a single archetype, presumably written in Greek
uncials[94] and that Georgian also shows some influence of the
Syriac text type.[95] In general his conclusions are:

1) Georgian was made from an Armenian translation which is
otherwise unknown. It is in no way connected with the extant
Armenian text.

2) This Armenian was a translation from Greek.

3) The Greek archetype of Georgian is also that of Ethiopic
and these two form a separate branch of the tradition (y).
The y group is free of interpolations, but its archetype had
lacunae. Georgian also shows some x type influence and the
archetype was much more damaged before Ethiopic was translated.

4) The existing Armenian is of x type and very inferior in
view of the evident interpolations and omissions.

5) Latin, Syriac + Georgian or Ethiopic is a strong combination showing, in all probability the reading of the archetype.
Armenian should only be used where its Greek original is sure.[96]

B. The Original of the Syriac

In an article published in 1956, Joshua Bloch suggested
that there was no Greek text of IV Ezra. According to this
theory the Syriac is a direct translation of either a Hebrew

or more probably an Aramaic original. Latin too is a direct translation from Semitic.[97] The existence of a Greek translation has been the basis of most past scholarly textual investigation.[98] Bloch would explain the Graecisms of the Latin as stylistic and regard the Greek quotations in Clement of Alexandria and other sources as ad hoc oral translations made from a Semitic text.[99]

He makes no attempt, however, to deal systematically or in any detail with the internal evidence for a Greek text adduced by Box, Violet and others from variations between the versions. There are many such, and they are to be explained most simply as inner-Greek corruptions. This evidence cannot be disregarded[100] and it is fatal to Bloch's theory. Further the differences between the Syriac-Latin tradition and the Ethiopic-Georgian are inexplicable on this theory. Thus, failing a more convincing demonstration to the contrary, the Greek basis of the versions must be asserted.

C. Aramaic or Hebrew? Gry's Theory

In his edition of IV Ezra in 1938, L. Gry introduced wide-ranging theories about the text of IV Ezra. He presumes a Greek text, but suggests that the translators of the versions also considered the original text when they were making their translations.[101] He thus undertakes the proof of an Aramaic original by showing that the variant readings of the versions can be attributed to variants in the Aramaic. This is conceivable, perhaps, in the case of the earliest versions such as Syriac and even Latin. In the case of Armenian it is so unlikely as to be, for all practical purposes, impossible.[102] The same is true of the Arabic versions. The whole presentation is rendered unconvincing by the lack of any attempt to deal with translation practices in the various languages as evidenced by other books, especially with respect to the use of the original Semitic text by translators of secondary versions.

He maintains, then, an Aramaic original. Not all of the many examples and proofs offered in support of this theory can be examined, but a few have been chosen and are set out here.

1. In 13:32 Armenian reads: եւ փշրեսցեն ի Հեթանոսաց զպատկերս պղծութեան իրեանց , "And they will abolish from among the heathen the images of their abomination."

According to Gry this goes back to an Aramaic gloss on the Armenian ויתבר' מארמאי צלמי תועי' which in turn is corrupt for an original gloss: "According to Aramaic (מארמיא):צלמי' יתבר', Erroneous (ותעי)." This he then takes as a proof that the Armenian translator knew an Aramaic text.[103] It should be noted, however, that the Armenian reads Հեթանոսաց = "heathens." Neither Aramaic nor Aramaeans are mentioned, nor is this an Armenian word for either. Further, it is hardly likely that the Armenian translator read Aramaic. Even if he did, it is most improbable that he noted variants in Aramaic in the margin of his own translation.

Even if he noted variants in Aramaic, it is even less probable that he commented on them in Aramaic. Even granting
all the preceding, there is no evidence for חוי׳׳ as an
abbreviation for חויבתהו or the like. Even accepting this,
Gry then asks us to believe that the gloss was conveniently
corrupted in Aramaic, mistranslated into Armenian and introduced into the text here.

2. As an example of the sort of putative readings supporting
an Aramaic original the following may be quoted: "P. xxvi,
7:21 פְּקֻדֵי des commandments (original); פַּקָדָא commander (most
versions)." The texts are: Latin mandans enim mandavit,
Syriac pwqdn' gr pqd, Ethiopic "For God commanded," Arabic[1]
"For God commanded with a command," Armenian պատուիրելով
պատուիրեաց Աստուած, Georgian "For God commanded with a
command." Armenian gives the standard reflex for Hebrew
infinitive absolute + finite verb, as does Latin. Syriac
can use a noun + a finite verb where Hebrew has infinitive
absolute + finite verb, cf. Gen. 2:7 mwt' tmwt. This may
also be the case in Greek, cf. Gen. 2:16,17, 3:4 etc. and
some such Greek probably lies behind Arabic[1] and Georgian.

3. If he wishes to use an Aramaic with 2 m.s. suffix conju-
gation ending in ṇ. . . (see pp. xxvi, 3:5, xxvii, 7:51),
then he cannot also suppose a 2 m.s. ending in אֵَ- (p. xxvi,
6:49).

4. The use of supposed abbreviations as the basis of readings is not justifiable unless some sort of support can be

offered. Thus, for example, on p. lxxvi to explain the readings which have been used to support a Hebrew hypothesis,
based on the use of וי'ה Gry says that this is a misreading
by the translator of the abbreviation וה' which really stood
for Aramaic והא'. P. lxxvii, No. 1. א' as an abbreviation for
Adam is not persuasive.

5. In general, his arguments against the strongest considerations urged for a Hebrew original are not convincing.[104] Some
of these have already been referred to. A further example is
p. lxxvii, No. 6 where for the suggested corruption יִרְאַיְ/יִרְאֻג
he offers the alternative יחמ(ני) being a corruption of
יתחמ(ני), a signally weaker hypothesis. To suggest that the
infinitive absolute + finite verb is a stylistic device does
not make it a possible construction in a text composed in
Aramaic.[105]

The discovery of the Qumran texts indicates the importance
of Hebrew as a literary language in the period of the Second
Temple. Gry's arguments based on differences between the
versions as reflections of Aramaic variants could only be
sustained on the basis of a theory of multiple Greek recensions. Since he does not show the variants to have any
pattern in relation to the major groupings of the versions
reached on other grounds, this seems unlikely. A theory
maintaining that the translators of the versions consulted
the Aramaic original but translated from Greek is not persuasive.[106]

D. Unexplained Variants

While it is thus inadmissable to base an argument for the original language of the book on variations between the secondary versions, there are a number of readings which seem to reflect precisely this. Gunkel observed in 14:3 that all versions read "thornbush" except Arabic[2] which has "Mount Sinai," perhaps reflecting סנה and סיני and that in 8:23 all versions read "for ever" except Arabic[2] which has "witness," perhaps reflecting לָעַד and לְעֵד.[107] Similar is perhaps the text of 12:47 which may show a double translation of לנצח.[108] In addition, in 6:20 Arabic[2] and Georgian read "appear," the other versions have "see," perhaps יֵרָאוּ and יִרְאוּ. A Hebrew variant may also lie behind the text of 6:28, see below, Chapter 2, n.217.

It is not valid to base any theory of multiple Greek translations or the like on such a small number of readings. Provisionally, they are best regarded as glosses on the Greek.

E. The Armenian Version

This version has peculiar characteristics and features of it should be mentioned. Preuschen maintained that it is based on an independent Greek text, so greatly does it differ from the other versions.[109] Marquart suggested that the Armenian is translated from extracts, but against this it should be noted that it does not have any major dislocations of blocks of materials.[110] Gry developed a complex view of the text. In his supposed Aramaic original he sees the use of an Aramaic Biblical text close to or identical with Targ. Jer. II. The first Armenian translator, he maintains, was

such an orthodox Jew that he rejected references to Memra
and other such features of this Targum and substituted for
them texts from Targ. Jer. I. The expansions are also in
part his work. He knew Latin, Syriac and Ethiopic and took
care to remove from his text anything that conceivably could
be thought to support Christianity. This corrected text, Gry
then says, came into the hands of a Christian scribe who
reworked it once again reversing many, but not all the
Judaizing features.[111]

This complicated theory is most unlikely. Leaving aside
the question of the Targumim, the improbability of an
Armenian translation being made by a Jew is enough to dis-
credit it. It is common knowledge that the Armenian alphabet
was developed by the Church and that the work of translation
was in the hands of a school of church scholars and clerics.
This renders the likelihood of a Jew having translated the
book very small. Much information is available in Armenian
sources about the character of the translators, the nature
of their work and so forth, all of which is ignored by Gry
and he adduces no similar phenomenon to support his theory.
To add to this the requirement that this Jew, presumably in
Armenia and interested in translating the book into Armenian,
would be so orthodox as to reject readings of the Targum,
and in addition to require that he know the book in Latin,
Syriac and Ethiopic is to make this theory incredible.

The Armenian translation is problematic, but it must be
approached in light of the historical situation in Armenia

and of available information about the techniques of the
Armenian translators. The problem arises because generally
the Armenian translations of ancient documents are remarkably faithful to their originals.[112] This raises the question, to which as yet no answer can be given, whether the
Armenian of IV Ezra is a faithful translation of a divergent
Greek original or whether it presents a translation technique
radically different to that found in the vast majority of
other Armenian translation texts.[113] This question must be
regarded as sub judice until further research has been
carried out on the Armenian text.

Some previously unobserved or unemphasized features of
this version may be mentioned.

1. In 7:75 a rare case of variation of textual tradition
within the Armenian may be observed.[114]

2. The reading "true Paradise" in 8:52, cf. 7:36 may represent a reflection of the old expression קושטא פרדס now known
from the Qumran Enoch fragments.[115]

3. The Armenian omits the words "Messiah" or "son" in all
but one of the passages in which the Messiah is called "son
of God."[116]

4. The concept of Paradise as prepared is to be observed in
Armenian and Arabic[2] of 7:38. The idea of the preparedness
of eschatological things may be further observed in Armenian
alone in 5:43. Armenian alone reads զպատրաստեալ նոցա բարիս
որ յառաջ քան զաշխարհ էր , "the goods prepared before the

earth was" in 7:14. This idea is also found in the Armenian expansion of 7:37.

5. Common readings of Armenian and Arabic[2] may be observed in 3:4, 7:38,95,.8:34, cf. also 7:104. Armenian, Ethiopic and both Arabic show a common base text in 8:9. Armenian and Arabic[1] both read "in truth" in 8:34.

6. In 13:31 Armenian reads alone "They shall plan to give battle with one another; place with place, tribe with tribe, kingdom with kingdom, people with people, leaders with leaders, priests with priests and the faith of worship shall be divided on each side." In 13:34 it introduces a phrase into the middle of the verse which, as a whole, reads, "And there will be gathered together at one time a very great (lit. such a great) multitude of the dwellers of the earth, to serve the Lord faithfully. And when the end draws near they will be divided from one another. This is the multitude which you saw and which wanted to do battle with him." Is it possible that these additions refer to contemporary events within the Armenian church?[117]

F. Quotation from the Bible

> 7:129 For this is the way of which Moses, when he was alive, spoke to the people saying: Choose life that you may live.

This is a quotation of Deut. 30:19. Syriac has a longer text which is a conflation of Deut. 30:15 and 19. In this, the text of Deut. 30:15 is drawn from the LXX with one reading represented only in LXX MS F (Ambrosianus). The texts of

30:19 are of interest. Latin reads <u>elige tibi vitam ut vivas</u>.
<u>Tibi</u> is present in the plural in Ethiopic and Syriac. In
Peshitta and Ethiopic Deuteronomy it is found in the singular
(one MS of Ethiopic omits). The major reading of LXX is
ἐκλέξαι τὴν ζωὴν . . . (without σύ which occurs in some
minor texts). The readings of the versions seem to show what
may have been a Greek ethical dative. The alternation of
singular and plural does not admit of any simple explanation.
Since the Syriac and Ethiopic texts in IV Ezra are not related
to the Peshitta and the Ethiopic Bible, they provide evidence
for a plural in at least some Greek tradition.

   This reading indicates that the translators were not, at
this point, influenced by their own Biblical texts, but
followed the text found in the MS which they were translating.

G. Concluding Remarks

   It therefore seems to be the case that, pending a thorough
and well based study of the nature of and relations between
the versions, the greatest weight must be given to the
closely related groups, Latin and Syriac, Ethiopic and
Georgian. The Arabic and Armenian versions are distinguished
by their distance from the other four texts and from one
another. Thus it is dangerous to argue for the originality
of their special readings.

Chapter II

THE TWO AGES

Preamble

Scholars since the time of Kabisch have distinguished
two main types of eschatological teaching in IV Ezra.
These are the so-called this worldly, particularist,
"national" eschatology and that of the other-worldly,
universalist, transcendental type. The special characteristics of these two eschatologies were set out schematically by Keulers and his scheme is reproduced here.

National-Earthly Eschatology	Universal-transcendental Eschatology
The nations	Man
Israel	The pious man
The hostile nations	The evil man
Israel's salvation from her enemies	Salvation of the pious from the troubles of this world
Annihilation of the enemies	Damnation of the wicked
Continued existence of the community of salvation	Continued existence of men after the resurrection
Jerusalem, Palestine, earth	New Earth, Paradise, Heaven
Valley of Hinnom near Jerusalem	Hell.[1]

This type of dual pattern, with greater or lesser variations, has been maintained to exist by nearly all major

scholars of IV Ezra.[2] It was used by the literary critics
as a basis for distinguishing various literary sources of
the book.[3] Hermann Gunkel, on the other hand, in 1891 in
his review of Kabisch's literary critical analysis, maintained the over-all literary unity of the book and gave an
explanation of the two eschatologies which has served the
scholars of tradition historical bent since then. He distinguished two types of material in IV Ezra, religious
problems and apocalyptic, especially eschatological ideas.
The latter, he maintained, serve as solutions to the former.
He also discerned two major religious problems, that of the
situation of Israel after the destruction of the Temple, and
that of the sinfulness and troubles of humanity. The
national eschatology is seen by Gunkel as the solution to
this first problem, and the universal eschatology the solution to the second.[4] The author himself, according to this
theory, held a more or less integrated eschatology which he
set forth occasionally.[5]

This same view was held in the course of time by
Lagrange,[6] and with rather more subtlety by Baldensperger.[7]
Porter recognizes three major eschatologies, the national,
the universal and "purely spiritual immortality"[8] and maintains that the apocalyptist is concerned with the first two
of these and does not really succeed in adjusting them to
one another.[9] Vagany also maintains a unity of authorship
and Gunkel's "two problem" theory, but sees this twofold

nature as reflecting different (oral ?) source documents.
The author's own unified conception, according to Vagany,
appears in 6:26ff., and 12:34.[10] Keulers' position is
similar to this except that he is less certain that the
integrated scheme is really the author's own view.[11]

It must be admitted that this type of patterning is a
moderately efficient way of categorizing elements of the
thought of the book. It is necessary to inquire, however,
whether it reflects accurately any sort of ancient reality.
If these two eschatologies were as distinct from one another
as these scholars maintain, if indeed the "spiritualism" of
the universal eschatology was as opposed to the "materialism"
of the national eschatology as some writers would have it,[12]
it is hard to conceive of a reason for them to be put in the
same book, even by a "non-logical" author like IV Ezra. If
they were not distinct from one another in the author's
thought world, then what reason can there be for modern
scholars to treat them as if they were?

This is to say that, while it is not a subject of
debate whether the elements distinguished as part of these
ideologies appear in some form or another in IV Ezra, their
supposed integration into two differing, opposed and equally
independent eschatologies must be subjected to further
examination. The following questions will be asked about
these elements and these "eschatologies."

1) Do these eschatologies appear as independent schemes in a

systematic fashion? Are they present in the book as two
self-sufficient options?

2) Are the general, metaphysical oppositions set up between
them borne out by the evidence, e.g. the materialism of the
national eschatology as opposed to the spiritualism of the
universal eschatology?

3) Is this two eschatology theory an adequate explanation of
the eschatological ideas of IV Ezra? Does it correspond to
the realities of the thought of the book?

The examination of these questions will be synchronic
for a diachronic approach seems, at the present stage of
knowledge, to be beyond the limits of judicious scholarship.
The origins of the apocalyptic are still too obscure and the
varieties of its later development too little understood to
make a historical assessment of these questions practicable.
It should, nonetheless, be possible to establish whether
these two eschatologies as they have been outlined by past
scholarship reflect any sort of reality in the thought world
of the author of IV Ezra.

I

Contrasts Between the Two Ages

This idea of the stark and indeed the utter contrast
between the two worlds or ages has been maintained to be a
sign of the universal eschatology. It has even been said
to show a dualism of the two ages, an anti-material bent, a

spiritual other-worldliness.[13] There is no doubt that IV
Ezra believed that there are two worlds or ages. They are
mentioned explicitly and implied directly or indirectly on
many occasions. An examination of the passages contrasting
them will reveal those features considered by the author as
crucial to the distinction between them.

A. Explicit Two World or Two Age Passages

6:7 7.I[14] answered and said: What will be the separation of
the times,[15] when (will be) the end of the former[16] and
the beginning of the latter?

8. And he said to me: From Abraham to Abraham,[17] since
from him Jacob and Esau were born;[18] but Jacob's hand
held Esau's heel from the beginning.[19]

9. For the[20] end of this age (world) is Esau and the
beginning[20] of the following is Jacob.

10. Since the end of man is his heel and his beginning
is his hand. Between the hand and the heel seek nothing
further, Ezra.

The passage is a fairly typical piece of apocalyptic exegesis.
It seems that Gen. 25:26 was, in this period, commonly interpreted in an eschatological fashion. Box discusses some of
the Rabbinic treatments of this verse, as does Violet II
ad. loc.[21] In addition to the tradition represented in Gen.
R. 63:9 and parallel in Yalqut Shimoni 110 which is quoted
either in the name of R. Gamliel (flourished 90-110) or of
the unknown חד מן אלין דבית סילנא noticed by Box and Violet,
there are two further traditions relevant to this, neither
of which has been discussed previously in this connection.
The first is an interpretation of the verse in Pirqe de R.

Eliezer in the name of R. Jehudah:

> "Hence thou mayest learn that the descendants of Esau
> will not fall until a remnant from Jaccb will come
> and cut off the feet of the children of Esau, as it
> is said: "Forasmuch as thou sawest that a stone was
> cut out of the mountain without hands." (Dn. 2:45)[22]

A third, most explicit tradition has survived in the

Midrash Haggadol:

> "And his hand seized on Esau's heel" for there is no
> further kingdom in the world after Esau's kingdom except
> Israel's alone. Therefore it says "on the heel" (b^cqb)
> i.e. immediately adjacent to it, and thus it says:
> "And it will be after this that I will pour out my
> spirit on all flesh (Joel 3:1)."[23]

This last passage not only confirms the Rabbis' knowledge of

the eschatological interpretation of this verse, according

to which Esau was Rome, but it also makes most emphatically

the point of the immediate succession of these two world

kingdoms central to IV Ezra 6:7-10. The identification of

Esau (Edom) with Rome has been seen to originate with

Herod.[23a] Although all the Rabbinic sources cannot be

stated confidently to be contemporary with IV Ezra, they

serve as evidence for the exegesis of this verse in Rabbinic

circles immediately subsequently to IV Ezra.

The scholarly interpretations of this passage have

varied considerably.[24] The direct historical identification

of Esau either with the Herodian dynasty or with Herod

Agrippa the Younger is unlikely.[25] The use of the verse in

Rabbinic circles with no such specific meaning and the

unclarity of the present passage mitigate against it.

The Kabisch-Box view is that Esau symbolizes this corruptible age and Jacob the incorruptible age to come.[26] This view as Keulers pointed out is conditioned by the supposed pecularities of the so-called S document's "universal" eschatology. Keulers thinks that the passage refers to the eschatological world empire of Israel as opposed to that of Rome which is to be overcome. Thus he sees it as belonging to the "national" eschatology. This view is also held by Gunkel and Vagany among others.[27] They base the identification of Esau with Rome rightly on Rabbinic use of the term and less convincingly draw support from the theory of the "national" eschatology.

The deliberately mystifying nature of both the angelic answer and its interpretation was noted by Gunkel.[28] Yet the fact that the passage is not located in a symbolic vision makes it likely that it was self explanatory to its circle of readers and that the mystery was a sham--a stylistic artifice. This justifies the use of the Rabbinic traditions which may thus be presumed to reflect a widespread interpretation of this verse. The first task is the exegesis of the plain meaning of the passage. This achieved, it may be possible to delve further into its implications.

In v.7 Ezra asks two questions: what will be the separation of the times? and when will one time end and the other begin? The answer to both of these is given in v. 8 "From Abraham to Abraham."[29] This is a rather mysterious reply and so immediately the Esau-Jacob reference is added as an explanation.

This Biblical incident is given an eschatological interpretation and this is done in two stages. The first stage, in v. 9, is the actual interpretation--Esau is the end of this world, Jacob is the beginning, perhaps by play of words the head or chief (ראשית/ראש), of the next.[30] This interpretation is then justified by reference to the general observation that the heel is the end of man and the hand is his beginning, implying that since Jacob's hand grasped Esau's heel, the beginning of the "following world" will come immediately on the end of "this world."[31] 10b. concludes the passage in the same cryptic vein.[32]

Thus both questions are adequately answered, the ages are consecutive and Esau is the end of this age and Jacob the beginning of the next. It is important to note that this is not an allegory using the closeness of the grasping of the hand on the heel as a symbol of the succession of the two ages. It is an eschatological interpretation of a Biblical incident and text, close in style and method to the Qumrän pešārîm. Like the sectarian commentaries it is based on the idea of the veiled eschatological meaning of the Biblical text and is carried out in terms of a clear and explicit eschatological hope.[33] It differs from the Midrash on this same verse in the degree of specificity of its eschatological urgency although the logic of exegesis is practically the same.

From this passage it may be observed that the ages are considered immediately consecutive. Further they may be called equally "times" (v. 7) and "ages" or "worlds" (v. 9). Moreover, if Esau is Rome then the rule of Rome is to be followed by Jacob—perhaps the rule or victory of Israel. No further kingdom will intervene. This is the point of the emphasis on the immediate succession of the kingdoms and is an element of hope for the author. Since Esau is the end of this age so Jacob will be the beginning of the age to come.

The passage is part of the body of the second vision. It is preceded (5:28) by Ezra's question about the sad fate of Israel. He is told (5:36ff.) that understanding of God's judgements is beyond him. He then proceeds to enquire about the end, whether judgement will be equal for all generations (5:41), whether it can be hastened (5:43), by whose agency God will visit creation (5:56) and then (6:7ff.) asks this question about the separation of the times. This is immediately followed (6:11ff) by a request for and a revelation of the specific signs, the Messianic woes which will herald the end. Thus it may be observed that the passage occurs in a part of the book which is greatly con-cerned with specific questions about the eschaton. The passage then offers a view of an immediate succession of the rule of Israel on the rule of Rome. There will be a

separation of the "times" or "ages," but no further heathen
kingdom will intervene.

6:34

> Hasten not to think[34] evil in the first times,[35] lest
> the consequences by upon you in the last times.[35]

The verse is the conclusion of the second vision. It
follows a short speech of angelic encouragement (6:30-33)
in which the angel assures Ezra that his upright conduct
has been noted and promises him further revelations. The
expression "last times" which is found in this verse is
common in the book. In IV Ezra, Latin novissimus is regularly paralleled by 'hr' or 'hryt' in Syriac, forms of the
stem dxr ($\Lambda \mathbf{\}\ell$) in Ethiopic and ψω[υ6ωՆ in Armenian.[36] In
the Hebrew Bible this usage represents אחרית / אחרון in Greek
ἔσχατος or ἔσχατον.[37] More difficult is the word tempus.
In IV Ezra Latin tempus is equivalent to Syriac zbn',[38]
Armenian dωՐωՆωկ,[39] and Ethiopic mawā‑cel.[40] The Biblical
situation is rather more complex. Greek καιρός which seems
to be the equivalent of tempus etc. can translate many
Hebrew words[41] and these words may occur with a variety of
meanings. The discussion here will be limited to phrases
which seem to show both novissimus and tempus or analogous
expressions.[42] In Daniel 2:28 for Aramaic אחרית ימיא and
Greek ἔσχατον τῶν ἡμερῶν, Latin reads novissimi tempores, but
Syriac has ywmt' 'hry', Armenian յωιniρu յեωի‑ Նu. Thus Latin
tempus in this phrase has no support in the other versions,

and must be regarded as a peculiarity of that version.[43] Dan.
8:17לעת קץ החזון in Hebrew has as parallels LXX ὥραν καιροῦ,
Th. καιροῦ πέρας, Latin in tempore finis, Syr. l^c dn swp'
dhzwn, Armenian ի ժամանակս վախճանի է ատելիղ. Thus עת--καιρός
--tempus seems to be one possible series. Dan. 8:19, however, produces a similar series with מועד,[44] and none of
these cases seems to reflect the type of steady usage which
would be required to explain the word tempus in IV Ezra.

In the Dead Sea Manuscripts the term קץ אחרון meaning
"last age" is coming into usage.[45] Here is an expression
which is ideally suited to the usage in IV Ezra where אחרית
הימים, overwhelming as it is in the Bible, has fallen into
the background.[46] The expression קץ אחרון is not found in
Mishnaic Hebrew where the word קץ is rare and does not
appear in combination with אחרון.[47]

The meaning of the verse is rather obscure, but it seems
to be a warning to Ezra not to doubt in this world lest he
be punished for it in the world to come or perhaps in the
period of disturbances to precede that world. The distinction of the two worlds or ages is clear in the expression
"last times" which evidently refers to the eschaton. The
world to come is the place where punishment for actions in
this world may take place.

7:12-13.

12. And the entrances (ways)[48] of this world[49] were
made narrow and sorrowful, difficult, few, bad, full
of dangers and greatly laborious.[50]

13. For the entries (ways) of the future world[51] are broad and safe and yield the fruit of immortality.

The first point to be noted is the contrast of "this world" and the "future world." This terminology is quite regular and probably reflects the same usage as Rabbinic העולם הזה and העולם הבא.[52] The confusion in the versions between "entrances" and "ways" may be an outcome of the extension of the language of the allegory related in vss. 3-9.[53] The meaning is clearly "ways" and the point of the passage is the contrast between the toilsomeness of this world and the ease and joy of the world to come.[54] In addition the world to come brings immortality and the assurance of this is the whole purpose of the angelic encouragement of which these verses form a part.[55]

The verses say that there is a straight, narrow and difficult way, beset by dangers and difficulties (cf. v. 3) which must be traversed in order to reach the broad, safe path which follows it.[56]

The idea of two ways, one good and one bad may be found in the Old Testament. The most explicit passage is Jeremiah 21:8 הנני נותן לפניכם את דרך החיים ואת דרך המות . This probably draws on Deut. 30:19 which is regularly interpreted in Rabbinic literature as referring to two ways.[57] The "way of the righteous" is also commonplace in the Bible and in the Dead Sea Scrolls.[58] The idea of the two ways may also be observed in the Qumran documents.[59] The relationship of

this to the Gospel of John[60] and to the later formulation of
the idea of the two ways in the Didache and other texts has
been noted.[61] The concept of the way found here arises out
of the contrast between the two ages,[62] and is to be seen
against the background noted.

The contrast of the two worlds is quite clear and the
toilsomeness of this world is contrasted with the safety and
especially the immortality which will be found in the world
to come. The latter is depicted to Ezra as the consolation
for the woes of the former. No hint of any other type of
distinction is found, in fact the parallelism between the
two worlds is somewhat emphasized by the path image.

7:29-31

29. And it will come to pass after these years[63] that
my servant[64] the Messiah will die[65] and all those who
have human breath.

30. And the world shall return to its[66] primaeval
silence for seven days, as in the beginning,[67] so that
no-one shall remain.

31. And it will come to pass[68] after seven days, the
age which is not now awake shall be aroused and corruption[69] shall pass away.

This passage clearly describes the end of one age and
the beginning of the next. The word saeculum and equivalents
in v. 31 denote "age" as is clear from v. 32 which implies a
continued existence of the earth and dust into the new age.[70]
The start of the new age is spoken of in terms reminiscent
of the creation. It is of note that the world or age returns
to silence as in the beginning. The view that one of the

peculiar characteristics of created beings is sound is noted below[71] and is also evident from 6:39 which speaks of the silence before the creation of man. Thus when v. 30 says that there will be seven days in which there will be silence, this means that there will be no men. This week is to be followed by the revelation or "arousal" of a new age.

The reading "corruption" in verse 31 is that of Syriac, Arabic and Georgian. Latin by implication and Ethiopic explicitly have a less likely reading "the corrupt age" or "world." The relationship between death and corruption, already pointed out,[72] is so close as to border on identity. The previous age has presumably passed away in v. 29 and what is asserted in v. 31 is that death will pass away also. It is no coincidence that v. 32 immediately follows this with the next stage of the drama--the resurrection of the dead.

In this schematic exposition of eschatology the Messianic kingdom is considered to be the end of the first age. The great transformation comes only subsequently. The distinction between the two ages seems, nevertheless, to be strong. In contrast to 7:12-13, the different nature of the new age seems to be quite emphatically stressed in v. 31 which speaks of the arousal of an age "not now awake." It certainly is quite distinct from that which has passed. Talk of the revelation of new and different things, however, is part of the apocalyptic style of the author. 7:26 speaks of the appearance of the "unseen land" and "hidden city" at the start of the Messianic kingdom which is, in that context, part of this world, and other examples of this type can be cited.[73] Thus while this expression does indicate the distinction between the two ages, it need not be construed as evidence of the utterly different nature of the new age. The major characteristic of the new age is that corruption will pass away.

There is then a clear distinction between the two ages in this passage. The new age will be different from that which has passed. Above all it will be without death.

7:50

> On account of this the Most High made not one world (age) but two.

The text of this verse is clear enough, but it is difficult in context. IV Ezra's question in 7:45-48 is concerned with the fewness of the saved. He feels that the evil heart has grown in men and estranged the majority of them from God and thus from eternal joy (47-48) and he asks how this can be. The answer is given in the parable of the rare and common minerals (51-59). In this context v. 50 can only be understood, and then not very well, as a general preamble to the following parable.

The verse does not occur in Armenian. Using this as an indication Violet persuasively suggests that it is out of

place here and really belongs after 8:1 and thinks that he
finds reflexes of it in the Armenian there.[74] While the
difficulty of the present context cannot be denied and the
verse may indeed be out of place, nevertheless the nature
of the Armenian translation is too little understood to
justify the use of its otherwise unsupported peculiarities
as precise indications of displacements.

In spite of this problem, the meaning of the verse is
patent. The exact connotation of saeculum is difficult to
determine, but the verse states that there are two saecula
and these are divinely created. If the verse is considered
to be original in its present context, it may be added that
the divine motive in creation of two worlds was to provide a
solution to the problems raised by the evil heart. This
incidentally would also be the case if the verse was placed
at 8:1.

7:112-113

112. And he answered me and said: The present world[75]
has an end,[75] glory[76] does not[77] remain in it continually,
therefore the strong have prayed for the weak.

113. For the day of judgement[78] will be the end of
this world (age)[79] and the beginning[80] of the future,
eternal[81] world (age).

Although the versions of v. 112 vary somewhat, these
differences are not of great significance for the exegesis,
since Latin, Syriac and Ethiopic all have readings implying
an end of this world.[82] As noted above the word translated
"world (age)" is Latin tempus. The readings of Syriac,

Ethiopic and Armenian make original עולם most probable, meaning either "world" or "age."

The context of this passage is Ezra's question whether
there will be intercession in the world to come as there is
in this world. The answer is that it has been necessary in
this world for glory does not remain in it continually, but
it will be otherwise in the world to come. There will be no
intercession of strong for weak or good for evil in that
world. The nature of this glory has been discussed at some
length. Violet observed that "glory" can have two major
meanings in this book, the glory of God and other glory.
The former is more frequent, but in accordance with the
latter usage the glory of Zion or in paradise may be referred
to.[84] Keulers has a similar analysis of this concept but he
perceives that the term "glory of God" may, in fact, be just
a name for God.[85]

A further comment should be added. Gershom Scholem
clearly established כבוד "glory" as a theosophic term for
He who sits on the Throne. In second century Jewish literature this term was to the fore and it was subsequently gradu-
ally replaced by the terms מרכבה and שכינה among others.
Thus, Scholem notes, in Jer. Hag. II:1 and Tosefta the
expression לדרוש בכבוד אנינו is found while the parallels
in Bab. Hag. read לדרוש במעשה מרכבה.[86]

This is clearly a development from the sort of use found
in IV Ezra. Divine glory seems to be connected in part with

the appearance of God on earth and this goes directly back
to Biblical usage.[87] Thus it descends on Sinai (3:19) and
the righteous already make God's glory prevail in the world
(7:60) and it will defend the righteous (7:77). Analogous
to this is the concept of the glory of God which is intimately
connected with judgement, the sight of which dismays the
wicked souls after death, and rejoices the righteous (7:78,
87,91). It alone will illumine the world on the day of
judgement (7:42). In all these cases "glory" is close to
being a name of God, and it is this last usage which is
perhaps best connected with the concept in the verse here
being discussed.

Violet, in his comment on this verse, notes that in the
Latin version the divine glory is always accorded an epithet.
Since none such is present here he considers this to be a
reference to that glory which will characterize the reward
of the righteous.[88] The close connection of the true and
final judgement with the full revelation of God's glory
(7:42) weighs against this conclusion. The verse surely
asserts that divine glory is not continuously in this world
and so judgement is not fully carried out in it and there
can, therefore, be intercession in this world. The nature
of the special revelation of truth and justice in the final
judgement which made intercession unnecessary will be discussed below.

In v. 113 the day of judgement is said to mark the

boundary between "this world" and "the world to come."[89] The
world to come will be eternal and perfect while this world
is imperfect for the divine glory does not remain in it
continually.

8:1

1. And he answered and said to me:[90] The Most High
has made this world (age)[91] for many but the future
world (age)[92] for few.[93]

Here again the two world or age theory is specific, and
it is once more mentioned in connection with the problem of
the fewness of the saved. The terminology of העולם הזה and
העולם הבא is also present. This verse is likewise followed
by the use of the rare and common minerals parable which was
observed to be connected (perhaps) with a two worlds proclama-
tion in 7:50.

8:46

And he answered me and said:[94] Those things which are
now[95] for those who are now.[95] Those[96] which are
future[95] for those who are future.[95]

This verse constitutes the answer to Ezra's repeated
questions about the fate of the multitude of men who are
sinners, and to his appeal that divine compassion be shown
to them. Its meaning in this context seems to be that Ezra,
living in the present, can understand the present, but he
cannot understand the future and thus questions about the
number of the saved should not bother him. The language
reflects the "this world--world to come" phrasaeology
observed above.[97] It again emphasizes the difference in the

world order which is to characterize the next age.[98] Beyond
the mention of that difference, however, the verse adds
little to the information already at our disposal.

B. Conclusions to Section A.

1) Terminology.

    A.   There are two worlds or ages. (6:7-10,34, 7:12f.,
        29ff.,50,112f., 8:1,46)

    B.   These may be referred to as "times" (6:34) or
        saecula (7:30f.,50,112f., 8:1 etc.)

        a.   In 6:7-10 both terms may be observed.

        b.   The terminology העולם הזה and העולם הבא
           is regular.[97]

    C.   There are fixed terminologies for expressing the
        contrast of the two ages.

        a.   "Former"--"latter" (6:7,34).

        b.   "This"--"the future" or "the coming"
           (6:9, 7:12f.,112f., 8:1,46).

    D.   The words saeculum and tempus and their equiva-
        lents are used equally of both ages. No dis-
        tinction between them is expressed by this
        terminology, nor can any indications of tenden-
        cies in this direction be observed.

2) Substantive Differences between the Two Ages arising out
   of Contrasts between Them Expressed in the Texts.

    A.   The world to come will be complete. Its ways
        are broad and safe (7:13); in it glory will be

fully revealed and judgement, by implication, perfect (7:113). It is for the few righteous alone (8:1) and its ways are comprehensible only to its denizens. (8:46).

B. It brings immortality (7:13,31) and is eternal (7:113).

C. These differences are noted in contrast to this world. They are differences of world order. No suggestion of a "spiritual"--"material" opposition was found.

3) The Place of the Separation of the Ages in the Scheme of Events.

    A. Three statements are made in these passages each of which offers a different view.

        a. In the scheme in 7:26ff. the new age arises after the death of the Messiah and all men (v. 29) and after seven days silence. It is followed by resurrection and judgement (v. 32ff.).

        b. In 7.113 in a somewhat similar fashion the day of judgement is said to mark the end of this world and the beginning of the new world.

        c. In 6:7-10 Esau (Rome) is said to be the end of this world and Jacob the beginning of the next.

4) Additional Note on Conclusion 3).

If "Jacob" means the Messianic kingdom of Israel[99] then the view of conclusion 3) A c above is in conflict with those of 3) A a and b. Keulers solves this problem by suggesting that the author sometimes reckons the Messianic kingdom in this age as in 7:26ff. and sometimes in the age to come as 6:7-10.[100] While it seems that this is the case, Keulers can offer no rationale for this inconsistency. The term "end" and its uses will be discussed below and this will throw some light on the problem. In general, however, it is important to remember that the author was faced with divers traditions and that his choice in a given case may have been conditioned by the context or the train of thought. The point to which Keulers' statements lead, but which he does not seem to perceive, is that in any given passage the omission of one or more elements of eschatology does not mean that the author of that passage did not believe in or accept that particular element.

C. Passages Dealing with this World and Implying the Future World.

4:26-32

26. And he answered me and said:
If you live you will see,
If you will remain alive you will be amazed
For the age (world ?)[101] is hastening to pass away.

27. Because it is not able to bear those things promised to the just (in their time(s))[102] for this world is full of[103] sorrow and weakness.

28. For the evil about which you asked me is sown and its in-gathering has not yet come.

29. If therefore that which is sown shall not be harvested and the place where evil is sown does not pass away,[104] the field where good is sown will not come.[104]

30. For a grain of evil seed was planted in Adam's heart[105] from the beginning[105] and how much evil fruit[106] has it produced until now and will it produce until (the time) when the threshing floor comes.[107]

31. Reckon then in your own mind how much fruit of wickedness a (one) grain of evil seed has produced.

32. When the ears of corn which are innumerable will .be planted what a great threshing floor they are destined to make.[108]

The image of sowing found in v. 28ff. is used by IV Ezra in a number of different fashions.

1) It is used in an allegory in 9:34 where men are likened to seed sown: some take root and grow while others do not. 5:48 describes man's being produced by the earth as sowing and this metaphorical use is found in fullest extension in 8:41 which states that many are sown but few are saved. Here the metaphor is used with the same point as the allegory in 9:34.

2) In 8:6 Ezra prays for "seed of new heart and cultivation of the mind whence fruit may spring." This is perhaps analogous to 9:31 which speaks of the sowing of the Torah in the hearts of men which sometimes gives fruit but sometimes is barren.

3) In 9:17 occurs what seems to be an utterance in the gnomic style, "as is the ground, so is the sowing . . . as is the husbandman, so is the threshing floor." The use of "threshing

floor" here clarifies its meaning in 4:35,37 where it signifies in context "the reward of the righteous." In general,
therefore, it signifies "harvest" which may be either good
or bad.

In short the image of seed and sowing is observed to
be used mainly as an expression of productivity and it may
be found in a number of different contexts. It does not
seem limited in use to one particular idea or referrent.
"Threshing floor" signifies the harvest, the total produce
and is often used of reward.

Ezra has enquired how it is that Israel suffers so
(4:22-25). The answer to this question, given in vss. 26f.,
is an eschatological prophecy, a statement of the imminence
of the eschaton. This age is quickly to pass away for it
is inadequate, full of sorrow and weakness.[109] The sowing
image is then introduced (v. 28). The evil about which
Ezra is said to have asked the angel and which is the starting point of the argument in this verse is not mentioned in
the questions immediately preceding. The evil heart, however,
does figure largely in the prayer which introduces this
whole vision.[110] That it is the evil heart which is
referred to here is made explicit by v. 30 which speaks of
the "grain of evil seed" planted in Adam's heart. In light
of this there can be no doubt that v. 32 refers to the
renewal of human hearts in the new age. In fact in 8:6
Ezra, using the same image, prays for the "seed of a new

heart." 6:26 speaks of the change of heart in the end-time which will result in the blotting out of evil.

"Threshing floor" in vss. 30 and 32 has the general meaning "produce" or "harvest." Its use in v. 30, of course, refers not to reward but its precise opposite, judgement or punishment. This is in complete accord with the usage of the book.

The remaining major exegetical problem lies in v. 29, specifically in the latter half of that verse. There, the passing away of the place where evil is sown is proclaimed. Coming as it does closely following vss. 26f. which prophesy the passing away of this age, it tempts the exegete to relate it to that pronouncement. Even the term "pass away" is identical in both instances. The context is, however, completely comprehensible only in light of the interpretation in terms of the "evil heart" expounded above. The ingathering of evil is indeed prophesied and the great pronouncement of the impending change of heart is set forth. The "passing away of the place where evil is sown" can only be interpreted as a perhaps not completely felicitous expression for this.

This is important, for here then is found another reference to the change of world order in the end; the passing away of the age seems to signify just this. This is not an outright statement of the material-spiritual opposition as might be otherwise maintained. While the age to

come is not mentioned explicitly in the passage, it is clear
that this age "full of sorrow and weakness" is to be succeeded
by a new age. In the context of the discussion of evil in
this vision the aspect of the new age which is emphasized
is the change of heart which is to take place in it.

6:20a

> And when the world (age) which is about[111] to pass
> away[112] will be about[113] to be sealed, I shall make
> you these signs:

This verse refers to the sealing of the age about to
pass away. The terminology of sealing occurs in three other
texts in IV Ezra.[114] Here it is used in a simple metaphorical way with the implication of final or definite
completion. This may also be the case in 6:5 and perhaps
in 10:23.[115] 7:104 is somewhat different in its usage and
will be dealt with below. In context, the reference to the
world which is about to pass away implies clearly that
another is to follow, but no further information is offered
about this.

6:25

> And it shall be that every one who shall have survived
> all those things which I predicted to you[116] will be
> saved and will see my salvation and the end of my[117]
> world (age).[118]

This verse implies the imminent end of this world or age.
The elements of danger, commonplace in IV Ezra's description
of the generation immediately before the end, are present.
Two characteristic features are found in contexts of this

type in the book, the element of danger which evidently refers to the Messianic woes[119] and the seeing or wondering at the great events which are to ensue.[120] The phrase "those who will survive the predicted woes" is, with slight variations, the typical language used in connection with this.[121]

In this passage the problem of the relation of the Messianic kingdom to the future age again arises.[122] The poetic section in vss. 27f. is typical of those used to describe the coming age,[123] and no explicit mention is made here of an intermediate kingdom. Nevertheless, the men who did not taste death mentioned in v. 26 should be identified with the company or companions of the Messiah. In 7:28 and 13:52 they are specifically connected with the Messianic kingdom.[124] Thus, while the intermediate kingdom is not mentioned, some of its most typical elements are seen to be present.

Any attempt at harmonization should be avoided, but this does not mean that the clear facts of the situation should be ignored. The presence and sequence of these traditional literary forms and elements connected with the intermediate kingdom and the future age cannot be disregarded. Here is another example of the non-logical approach of the author to the eschatological events. It is of note too that the new age itself is not mentioned, all that is described is the change in the human and moral world order

which will come "after the end of my age." This brief and
allusory style strengthens the view stated above[125] that the
argument e silentio in these matters is precarious.

14:9

> For you will be taken up from men and you will be
> henceforth[126] with my servant[127] and with such as
> are like you until the times (of the world ?)[128]
> are ended.

If our reconstruction of the end of the verse is correct
then here too is a reference to the completion of the times
of this world. "Times" alone may refer to a world-age.[129]
Thus whether the phrase "of the world" is original or not,
the end of this world or age is implied in the verse. Of
note again is the fact that Ezra is to remain with the
Messiah and his companions only until the end of the times.
This is another example of the placing of the decisive
division of history at the beginning of the intermediate
Messianic kingdom, not at the start of the new age.[130]

Excursus

The Messiah as the Son of God in IV Ezra

In the verse just considered (14:9) and on five other
occasions some or most of the versions refer to the Messiah
as the son of God. This terminology which seems strange in
a Jewish eschatological context will be examined here. First
the readings of the versions in all these instances will be
set forth schematically.

Verse	Latin	Syriac	Ethiopic	Arabic¹	Arabic²	Armenian	Georgian	Sahidic
7:28	filius meus Iesus	bry mšyḥ'	masiḥeya	وادي المسيح	المسيح	o ʃ ɫ ʉ ɾ_ Ʉʊʊ ɳ ɾ ɾ ɳ ᵣ	electus unctus meus	L A C K I N G
7:29	filius meus Christus	bry mšyḥ'	qʷelʿēya masiḥeya	OMITS	OMITS	OMITS	electus unctus meus	L A C K I N G
13:32	filius meus	bry	weʾetu beʾsi	فتاك	فتاى	ɾ ʉ ɾ ʒ ɾ ᵤ ɪ ᵤ ᴸ ᴋ̌		my son
15:37	filius meus	bry	waled	فتاك	فتاى	OMITS	L A C K I N G	L A C K I N G
13:52	filium meum	bry	waled lawaleda (DPRX)laʾuda ʾemaʾbryʾu(s)	فتاى	عبدى (amended) ms ق. فتاى	ᵹ ʉ ɾ ʉ ɾ ᵤ ᵣ ᵣ ᵤ ᵣ ʒ ᵣ ʒ ᴸ ᴋ̌ ᶜ̌		L A C K I N G
14:9	cum filio meo	bry	waledeya MSS BFOR weḥideya	فتاك	عبدى	ᵣ ʉ ᵣ ʒ ʉ ʊ		L A C K I N G

1) Notes on the Versions.

    a. Latin: Iesus in 7:28 is regarded by all scholars as secondary.

    b. Ethiopic: 7:20 q^uel^{c}ēya--my servant, my young man.

               13:36,52, 14:9 waled--child. This word is used in N.T. for "son" in expressions "son of God" etc.

               13:52 variants lawaleda (DPR) + (la)'eg^{w}ala 'emaḥeyāw (BF) is the regular translation of "son of man" as in Ezekiel etc.

    c. Arabic: فتًى means "youth" or "young man." It does not mean "son," nor does it translate the set phrases employing that word.

               13:52 Arabic[2] reads عنديٰ which is emended by Gildermeister to عبديٰ. MS B reads فتًايٰ. Compare 14:9.

    d. Armenian in part follows its practice of transferring first person phrases used of God to the third person. This may be observed here in 7:28, ?13:32,52. See also the Armenian of 5:41, 7:27, 8:7,13 etc. Further, in all cases except 7:28 the word "Messiah" or "son" is omitted.

    e. Georgian and Sahidic are both fragmentary texts.

2) The Readings of the Versions

    a. 7:27. Ethiopic, Arabic[2], Armenian and Georgian all show texts without the word "son." It seems that the

reading "son" or "child" is secondary here, perhaps a
dittography in the Greek text behind Latin, Syriac and
Arabic[1]. This is especially likely since Latin and Syriac
reflect the same textual tradition.

   b. Drummond[131] suggested that the readings of the
various texts here reflect παῖς translating Hebrew עבד .
That a Christian translator should render παῖς as "son" is
clearly more probable as a source of variations than the
assumption that he translates υἱός as something else. Further
the variant readings all fall within the semantic range of
παῖς but not of that of υἱός. The evidence is as follows:

   1) Ethiopic 7:29 reads q^{u}el^{c}ēya which regularly translates παῖς or παίδιον.[132]

   2) Arabic[1] reads فتای "young man" in 13:32,37,52, 14:9.

   3) Arabic[2] reads فتای in 13:32,37,52, 14:9.

   4) Arabic[2] reads عبدی in 13:52 and 14:9.

These readings cannot be explained if an original υἱός is
posited. On textual grounds it is difficult then to assume
any reading other than παῖς in the Greek, and it is most
likely that this in turn translates עבד in Hebrew. The readings of the Armenian reflect one of the peculiarities of
that version for which no explanation has yet been found.

   Box suggests that the reading "son," in particular in
Ch. 13 is original. He sees it as based on the Messianic
interpretation of Ps.2. He admits that this is rare in
Jewish literature and cites three texts Ps. Sol. 17:26,

Sukkah 52a., Targ. Ps. 80:16.[133] While Ps. Sol. 17:26 and
Targ. Ps. 80:16 show an eschatological interpretation of
parts of Ps.2, only in Sukka 52a do we find a reference to
Ps. 2:7 which might provide a background for the "son of
God." This is, however, clearly later than our source
based as it is on a tradition of the Messiah b. Joseph.

It is quite possible that a Messianic title "son of
God" existed among Jews in the first century C.E.[134] and it
is also possible that this title could have come from the
Messianic interpretation of Ps.2. As far as IV Ezra is concerned, however, the textual evidence is compelling and it
is clear that the versions must represent an original παῖς.

D. Conclusions to Section C

1) Terminology

    A. This age has an end (4:26, 6:20^a,25, 14:9) and
        by implication will be followed by another.

    B. This age may be referred to as "times (of the
        world)" (14:9) or as saeculum (4:26f, 6:20^a,25).

        a. The term העולם הזה is not used of this
           age alone.

2) Substantive Information about the Ages Arising out of
Contrasts between them Expressed in the Texts.

    A. The evil heart, present in this age, will be
        removed (4:28-30).

    B. This age "is full of sorrow and weakness" (4:27).

    C. Ezra and other holy men will appear with the
        Messiah after the end (14:9).

3) Separation of the Ages: the End, its Place in the Scheme
of Events.

       A. The end of this age will be soon (4:26, 6:20[a]).

       B. It is preceded by signs (6:20[a]) and dangers
          (6:25).

       C. It will be seen by those who survive (6:25).

       D. 2) c and 3) c tend to indicate that the end is
          placed at the start of the Messianic Kingdom.
          See discussion pp. 69, 70.

E. Passages Dealing with the World to Come in which this
    World is Implied.

7:47

And now I see how the future world[135] will[136] make joy
for few but tortures[137] for many.

In 7:45f. Ezra is concerned with the fewness of the
saved and this verse is the conclusion of his question about
the fate of the sinners, in which category he includes
nearly all men. The expression "future world" once again
reflects the standard terminology of the book. The term
העולם הבא is even more explicit in the Syriac, Ethiopic and
Arabic2.[138]

"Joy" and "torment" are among Ezra's standard terms for
reward and punishment. Joy signifies eschatological reward
and is especially connected with paradise. This may be due
to the widespread interpretation of Hebrew גן עדן as "garden
of delight."[139] Further the Messiah is said to make those

who survive into his kingdom rejoice.[140] Joy is also one
term used to describe the intermediate state of the
righteous souls.[141]

"Torment" or "torture" on the other hand describe the
ultimate fate of the wicked[142] and Gehenna is called the
"place of torment."[143] Torture may also refer to the
intermediate state of wicked souls.[144] Thus this usage
does not just describe the nature of the world to come or
the intermediate state, but it constitutes an element of
the technical language of reward and punishment and is
flexible in its application to a particular eschatological
state or period.

Since the text speaks of the world to come it is clear
that two worlds are implied. Further, the future world will
be the place where the righteous and wicked will receive
their due; there few will be rewarded but many punished.

7:75

> And I answered and said:[145] If I have found grace
> before you, O Lord,[146] show to your servant whether
> after death, now when each of us gives back his
> soul[147] we shall surely[148] be preserved in[149] peace
> until those times come in which you will begin[150] to
> renew your creation[151] or shall we suffer tortures
> at once.[152]

This verse introduces the lengthy section (7:75-101)
which deals with the intermediate state of the soul. In it,
however, a clear distinction between this world and the world
to come is implied. The end time and the period of judgement
are evidently meant by the phrase "those times . . . in which

you will begin to renew your creation." The element of
peace or quiet in the context of reward, noted above, characterizes both the intermediate dwellings of the righteous
souls and the new age.

The end is evidently called a renewal of creation. The
creation elements in 7:29-31 were analyzed above.[153] In the
verse here being considered the Armenian and Ethiopic do not
have this reading and it is also omitted by Arabic[2]. It is
present in a verbal form <u>creaturam renovare</u> and <u>thdt bry'tk</u>
in Latin and Syriac. Arabic[1] which is expanded here speaks
of "a new creation." The form of the text in Syriac and
Latin is to be preferred.

The Syriac and Latin verbs both mean "to restore" or to
"renovate." Hebrew חָדַשׁ which lies behind them, means in
Biblical Hebrew "to renovate,"[154] "to restore."[155] In Qumran
the most interesting uses of the root are not verbal.[156]
In the Mishna the verb means "to renovate"[157] or "to
innovate (a point in Halakha)."[158] In the Talmud a number
of interesting references may be discovered. The most
fascinating has the phrase "the Holy One is going to renew
his world" עָתִיד הקב"ה לחדש את עולמו,[159] almost word for
word as in IV Ezra.

It is difficult to decide whether the expression here means
"to renovate" the world or to create a new world. There is
no doubt that the major meaning of the verb חָדַשׁ is "to
restore," "to renovate." The suffix on "world" in the

Talmud and "creation" here tends to point to the former
meaning. The nature of the process described in 7:29-31
could also be interpreted to support this view. Either way
the typology of the creation is at work. Involved in the
discussion, however, is the question of whether this implies
for the author of IV Ezra the restoration of a specific
creation state which had existed in the past and will exist
in the end of the world. Of this, other than the phrase
here and the passage in 7:29-31, there is little evidence in
the book. Even the eschatological paradise is to some
extent distinct from Adam's Garden. This may be to employ
an argument from silence, but there are many descriptions
of and references to the new age in the book, and only once
is it called a "renewal of creation." Since "creation" may
simply mean the world, it is at least possible that all
this expression means is a setting in order, an establishment of the full divine constitution of the world. If this
is so, then the reference to an ideal past state is absent.
The importance of the Urzeit-Endzeit pattern, however, has
been pointed out, and it is impossible to ignore it.[160]
Thus it seems better to say that in IV Ezra only traces of
this pattern are found; for the author of the book it does
not seem to have played a significant role in his thought
about the establishment of the new age.

8:52-54

52. For you[161] Paradise[162] is opened, the tree of life

is planted,[163] the future world[164] is prepared,
delight[165] is prepared, the city is built, rest
is appointed, goodness is established, wisdom
(pre)[166] constituted.[167]

53. The root is sealed up from you,[168] infirmity is
blotted out before you[169] and death is hidden.
Sheol has fled, corruption is forgotten.[170]

54. Distresses[171] pass away and in the end[172] the
treasure-house of life[173] appears.

This passage is one of the poetic descriptions of the
world to come and contains many highly interesting elements.
Full consideration will be given them below. For present
purposes it is adequate to note the contrast between the
two worlds made in these verses. They form a prophecy to
Ezra and to those who are like him and are designed to con-
sole him for he is disturbed over the fate of the wicked.[174]

V.52 and 54 are statements of elements which are present
in the world to come, while v.53, deals with elements which
are absent from that world, and thus are presumably present
in this world. The relationship of death and corruption has
been dealt with above.[175] It is corruption, death and
infirmity which are to be removed in the world to come.
The elements of joy and delight are as typical of the
eschatological reward of the righteous as is immortality.
Here again the contrast of the two ages is clear. It is
further significant that it is precisely the death-corruption
elements the removal of which is stressed in v.53.

F. Conclusions to Section E.

1) Terminology

A. Another age is expected to follow this (7:47,75).

B. It may be called the future world (העולם הבא) (7:47, 8:52) or the time of renewal of creation (7:75).[176] Latin reads tempus (8:52).

2) Substantive Information about the Ages Arising out of Contrasts between Them.

A. The future world brings reward and punishment (7:47,75).

B. Few are rewarded and many punished (7:47).

C. To the righteous the future age brings life, joy etc. (8:52).[177]

D. The future world is to be free of corruption, death and infirmity (8:53).

E. No suggestion of the time or place of the division of the ages was found in these passages, nor was any information about the relation between the Messianic age and the world to come forthcoming.

G. General conclusions, based on sections B, D, and F. above.

1) Terminology

A. There are two ages or worlds.

B. These may be called "times" or saecula.

C. The contrast between them is expressed by the terminology "former"--"latter" or "this world"-- "the future world."

> a. This latter probably reflects Hebrew העולם הזה, העולם הבא.

      b.   The term העולם הזה is not used of this
          world alone.

      c.   The term העולם הבא may be used of the world
          to come alone.

2) Information

    A. About this World.

         a. It has corruption, death and infirmity.

         b. The evil heart is present in it.

    B. About World to come.

         a. It is complete.

         b. Glory and full judgement will appear in it.

         c. It brings immortality and is eternal.

         d. The evil heart will be removed.

         e. Ezra and other holy men will appear at its
           start.

    C. Differences as expressed in the passages contrasting
       the two worlds were found to be differences of
       world order rather than "spiritual"--"material"
       oppositions or the like.

3) Thus it is clear that IV Ezra has a view of two ages. As
became evident in the discussion, however, the nature of
these ages is described differently by him in different
places. Thus the relationship of the Messianic kingdom to
the world to come was ambiguous, the end could refer either
to the end of this world or to the end of the Messianic
kingdom. Since this section has been concerned only with

passages mentioning contrasts of the two ages, the information it has given us on both counts has been incomplete. In order further to understand the problems and to answer the questions raised in the Preamble to this section it is necessary to examine in greater detail Ezra's concept of the end and what will follow that end. To this task the next two sections will be devoted.

II

The End

Two main questions arise with respect to the end. The first is the problem of its place in the eschatological scheme: what precedes it and what follows it? The second is the question of the nature of the end: what does the book say about it as an eschatological event? Neither this nor the study of the two ages above can in itself answer the basic questions posed in the Preamble, but the combination of them will give a clear indication of the direction that must be taken in giving that answer.

A. The Place of the End in the Eschatological Scheme

The governing interest of this section is the specific question: when is the end said to occur? This excludes from the immediate realm of investigation passages dealing with "eschata" or last things in general and delimits it to the end itself. Thus the terminology involved in Latin novissimus and parallels is not relevant for it refers to

the "eschata" in general and not specifically to the
temporal point, the end itself.[178]

The term involved here is _finis_, Syriac šwlm' and
parallels. That this was a _terminus technicus_ not only of
IV Ezra's eschatological language but of that of his con-
temporaries is clear. Had it not been readily understood
by his readers he would not have used it alone, without any
referrent. The fact that he did so[179] indicates that, in
an eschatological context, its meaning was unmistakable.

The word "end," however, is not only an eschatological
term. It may be used in a non-technical sense in both
eschatological and non-eschatological contexts and a careful
examination is necessary in order to distinguish which use
is found in any given instance. Many examples of _finis_ and
parallels in a non-technical sense occur and this is perhaps
best illustrated by an example such as 6:1--a non-technical
use in an eschatological context.

The verse is the answer to Ezra's question: by whom
will you visit your creation (5:56)?[180] The answer is:

The beginning[181] is by (through)[182] man[183] but the end
is by (through) myself.[184]

In spite of the difficulties which scholars have found,[185]
this verse need raise no problems. Since "visitation" here
implies punishment, the most likely interpretation is that
the "beginning" is the troubles caused by the enemy nations
which will be part of the "birth pangs of the Messiah," the

onset of the divine visitation which will conclude in judgement. Of interest is that "end" here clearly means "end
of the visitation" as opposed to its beginning. Thus it
is an example of the non-technical use of this word
occurring in a highly eschatological context.[186] It is
not always completely clear whether a given use is technical
or not, and sometimes the total interpretation of a chapter
or vision must be employed in determining this.[187]

There are two outright statements of what the end is.
7:113 and 12:34 both say that the end is the day of judgement.
The text in 12:34 is not as firm as could be desired but the
best reading is without doubt ". . . until the end comes,
the day of judgement. . . ."[188] In light of these two
explicit statements, then, it must be concluded that the
day of judgement is the end.

In 11:39-46, however, equally clearly the end is said
to come with the destruction of the fourth heathen empire
and to be followed by the Messianic kingdom. In v. 39 the
eagle is said to be the last of the beasts which the Most
High made to reign in the world "and through which the end
of times (Latin: my times) might come." This statement
occurs in the lion's indictment and is followed by a list
of the wicked actions of this kingdom (vss. 40-43). It
continues (44) with the statement that the times are ended,
the ages filled and that (45) the eagle will disappear "so
that all the earth shall be at rest (again) relieved of your

violence and await the judgement of Him who made her" (46).
The decisive point, the end is here clearly the destruction
of the eagle and there is an intermediate period between
the destruction of the eagle and the judgement, which period
is the Messianic kingdom.

Similarly in 6:25 the end comes following the Messianic
woes[189] and is followed by a period of peace for the survivors, the appearance of those "who have not tasted death
from their birth" and other such events (6:26ff.). There
is no reference at all to judgement, but in the description
the "survivors,"[190] the appearance of the assumed,[191] and
certain other elements are specific to the Messianic kingdom.[192] 6:7-10 also has the Messianic kingdom view.[193]

In 5:41 the exegetical problems are more acute. Ezra's
question in v. 41 is about the inequality of reward if the
future kingdom is to be populated only by survivors. It
is the first of a series of enquiries dealing with judgement and seems to be talking of the Messianic kingdom which
precedes resurrection for it has the language and ideas
typically used of this kingdom. The angelic response is
that judgement is final and equal for all (v. 42). This
implies that the Messianic kingdom is not final and as a
corollary of this deliberately shifts the ground of discussion from that kingdom to judgement and resurrection.
Ezra accepts this as an adequate answer and continues the
discussion about judgement and resurrection (v. 43ff.).

The connection of thought in the text is not as clear
as could be desired and this interpretation is offered with
diffidence, but in light of the text as it stands, it seems
to be the most reasonable. The argument is not strictly
logical, Ezra enquires in terms of the promise of felicity
given to those who will survive and is answered in terms of
final judgement. The connecting link is reward, although
this is not made explicit. V. 42 introduces new terms of
reference into the discussion--judgement and resurrection.
Ezra clearly knows these (v. 45) and thus once v. 42 has
stated, in fact, that ultimate reward is only to be found
at judgement, he pursues the discussion with no further
reference to the felicity of the survivors after the
Messianic woes and the problems of inequality which it
raises. This is not necessarily to be seen as a rejection
of the idea of the Messianic kingdom for had open opposition to or rejection of this concept been intended, it
would surely have been made explicit.[194]

Here is a clear example of how the reigning interest
of a given passage provides coherence despite the varied
and unreconciled concepts involved. It seems that IV Ezra's
interest is in reward, not in the inequalities of the survivors. Thus he does not try to solve the problem of
inequalities as does the author of I Thess. 4:13ff. by
producing two groups, the survivors and the resurrected.
Instead, he just disregards the specific question of v. 41

which is never answered in the terms in which it is asked,
for this is not the problem that concerns him and he follows
his interest in reward through the questions in vss. 43ff.[195]
In view of this, then, the end referred to in v. 41 may be
seen to be part of the complex of ideas called the
Messianic kingdom.

14:9 is a prophecy of Ezra's assumption.[196] He is to
be with the Messiah until the times are ended. Since the
Messiah is to be connected with the Messianic kingdom this
too may be a reference to the end coming at the start of
that kingdom. In this verse, however, a verb and not a
noun is employed and thus it can only serve as supporting
evidence in the discussion, not as a proof text.

There are a number of further passages which mention
the end but which either do not supply any information about
its place in the scheme of events or are too general to be
of value. Two of these, 3:14 and 14:5 discuss the secret
revelation of the end to chosen figures, Abraham and Moses
(cf. Ap. Bar. 4:3ff.). In 12:9 Ezra, evidently referring
to the vision in chapter 11, asks God for its exact interpretation (v. 8) for "you have considered me worthy to show
me the end of times and the last of the periods."[197] Box
says that this verse is the work of the Redactor (R) for the
A document (the Eagle Vision) is not concerned with the end,
but in 11:44ff. the lion speaks of the end in a passage
whose originality Box does not doubt.[198] While in view of

the whole vision and its interpretation, especially in light
of 11:39-46, "end" probably means the beginning of the
Messianic age, this is not sure enough to constitute a
basis for argument. It is significant, however, that as
in 3:14 and 14:5, here too knowledge of the end is a special
privilege. This is part of the book's apocalyptic ideology.

The passage 4:26-32 was discussed above[199] in detail.
v. 26 which speaks of the passing away of this age, may be
referring to the end. If so, the problem of the eschatology
of this passage arises. It is far from as clear as Kabisch
would have it that this refers to the "new age" concept and
that the author of this could not have held simultaneously
a view of a Messianic kingdom. It is not insignificant
that here and in 5:42, the two classical passages for the
theory that the S author held a pure otherworldly eschatology,
the deepest concern is with the question of reward, or
theodicy and both express a sense of great urgency. It
was seen above that 5:41 shows the stamp of the concept
of the Messianic kingdom. This is equally true of the
elements of survival and wonder here in 4:26.[200] It is
illuminating to observe that while in the former case the
succeeding questions, 5:43ff. are occupied with reward,
4:33 takes up the matter of haste. These are in fact the
Janus-faces of one of Ezra's great problems.

Keuler's theory is that the fundamental conditioning
element in the choice between "national" and "universal"

elements in eschatology is whether the problem of Israel or
the problem of man is central.[201] It is surely significant
that this passage, perhaps the key parade example of the
"universal" new age eschatology, comes as the answer to the
very "nationalistic" question of how God's chosen people
and his Law have been brought to destruction, given up, in
the words of Box' translation "to godless tribes." 5:41 has
a similar prelude (cf. v. 35). If the two clearest examples
of the pure "new age" eschatology are answers to "national"
problems, then this tends to indicate that the conditioning
element of choice is not in fact "national" vs. "universal"
but, as is here being maintained, a matter of context,
association and purpose. In these terms it makes sense
that passages responding to Ezra's urgent questions about
reward will tend to highlight the decisive and final
reward of judgement and the new age. But it should not be
surprising if elements drawn from the Messianic kingdom
concept also creep in, as proves to be the case. It will
be observed as a result that, even if 4:26 does refer to
the end it is difficult precisely to fix the point in the
scheme which it represents.[202]

Thus while "the end" is a technical term in eschatological contexts, this examination indicates that it can have
at least three specific connotations. First, it may be the
day of judgement (7:113, 12:34). Second, it may occur
immediately before the Messianic kingdom (11:39-46, 6:25,

6:7-10, 5:41, 14:9). In 11:39-46 this intermediate period is explicitly followed by judgement. This too may be the implication of 6:7-10 where Jacob is said to be the beginning of the age to come. Third, it occurs as a general term with no indication of its precise meaning in 3:14, 14:5 and perhaps in 12:9; 4:26, 6:15, 12:21-30 all presented problems which did not permit their use here.

B. Meaning and Use of the Term.

Thus, in the matter of the point of time signified by the specific eschatological terminus technicus "the end" the same problem occurs as with the point of separation of the two ages in passages expressing the contrast between them.[203] It could therefore be concluded, as in fact Keulers implies, that the author is more or less inconsistent.[204] It is possible, however, that since "end" was a technical term in an eschatological context, it did not always refer to the same specific point in any given eschatological scheme, but rather had come to signify something like "the decisive point in the eschatological sequence." If this is so, then variation is to be expected as to its precise location within that sequence of events, a variation conditioned by the context and purpose of the passage in which the term is employed.

Two of the passages, 5:41 and 4:26 have already been examined from this point of view. In 5:41 the term "end" was connected with the Messianic kingdom. This was determined primarily through the association of ideas.[205] On the other

hand, it became evident it was impossible to fix its precise
connotation in 6:25.

In 7:112-113 the first explicit statement that the end
is the day of judgement occurs in the context of a discussion
of intercession and its place in final judgement.[206] In vv.
106-111, Ezra is responding to the angelic statement that
there is no intercession in final judgement. He argues that
if there is intercession in this imperfect world then it
should exist in the world to come which is perfect. In
7:112-113 the angel points out to him that it is precisely
because this world is imperfect that there is intercession
in it. The day of judgement is said to be the end of the
imperfection of this world. Thus it seems that the purpose
of the use of "end" is to emphasize the difference of this
world order from the future, especially in the area of judgement. In light of this it is clear why the "decisive point
of history" should be said to be the day of judgement.

In 12:30-34 there are three references to the end. V.
30 says, probably, that the last two little wings are kept
for the end of days while v. 32 says that the Messiah is
preserved for the end of days. V. 34 equally clearly states
that the Messianic kingdom will last until the day of judgement which is the end. Thus here, in the space of four
verses, the end is said to be both the day of judgement and
the start of the Messianic kingdom. Box[207] says that the
end for the A document is the introduction of the Messianic

kingdom. Therefore v. 34 is redactoral and secondary, an attempt, Box says, to unify this eschatology with the concept of final judgement. It might be suggested that a terminological distinction exists, v. 32 speaks of "the end of days" and v. 34 just of the "end." In 7:113, however, the end is the day of judgement and is in Latin _finis temporis_, while 12:30 has just _finis_ of the Messianic kingdom. It should be added that if this verse is secondary it could not have been introduced for consistency since the whole reason for suggesting its secondary nature is precisely a supposed inconsistency about the end.[208]

In the area of context and purpose the most important thing to observe is the change of temporal viewpoint between the verses. V. 30 speaks of the situation before the end of the fourth kingdom and is concerned with why the two little wings are reserved and in 12:32 there is a specific tradition of the preservation of the Messiah for the end,[209] presented in a verse describing the Messiah and the time of his coming. 12:33f. on the other hand tell of the actions of the Messiah and of his kingdom, and from the point of view of the Messianic kingdom the decisive point is judgement.

This argument may appear to be circular, obviously the Messiah is the subject when he is said to be preserved for the end and so forth. In fact, it is not, for there is no necessity that the term end be used here and if it is, it is because it is associated in the author's mind with these

events. Thus it is evident from this passage that the term
has a number of possible connotations and that the choice
between them is, in fact, conditioned by context and association. This variation is quite comprehensible once the term
is seen to have the meaning "the decisive point" in an
eschatological context.

The occurrences in 6:7-10 and 6:25 are best understood
in the light of the total development of this particular section of the vision. The difficult passage in 5:41ff. was discussed above.[210] Ezra's haste and urgency to see the solution to the problem of reward was found to be the basis of
the development of the thought there. It was observed
that there is unclarity in the expression of the eschatological
events conditioned by this basic problem and that this
interest carries through to 5:55. In 5:56 a new problem is
raised--that of the agency of the divine visitation. Its
beginning is to be through man and its consummation through
God alone. He alone had pre-created the eschatological
climax.

In 6:7-10 Ezra proceeds to ask about the sign of the
decisive point and its time and is told that its beginning
is Israel's kingdom which will follow that of Rome.[211] This,
as it were, complements the information that the visitation
will start with man (Messianic woes?) and end with God alone
(judgement?). Ezra's interest in the signs together with
the current interpretation of the verse Gen. 25:26 which is

here employed set the context of the passage. That questions
about the signs brought to mind the materials dealing with
the Messianic woes is also clear in 6:13-25 when in response
to a question about the signs, a full and detailed listing
of woes is given, concluding with a vague description of the
future state composed of elements drawn primarily from the
concept of the Messianic kingdom, and partly from the new
age. The focus is on the signs, the end comes after them
and what follows that is barely described.

Inasmuch as the Messianic woes seem to imply the idea
of the survivors and that in turn is connected with the
Messianic kingdom, the relation of the end with the Messianic
kingdom is clear in this passage. These elements condition
which point is here considered decisive. The element of
empire introduced by the Esau-Jacob interpretation similarly
explains the use in 6:7-10.

14:9, the promise of assumption made to Ezra, shows the
connection by association in an ideal way. The assumed are
said to be with the Messiah who is pre-existent in heaven,
and immediately the idea of the appearance of the Messiah
at the end to inaugurate his Kingdom is introduced. This
association not only determines the introduction of the last
phrase of v. 9 but is also the connection for the introduction of vss. 10-12 which are not otherwise part of the
structure of thought of this section.

11:39-46 also focus on the destruction of the heathen

empire. The four empires are created so that they may bring
the end into being. From this point of view it is quite
natural that the decisive turning point is the destruction
of the last empire although from v. 46 it is clear that this
is to be followed by some sort of intermediate state and
then judgement.

Thus it may be observed that this term does not always
refer to the same point in the eschatological scheme. There
is, however, a consistency in its use, for it always seems
to refer to the crucial turning point of history. What is
crucial is determined by the context and purpose of the
particular passage. Its introduction and connotation may be
almost totally conditioned by the association of thought in
the particular passage and are not, it seems (cf. 12:30-34),
necessarily determined by what has preceded or followed it.

This leads to the conclusion that, indeed, the theory
proposed at the beginning of this section is valid. The term
"end" means primarily "the decisive turning point of history."
Just which point this is, the start of the Messianic kingdom,
or of the new age, or of some undefined future state, seems
totally dependent on the three considerations of context,
purpose and association. The intertwining of themes in the
descriptions of the future world is such that sometimes it
is almost impossible to determine which particular referrent
is intended, although often a preponderance of themes in one
or another direction may be observed. This was seen to be

especially true in passages whose main interest was neither
in the description of the course of events nor of some
aspect of those events.

III
Descriptions of the New World

In the course of the researches of the last two main
sections an unclarity was found to exist in the view of the
nature of the future state expressed in the book. Sometimes
it seemed to be the Messianic kingdom, sometimes the world
to come and sometimes elements of both were involved. This
was seen to depend, to some extent at least, on context and
purpose--a fact which weighs against the clear, two-eschatology
theory of Keulers. This situation demands a fuller examination of those passages in which the events following the end
of normal human history are discussed. This will be carried
out in light of the following considerations:

a. In view of the complex situation revealed by the study
of the contrasts of the two ages and of the end, does Ezra
have a stock of ideas about the new world which can be
isolated? Are there specific literary forms, images or
linguistic usages connected with these?

b. Is it possible to isolate those ideas central to Ezra's
conception from those which he merely accepted from tradition,
especially through the application of the criteria of context,
purpose and association?

The signs preceding the inauguration of the new world, the Messianic woes, fall beyond the direct interest of this section and will be treated only as they bear on the above problems.

The passages dealing with or referring to the future state are numerous. Any attempt to give a consolidated view of the eschatology without treating different types of usage separately would presuppose a consistency of thought the existence of which above discussion has shown that there is reason to doubt. 7:26-44 is the fullest description of the eschatological events given in the book. It is of advantage, therefore, to use it as a basis for the study of the descriptions of the new world. Each of the central elements mentioned in this passage will be analyzed as it is employed in the book as a whole. This is not to assume that these verses represent a scheme utilized consistently by the author, but simply to treat them as a convenient catalogue of the elements which constitute his eschatological views.

A. Text of 7:26-44.

26. Indeed, behold a time[212] is coming, and it shall be, when the signs which I predicted to you come, the city, now unseen, will appear and the land which is now hidden will be seen.[213]

27. And everyone who will be saved from the predicted evils will see my[214] wonders.[215]

28. Then my Messiah[216] will be revealed with those who are with him, and he will make rejoice those who remain,[217] for four hundred years.[218]

29. And it will come to pass after these years[219] that my servant[220] the Messiah will die[221] and all those who have human breath.

30. And the world shall return to its[222] primaeval silence for seven days as in the beginning[223] so that no-one shall remain.

31. And it will come to pass[224] after seven days, the age (world) which is now not awake shall be aroused and corruption[225] shall pass away.

32.   And the earth will give back those who sleep in it,
    And the dust will return[226] those who rest therein,
    And the chambers will give back those souls which
        have been entrusted to them.

33. And the Most High will be revealed on the Throne of Judgement,[227] [228]
    [229]And mercy will pass away,[229]
    [230]Grace (?mercy) will be made distant,[230]
    Longsuffering will be gathered up;[231]

34. But judgement[232] alone will remain,
    And truth will be established,
    And faith will increase;[233]

35.   And reward[234] will follow,
    And recompense will appear,
        And justice will awaken,
    And injustice will not sleep.[235]

36.   [236]And the pit[237] of torment (s)[238] will appear,
    And[239] opposite it will be[239] the place of quiet,[240]
        And the furnace of Gehenna[241] shall be revealed,
    And opposite it the Paradise of delight.

37. Then the Most High said to the aroused nations:[242] See and understand whom you have denied[243] or whom you have not served[243] or whose commandments you have spurned.

38. Look before[244] (you);[245] here are delight and rest[246] and there, fire and torments.

39. The day of judgement will be thus:[247] it has
        no sun,[248] nor moon, nor stars,[249]

40.   nor cloud, nor thunder,[250] nor lightning,
        nor wind, nor water,[251] nor air,[252]
    [253]nor darkness, nor night, nor morning,[253]

41.   nor summer, nor spring,[254] nor harvest,[255]
        nor heat, nor frost, nor cold,[256]
        nor hail, nor rain, nor dew,

42.   [257]nor midday, nor night, nor dawn,[257]
            nor brightness, nor clarity, nor light,[258]
But only the glory of the brightness of the Most High,[259] by
which[260] all shall see[261] that which has been established.

43. For it[262] will last for a week of years.[263]

44. This is my judgement[264] and its nature[265] but to you
alone have I shown this.

B. The Messianic Woes: "the signs which I predicted to you."

"Signs" is the technical term used in IV Ezra to desig-
nate those events called elsewhere the Messianic woes. Thus
it is used in 4:52, 5:1,13, 6:11,20, 8:63, 9:1, 13:32, all
of these in the context of predictions of the woes. The
term is also found in other books with the same meaning.[266]
The actual events constituting the woes are listed in IV
Ezra 5:1-12, 6:13-24, 9:3, 13:29f. They are also mentioned
or referred to on a number of other occasions.[267] Aspects
of the woes cycle and of the anti-christ materials are
probably crucial formative elements in the description of
the activities of the last kings of the fourth empire in
chapters 11-12.[268]

The woes are followed in 6:25, 9:8 and 12:34 by the
Messianic kingdom.[269] 8:50 is not clear and it may be sus-
pected that the materials in v. 52 do not represent a consistent description of any given eschatological state.[270]
The woes are never said to be followed directly by judgement.
Thus it may be concluded that where the text is explicit the
woes are followed by the Messianic kingdom (8:50 remaining
problematic). In 11:46 and 12:34 as in 7:26-44 this Messianic
kingdom is succeeded by judgement. 9:7 is not explicit.

C. The Heavenly Jerusalem: "the unseen city" (v.26).

The concept of the heavenly Jerusalem is found in 8:52 and in Vision IV, especially in 10:27,42,44,54, etc., in 13:36 and in Armenian 6:25. The especial holiness of Zion is mentioned in 3:24 and 5:25. The notion of the ideal, future Jerusalem has its origins in the Hebrew Bible,[271] and it is widespread in the Apocryphal and Pseudepigraphical literature.[272] It is also found in the New Testament,[273] in the Dead Sea Scrolls,[274] in Rabbinic literature[275] and in the later Jewish apocalyptic.[276]

In IV Ezra its pre-existence is implied clearly here, in Vision IV and in 13:36 and this may also be the case in 8:52. Here and in 13:36 it is clearly stated that this city will be revealed at the end.[277] It is connected here with the unseen land. In 8:52 it is found in a catalogue of elements which also includes paradise, the tree of life, the future age and rest. The connection between the city and paradise may also be observed in IV Ez. Arm. 6:25, Ap. Bar. 4:2ff., cf. Ap. Jn. 22:1f. Here and in 13:35 it is said to appear at the start of the Messianic kingdom. Against the views of Kabisch[278] and Gunkel[279] who say that this represents Jerusalem in heaven[280] Keulers, following Vagany, argues cogently that the city is heavenly inasmuch as it is marvellous and appears from heaven, but it will manifest itself in the Messianic kingdom and this in fact is the meaning of the references in Vision IV.[281]

The heavenly Jerusalem is generally referred to in IV
Ezra simply as "the city"[282] and twice it is called Zion.[283]
Thus in IV Ezra the new Jerusalem is connected specifically
with the Messianic kingdom. It is pre-created, has a special
holiness and will appear at the end.

D. "The Hidden Land" (v.26)

The expression as such is unparalleled in comparable
literature. "Land" alone, however, refers to the land of
Israel chosen by God (5:24) and given to Israel for an
inheritance (14:31). The word "hidden" is problematic but
it may best be explained by the apocalyptic penchant for
speaking of hidden things which are to be revealed at the
time of the eschaton.[284]

The meaning of this phrase has been much debated.
Gunkel[285] and Box[286] consider it to be a reference to paradise
which is found alongside the heavenly Jerusalem in Ap. Bar.
4:6 and Ap. Jn. 22:2. To these two references, first cited
by Gunkel, might be added IV Ezra Arm. 6:25. In none of these
instances nor elsewhere is paradise called "land" nor is the
phrase "hidden land" found, which is a weighty objection to
this theory. Keulers and Vagany[287] both argue that this
phrase refers to Palestine which is frequently called "the
land" in IV Ezra and elsewhere.[288] In 13:48, 12:34 as in Ap.
Bar. 29:2 the land is intimately connected with the survivors
and figures as the locale of the Messianic kingdom.

Although this seems to be a more plausible solution to

the problem than that of Gunkel and Box, it is not absolutely
convincing. The expression remains unparalleled and difficult, in spite of the explanation of "hidden" offered above.
It may be tentatively accepted, however, that this is a
reference to the land of Israel but it is better to base the
role of the land in eschatological contexts on texts like
12:34, 13:48. There it is clear that the land of Israel is
indeed the venue of the Messianic kingdom.

E. The Survivors

In 7:27 as in 6:25, 9:8 and 13:19 the term "the survivors"
means those people who survive the Messianic woes. Even more
specifically in 12:34, 13:26, 48f. it means those who survive
the great eschatological battle waged by the Messiah. The
term is also used in contexts which do not make clear what
the remnant is surviving from, thus 4:26, 5:41. These, however, must gain their meaning from the context of the Messianic
woes tradition, and this is a clear indication that this had
become a terminus technicus. The concept, but not the term,
is encountered in Ap. Bar. 29:1f., 32:1, 71:1 and there survival is limited to those dwelling in the land, cf. IV Ez.
12:34, 13:48. The term is used of the last generation also
in 1 Thess, 4:15 in the context of a different eschatological
view[289] while in Mk. 13:13 it occurs in precisely the same
sort of context as here.

Box points out that this expression is paralleled by the
Rabbinic נצל. Thus Sanh. 98b. מה יעשה אדם וינצל מחבלו של

‏משיח יעסוק בתורה ובגמ"ח‎.[290] The Biblical doctrine of the remnant is well known.[291] At Qumran the sect evidently applied to themselves the idea of the righteous remnant eschatologically conceived, thus, for example CD i:4f., 1QM xiii:8, 1QH vi:8. 1QM xiv:8 bears a close relation to Isa. 11:11, a verse used frequently by the sect.[292] This sort of application of eschatological ideas is one of the features which distinguishes the sectarian writings and its absence from IV Ezra is significant in illuminating the religio-sociological differences between his background and that of the sect.

On the other hand in CD vii:21 ‏אלה ימלטו בקץ הפקודה‎; although probably also referring to the sect, is more analogous to the uses in IV Ezra, for it refers to the men of the sect in the future, after the time of visitation,[293] not to the sect of the present. The use of this expression for the future remnant is found elsewhere in the Intertestamental books.[294] It is the formulation of the notion of the righteous remnant in an apocalyptic setting.

It may thus be concluded that "survivors" is a technical term used of those who survive the Messianic woes.[295] It is connected with the biblical idea of the remnant. The fact that this term is not found in Ap. Bar. in spite of its close relationship to IV Ezra is significant.

F. "The Predicted Evils" (v.27).

The whole phrase "those who survive the predicted evils"

is a cliché in IV Ezra and is found three times, 7:27, 6:25
and 9:8. It is neither frequent enough within the book, nor
widespread enough outside it to be considered as more than a
standard feature of IV Ezra's style.

G. "They will see my Wonders" (v.27).

What the remnant survives for is described differently
in different texts. Here it is called the "seeing of wonders."
The use of the phrase is parallel to 13:50 where the Messiah
shows wonders to the survivors. "To see," as was pointed
out by Volz, is used in Rabbinic literature of the end, mainly
in the phrase לראות בנחמה.[296] It is also found in Ps. Sol.
17:50, 18:11. The verb is used with the object "salvation"
in Ps. 91:16 and this was interpreted eschatologically in CD
(MS B) xx:34. Terminologically speaking this latter usage is
far closer to IV Ezra than that of Rabbinic literature for it
is salvation that is seen in 6:25, 9:8.

Box suggests that in these cases the verb has the meaning "to enjoy."[297] The use in 13:50, however, weighs against
this, for here we have "to show" clearly a Hif̂^{c}îl of r'y
which tends to indicate that the verb retained the meaning
"to see" although this may have been somewhat extended.[298]

The element of wonder is present in 4:26, 7:27 and 13:50
parallel to "salvation" in 6:25, 9:8 and 13:48. "Wonder" in
IV Ezra refers primarily to eschatological acts or to the
revelation of those acts.[299] It is found once of creation[300]
and once of the miracle performed for the returning ten

tribes.[301] In Ap. Bar. a similar situation prevails.[302]
These wonders are interpreted by Keulers as various particular events of the Messianic time,[303] but since there is no
indication of this in the text, the reference may be simply
to the eschatological events in general. The parallel position of wonder and of salvation in the sort of sentence here
under discussion tends to suggest that these terms may be
largely synonymous in such contexts.

It is significant that neither the survivors nor the
seeing of wonders are found directly connected with the
resurrection-judgement material. It is of further importance
to notice the correlation between the survivors and the
seeing of wonders. The connection with the Messiah and his
activity is most explicit in 13:48-50. The problematic
passage, 6:25ff. was discussed on p. 86 above and it is
amply clear that the Messianic kingdom language is involved.
This meaning of the term "survivors" also strengthens the
argument for the interpretation of 5:41ff. suggested above.
This passage neither represents two classes of men, the
survivors and the resurrected, nor, probably, does it describe
judgement immediately following the end. It employs the
problem of reward, not the sequential structure of events
as its organizing principle.[304]

H. The Messiah (v.28ff).

Three major questions must be asked about the concept
of the Messiah as expressed in the book:

1) What nature and functions are attributed to him?

2) Are these common to all passages dealing with him?

3) What function does he play in the total eschatological thought of the book?

1) The Messiah is definitely referred to in 7:28f., 11:37-12:1, 12:31-34, 13:3-13, 25-52, 14:9. It has been suggested that the son in Vision IV is the Messiah but this seems unlikely.[305]

2) 7:28ff.

The Messiah is here called "my Messiah" and "my servant the Messiah."[306] He is said to be revealed together with his company, which suggests pre-existence. He makes the survivors rejoice for four hundred years and at the end of this period he dies together with all men. There is no indication that he plays any part in the events preceding the end of this world.

3) The Messiah in the Eagle Vision (11:37-12:1, 12:31-34).

a. Contents of the Vision

In chapter 11, the lion, speaking in a human voice (37) indicts the eagle (38-43) and pronounces punishment on it (45f.). As the lion speaks, the last head and the last two little wings disappear, the body of the eagle is burnt and the earth greatly rejoices (12:1-3). In the angelic interpretation the lion is identified with the Davidic Messiah, preserved by the Most High for the end (12:32). He will come and rebuke the last of the four world empires, "he will first

set them up in judgement (Syriac, Arabic[1], Armenian: his
judgement) while they are alive, and it shall be when he will
have rebuked them he will destroy them" (12:33). He will
then deliver the rest of the people in the land of Israel
and rejoice with them until the time of the end and the day
of judgement (12:34).

b. Nature and Functions of the Messiah

The most important function here attributed to him is
indictment and punishment, referred to in the interpretation
as judgement. The Messiah is pre-existent, he will rule over
the people in the land for a time and then the end will come.
In contrast to 7:28ff. where the Messiah plays no part in
the events preceding the end, here his role in these events
is central. On the other hand, his rule over the temporary
Messianic kingdom is clear in both passages and the language
of rejoicing and the term survivors are common to both.
Additional features presented here are the Davidic geneaology,
the Palestinian locale of the kingdom and the forensic aspects
of the description of his activity. Pre-existence which was
only hinted at in 7:28ff. is made explicit.

c. The Vision as an Independent Source?

Box, the most recent major source critic, claims that
chapters 11-12 constitute an independent source. His bases
for this are:
a. They have a political eschatology while that of S (Vis.
I-IV) is transcendent and dualistic.

b. Thus the annihilation of the eagle will be the beginning
of the day of judgement on this earth. Therefore there
is no resurrection and general judgement.

c. The author of S could not have combined the political and
the transcendent eschatologies for he despaired of this
world.[307]

In his reply to this Keulers adduces the following considerations:

a. The S source does in fact recognize the Messianic kingdom.
This contention is based on his interpretation of 6:7-10,
on the Messianic kingdom features, Behemoth and Leviathan
in 6:25 and on the fact that the heavenly Jerusalem in
Vision IV belongs to this cycle of ideas.

b. S is not as mild to the heathen as Box would have him nor is
A as vicious. The annihilation of Rome is to be seen
more as a fulfillment of divine promise than as an expression of hatred.[308]

To these points the following should be added:

a. The situation in 6:7-10 is indeed as Keulers maintains.
The new considerations brought to bear above on the
interpretation of this passage are conclusive.[309]

b. 4:26ff., a key passage for Box in the establishment of
the transcendent and dualist eschatology of S does not
support this theory.[310]

c. In IV Ezra the heavenly Jerusalem is clearly part of the
terminology of the Messianic kingdom and Keulers'

statements are supported by the examination of the concept here undertaken.[311]

Thus the supposed contrasts between the documents are not as sharp as Box would maintain and therefore this is not an adequate basis for seeing A as a separate source.[312]

d. Editorial Adjustments within the Vision?

Box further maintains that the following editorial adjustments were made to the "original" eagle vision:[313]

a. The phrase "whom the Most High hath kept unto the end of days" in v.32 is secondary because this implies transcendence which contradicts Davidic descent.

b. All of v.34 referring to the deliverance of the survivors and their joy in the Messianic kingdom until the end is an addition for it is "out of harmony" with the views of the vision.

c. Box characterizes the views of the writer as follows: an obsession with the might of Rome and purely political hopes centered on this world whose consummation will be the overthrow of the Roman empire. Thus the end comes with the annihilation of the eagle. Therefore in 11:46 "the judgement and mercy of him that made her" is not the day of judgement but the character of the rule of God which is to follow the overthrow of the Roman empire.[314]

Keulers makes the following points:

a. Alongside 12:1-3, 12:32f. must speak of the leaders of the Roman Empire, for the empire itself had already disappeared. Thus there is a combination of the Messiah as judge and the Messiah as king.

b. The Davidic geneaology is traditional so it is introduced in spite of the apparent anomaly.[315]

To these should be added:

a. It is interesting to compare the arguments about the supposed incompatibility of heavenly origin and Davidic descent with the treatment of the Melkizedek figure in the materials associated with II Enoch. There Melkizedek is born before the flood and assumed to heaven in order to appear later at the appropriate time.[316]

b. Keulers does not really come to grips with Box' basic contention about the eschatology of A which in fact determines these other matters.

c. 11:46 according to Box cannot refer to final judgement for the end has already taken place. This is based on the unstated premise that the end = the day of judgement. Above it was established that which particular event is called the end is determined by the immediate context.[317] Now as Box himself rightly notes, the main prepossession of this vision is with the Roman empire and of necessity its climax is the overthrow of that empire. This is thus called the end, but it does not follow that this is the day of judgement.[318] Were there further support in the vision or in its interpretation for the view that 11:46 refers to the theocratic rule of the Messianic kingdom, Box' view might be acceptable, but such support is lacking.

d. The awkwardness of Box' interpretation is highlighted by his own confusion. On the one hand he says that "judgement" in 11:46 "means the judicial process by which the Roman Empire is condemned and destroyed,"[319] while on the other he claims that it "suggests the mild rule of the theocratic king, i.e., God himself."[320] If 12:34 is genuine then there is no doubt whatsoever that 11:46 refers to final judgement after the end of the Messianic kingdom.

e. If 12:34 is secondary, as Box would have us believe, then in the interpretation of the vision there is no reference whatsoever to the nature of the Messianic rule. In this case in chapters 11-12, only 11:46 would give information about the nature of the future kingdom.

f. It has been shown that Box' interpretation of 11:46 can only stand up if there is other evidence to support it. In his "original" vision there is nothing. Thus, in fact, there is no representation of the Messianic age in the "genuine" vision with which 12:34 could be out of harmony. Therefore there seems to be no basis for considering 12:34 as secondary.

g. To this one further consideration may be added. In Daniel 7, for example, where the eternity and universality of the Messianic kingdom of Israel are proclaimed, they are

made explicit both in the vision and in its interpretation.[321] To this the situation here stands in stark
contrast. If 11:46 is proclaiming the eternal kingdom
of the Messiah it is obscure and misleading. 12:34
excludes this concept and if it is secondary then that
kingdom is ignored altogether in the interpretation.

h. Therefore 12:34 is original and "judgement" in 11:46
refers to final judgement to follow the Messianic kingdom.
To summarize:

i. If 12:34 is not original, then in the text there
is no interpretation of 11:46 at all.

ii. It is not in conflict with the views of the
"genuine" material, for that material expresses no
views.

iii. In light of the main interest and emphasis of
the vision, the placing of the climax at the destruction of the empire is not anomalous, even though the
author also believes in a temporary Messianic kingdom
and day of judgement. The perfunctory nature of the
description of the events following this destruction
emphasizes the almost exclusive preoccupation with
Rome in the vision.

e. The Pre-figuring of Final Judgement

The judicial aspect of the function of the Messiah and
yet the distinctness of his activity from the final judgement
raises the problem of the relationship of that judgement to

other events which involve the separation of the righteous
from the wicked. Here this is done for the last generation
by the Messiah. In 7:27ff. it is effected by the woes--the
concept of the survivors presupposes this. Another case in
which this problem arises is in the separation of the souls
of the righteous and the wicked after death in 7:75ff. The
question of the relationship between the pre-figuring of
judgement in the form of the survivors concept and final
judgement is one of the factors at play in 5:41ff. There
the answer was, in effect, that the day of judgement has a
decisiveness and a permanency unlike any other event.[322] It
will become clear in the course of our examination of it that
the day of judgement is primarily characterized precisely by
these features of permanency, truth and decisiveness. In
light of this the apparent anomaly of the judicial function
of the Messiah need not be seen as an obstacle to the
eschatology put forward by this chapter.

f. The Forensic Features of the Messianic Figure

Box' point about the different functions of the Messiah
here and in 7:28ff. is quite valid. There the Messiah
appears after the end of the convulsions which precede his
kingdom. Here, however, he appears as the wickedness of the
last heathen empire reaches its peak and is directly
responsible for its overthrow. Further his activity is
described in legal terms, reminiscent of the language of
God's judicial activity, for example in 7:37.

Baldensperger pointed out that in Daniel 7 the eschatological battle is given a forensic formulation and sees this
as relevant to the language used here of the Messiah.[323]
The Son of Man as cosmic judge is one of the most remarkable
features of the Similitudes of Enoch. The comparison with
Daniel 7 on the one hand and the Similitudes of Enoch on the
other will help us better to evaluate the significance of
the legal formulation applied here to the activity of the
Messiah.

In Daniel 7, of course, the theme of judgement is
explicit. It is judgement by the Ancient of Days = God and
is cosmic in nature. He sits on the Throne with His attendant
hosts before Him, the heavenly books are opened and judgement
is given.[324] This is judgement of cosmic extent, performed
by God and described in language which makes this unmistakable. In the Similitudes, judgement, although performed by
the Son of Man, has the same cosmic, universal aspects. He
sits on the Throne of Glory,[325] as judge over the sinners.[326]
The universal and ultimate nature of his function is greatly
stressed.[327]

In our vision the elements of judgement are also clearly
present. 11:38-43 are the indictment, 45-46 the pronouncement of sentence and 12:1-3 its execution. In the interpretation, 12:33 is even more explicit. The Messiah will set up
the leaders of the fourth kingdom in judgement while they
are still alive and then he will destroy them.[328] Yet the

elements of universality and resurrection generally associated
by IV Ezra with final judgement do not appear, neither do
those features which serve to highlight the cosmic nature of
judgement in Daniel 7 and in 1 Enoch. There is, for example,
no enthronement. This vision is greatly influenced by Daniel
7 as is evident not only from the explicit reference to that
chapter in 12:11 but from many other elements in the structure of the vision.[329] This renders the lack of these cosmic
features the more striking.

The question must now be raised whether the Messiah's
function of judgement in the form in which it is presented
here is a modification of the concept of the Messiah as
cosmic judge as it occurs, for example, in 1 Enoch or
whether it is to be seen as one result of the legalizing of
the eschatological cosmic battle, another of which is the
concept of the Messiah as cosmic judge. In this connection
it is important to examine the vision in Ap. Bar. 39-40.
Although the Syriac Baruch has many connections with IV
Ezra, there is clearly no literary connection between this
vision and IV Ezra 11-12. It is, like IV Ezra 11-12, a four
empire vision. The anti-christ features which influenced
the indictment in IV Ezra 11:38-43 are also evident in Ap.
Bar. 39:5,[330] and both stem from the characterization of the
little horn in Daniel 7. Here, strikingly, the legal form,
in particular the judgement of the leader of the last empire
(41:1), and the temporary Messianic kingdom until the end

(41:3) occur. The cosmic and universal elements are also totally absent.

This tends to indicate that the cosmic judgement of the Messiah is not the background of these visions. Had some hint of this appeared in either of these two visions unrelated to one another in their literary form, the situation would have been different. Here the features of judgement must be seen as a function of the legalizing of the eschatological battle leading to the description of the activities of the Messiah in legal terms. This is seen as the introduction to the Messianic kingdom. For Baruch and for Ezra final judgement is the realm of God. When the eschatological battle became separated from final judgement as is the case in Ezra and Baruch, the Messiah as warrior took over some aspects of the judgement language, but final judgement remained the preroga- tive of the Most High.[331]

The coincidence of a number of common elements in the visions of Ezra and Baruch tends to suggest a distinct associational complex. The two visions have in common first the vision form and the use of nature symbolism, second the four empires theory, third the last, most wicked empire and its overthrow by the Messiah, fourth the formulation of the Messianic activity in forensic terms, fifth the judgement and destruction of the leaders of that empire and finally the concept of the temporary Messianic kingdom. Yet, in spite of all this there is no literary interdependence.

The roots of most of these elements lie deep in apocalyptic tradition and especially in Daniel 7, and it is quite
possible that there developed in the two hundred and fifty
years after the composition of Daniel, a traditional complex
which might be called "The Four Empires Vision Complex" and
which was characterized at least by the basic elements of
the symbolic vision form, the four empires and the military-
legal function of the Messiah. IV Ezra in 12:11 makes it
evident that he is dependent on a tradition of interpretation
or rather re-interpretation of Daniel 7 and he may not have
been the first. In any case, the deeply traditional nature
of the materials in this chapter may be the explanation of
the introduction of the forensic features of the Messiah,
whether or not a crystallized complex such as that suggested
here actually existed.

Thus it may be concluded that the legal language used
here to describe the Messiah's activities is not to be seen
as the prime characteristic of that figure. The prime
features are still military, the overthrowing of the great
Roman Empire and the description of this activity in legal
terms is one of the elements of the tradition here involved.

g. The Question of Originality

It is clear, then, that this vision is drawing on traditional materials. In this no doubt lies the explanation of
those differences from the first part of the book which have
led many scholars to posit an independent source for the

vision. It seems clear, however, that the vision is not an adaption of a written source. The overall congruence of vision and interpretation, in spite of minor problems, weighs against this. This is especially so if the situation in chapter 13 is borne in mind. There the vision and interpretation are far from harmoniously related and it will be seen that there is reason to think that the vision is an independent piece, while the author tried to write an interpretation to it.

Here both unevennesses and differences from other places in the book are best regarded as the result of the author's employing a highly traditional complex of ideas, a complex which probably imposed certain features, such as the function of the Messiah, on him who employed it. It is easier to see the divergences in the concept of the Messiah between this vision and 7:28ff. in these terms than to explain their similarities as Box does, as the result of editorial adaption of a divergent eschatology to that of the first part of the book. If the similarities are the result of an editorial adjustment, then it must be admitted that this adjustment is unbelievably clumsy. After all, the Messiah does not fit that of 7:28ff., the warlike and judicial functions have been left and the "new" eschatology is most inadequately affirmed. It is best, therefore, to see the vision as the composition of the author, employing a literary form well known to him from tradition.

4) The Son of Man Vision: Chapter 13

a. The Contents of the Vision

The Seer saw that the wind (2) brought up "as the form of a man" from the heart of the sea (3). This man flew with the clouds, his glance caused trembling (4) and all who heard his voice melted (5). A great, hostile host gathered against him and he cut out a mountain and flew on it (6). The place from which the mountain was cut was not to be found (7). The multitude was afraid, but they fought him (8) and he, without weapons, (9) destroyed them with his fiery breath (10). He then descended from the mountain and called to himself another, peaceful and joyous multitude (12-13a).

This, the angelus interprens tells Ezra, is the Messiah who was preserved by the Most High for many times to deliver creation and set those who remain in order (26). The signifi-cance of his fiery breath and weaponlessness is (27f.) that the time of deliverance is coming (29), the woes will commence (30f.) and then the servant will be revealed (32). The nations will unite to fight him (33f.) but he will stand on Mt. Zion (35) and the heavenly city will appear (36). The fiery elements are the rebuke, reproach and destruction of the enemy (37f.). The peaceful multitude (39) is the ten tribes whose story is then told at some length (40-47) and the survivors in the land (48). He will destroy the nations, defend the survivors and show them many wonders (50). He ascended from the sea because no-one except his companions can see him until the time is ripe (51f.).

b. Nature and Functions of the Messiah

The Messiah is called "as the form of a man" or "the
man" in both vision and interpretation. It is clear that
the former title is simply a function of the mysterious
style that the apocalypticists liked to affect for in the
overwhelming majority of cases he is called just "the man"
or "that man."[332] In the interpretation he is also called
"my servant."[333] He is pre-existent and, as in 7:28, he is
revealed, according to the interpretation, together with his
companions. He delivers the survivors and presumably rules
over them, but the element of rejoicing common to 7:28f. and
12:34 is not mentioned. As in A he plays a central role in
the events preceding the end. He is not said to be of
Davidic descent, but as in A, in the interpretation his
kingdom is in Palestine and the forensic features appear
only in the interpretation.

c. Vision and Interpretation

H. Gunkel, in his treatment of Visions IV, V, VI pointed
out the need to distinguish between materials composed by an
apocalypticist as allegories and materials which existed
previously, often in mythical form, and which are employed
by the apocalyptic writer as allegories. The former, he maintains, have no independent meaning while the latter do. He is
not certain into which category Vision VI falls.[334] It seems
possible that a third class of materials exists, original
allegories used by a later writer with a new interpretation.

If either the second or the third situation occurs, then
it is important to bear in mind that, even if the vision was
originally an independent piece later employed by the
apocalypticist for his own purposes, from the point of view
of the student of the thought of that writer, what is significant is the understanding of the vision offered in his interpretation. The independent meaning of the allegory, if such
be present and can be determined, may well be important from
other points of view but not from that of the thought of the
author. The author is using this allegory to convey his
ideas and he provides an interpretation to make these ideas
explicit.

   d. Unity and Authorship

   Box maintains that this is an independent source and
that the redactor is responsible for 13b-24, the middle
phrase of 26, all of 29-33,36,48 and the reference to the
companions of the Messiah in 52.[335] The arguments against
it being an independent source are in general the same as
those brought to bear in the case of the eagle vision and
as there, the crucial question is one of eschatology. Box
points to the following distinctive features of this source:
the fact that all the heathen powers and not just the Roman
empire are involved, the transcendental Son of Man as opposed
to the Davidic Messiah and the ten tribes tradition which he
claims implies a pre-70 C.E. situation.[336]

   The first and third of these features are not really

convincing. In Vision V the author is in the context of a
four empires vision and thus must talk of the Roman empire,
while here he is talking about the eschatological war.
Besides, it may be questioned whether to an author of the
first century C.E. there was a great distinction between the
Roman empire and all the heathen world. The ten tribes tradition is combined here with the survivors in the land and is
only isolated because Box excises v. 48. The features of the
Messianic figure will be discussed below and then an assessment of Box' second proposition will be made.[337]

There are, however, severe literary problems which are
not adequately treated by past scholars of the book. The
chapter falls into three sections: the vision (1-13a), the
seer's thoughts about the vision (13b-24) and the angelic
interpretation (25-53). The structure of the vision itself
is fairly clear. Some seemingly anomalous features have been
pointed out by past scholars, but they are no more problematic
than those found in other apocalypses.[338] Problems of far
greater gravity arise, however, in the interpretation.
1. The interpretation of the man is given in v.25 while that
of his rising from the sea is added only at the end of the
interpretation in v.51ff.
2. Vss. 27f. state that the weaponlessness of the man and
his fiery breath are to be interpreted. Instead of the
explanation of these elements which should follow immediately,
in vss. 29-36 there is a prophecy of the woes, the gathering

of the host including a reference to the man's voice which
was mentioned in v.4 and which is not interpreted elsewhere,
and the mountain. Only in v.36 does the interpretation mentioned in v.28 finally appear.

3. The ten tribes material seems to be an originally independent and from the point of view of the vision unnecessarily
detailed pericope. V.48 shows signs of its integration into
the interpretation.[339] It is, however, clearly original in
the present form of the piece.

4. The companions of the Messiah introduced in v.52 are not
mentioned elsewhere in the vision or in the interpretation.

These considerations lead to the conclusion that the
author is here writing his own interpretation to a previously
existent allegory. This seems more likely than the interpolation theory developed by Box, for his hypothesis does not
really solve the problems of the interpretation: his
"original" displays much the same problems as the text as it
now stands. One other possibility is that of a radical
reworking of an original interpretation which is suggested by
two features. The first is the separation of the two parts
of the explanation of the man rising from the sea. The other
is the evidently double explanation of the mountain.[340] If
this is so, then in any case it must be admitted that the
original interpretation is so reworked that it is impossible
to recover it. Only the attempt to give a new interpretation
to a vision which he had before him can explain on the one

hand the contrast between the closely structured allegory and the confused interpretation and on the other the general contrast between this interpretation and the clearly formulated interpretation of the Eagle vision whose originality there is no reason to doubt.

If this theory is correct then of primary interest in our study will be the view of the Messiah given in the interpretation. It will become clear that there are differences between the views of the vision, at least as far as they can be reconstructed, and those of the interpretation and this supports the theory of the literary structure here being put forward.

e. The Man

It was observed in section b. above that the Messiah is called "man" both in the vision and the interpretation while the title "my servant" is found only in the interpretation. The name "Messiah" is not found at all. The man is identified in the interpretation as "my servant" in v.32 and "my servant" continues as the subject of action in v.37. The figure of the "man" in the interpretation is treated as a symbol used in the vision for "my servant." Thus it occurs twice of the three times in the interpretation in the expository formula which first mentions the symbol to be interpreted and then gives the interpretation[341] and the third occasion, 13:32 is also an identification. "The man" is never the subject of action in the interpretative sections.

This is significant for the understanding of this figure in the vision as a whole--"man" seems to be treated in the interpretation as a symbol just as the lion was in chapter 12, it is the symbol of the Messiah who is called "my servant."

This clearly bears on the problem of the Man in the vision. Although the representation in the vision is of a man, for the author of the interpretation this figure has to be identified as "my servant." Box, as already noted, characterizes the Messiah in this chapter as the transcendent Son of Man. Box, Volz and others have suggested, on the basis of the title, that this man is to be identified with the Urmensch.[342] In his treatment of the much more clearly defined Son of Man in 1 Enoch, Sjöberg concluded that while the figure was influenced by the Urmensch, it was not identified with him. Adam, he pointed out, takes over some of the primary features of the Urmensch, but the Son of Man is identified neither with Adam nor with the Urmensch.[343]

The actual form "Son of Man" is not found in this vision and although originally this title probably means simply "man" the consistent use of the formula "Son of Man" in the Similitudes and the New Testament clearly shows that it early became formulaic. The major feature of the figure in the vision is as warrior. The martial aspect of his function is far more emphasized in this chapter than it is in Chapters 11-12. Contrariwise the judicial aspect is completely absent from the vision and is introduced only in the interpretation.

The symbolism used to describe this figure in the vision is
ancient cosmic symbolism largely drawn from the language of
Yahweh's epiphanies, especially of his epiphanies as Divine
Warrior. The winds regularly precede epiphanies of Yahweh,[344]
the clouds come before him or are his chariot.[345] These
elements also feature in Daniel 7 and of course this may be
their direct source. Fire is also typical of Yahweh's
appearance and is one of his main instruments for the destruction of his enemies.[346] The "melting" of the enemies in v.4
is also a function of the Divine Warrior.[347] All of these
elements had been freed from the complex of Yahweh's Holy
War by the time of IV Ezra, but doubtless the cosmic aura
still surrounded them. It is therefore significant to note
that none of them except the fiery elements is mentioned in
the interpretation and there the fiery elements are interpreted in judicial terms. The mountain may also be originally
connected with cosmic war as Box points out, but the interpretation clearly thought of it as Mt. Zion.[348] Further the
figure of the mountain is obviously derived from Dan. 2:45
as the element of its unknown origin (v.7) indicates.

The cosmic features of the Son of Man in I Enoch have
been mentioned. Inasmuch as the Messiah acts as warrior in
the cosmic war, it is natural that the symbolism connected
with the Divine Warrior be transferred to him. Yet it may
be observed that one significant feature of the interpretation
is the exclusion or re-interpretation of all the cosmic

elements of the vision. The forensic aspect is less prominent here than in the Eagle vision, but the treatment of it in the interpretation is virtually identical with the description there, both rebuke and destruction are present. The element of sentencing seems to be absent although this may be the meaning of v.38.[349] In any case the righteous word as an instrument of destruction is well known.[350]

Therefore it may be that in view of the title "man" and of the cosmic imagery applied to this figure in the vision, that the Son of Man is here involved. The understanding of this man in the interpretation, however, is substantially that of the Messiah in Chapters 11-12. The cosmic aspects are played down, the judicial element is introduced, and features connected with the intermediate kingdom appear, such as the woes, the survivors in the land and so forth.

f. The Messiah of the Vision and of the Interpretation

Thus although the man is central to the vision, he does not seem to have played any major role in the interpretation. Further there are features of the Messiah as presented by the interpretation which are not hinted at in the vision. Some of these have already been noted, such as the judicial language of vss. 37ff. These legal features are only present in the interpretation of Chapter 13, while in Chapters 11-12 they are represented in both vision and interpretation and are more strongly emphasized.[351] The showing of wonders (v.50) has no parallel in the vision nor do the companions (v.52). The cosmic features of the vision, as noted in the preceding section, are suppressed in the interpretation.

Further the interpretation adds certain other elements of eschatology which are absent from the vision. The function of the Messiah after the destruction of the host is described (vss. 26,49f.). There is no hint of this in the vision which stops with the approach of the joyous multitude in v.13. The woes in vss. 29ff. are not hinted at in the vision. Further there are elements such as the heavenly Jerusalem in v.36 and the survivors (vss. 26,48) which are, at most, only implicit in it.

Now it is surely significant that it is those elements either not mentioned or only implicit in the vision which show greatest connection with the rest of the book. In the case of certain of these this may simply be because the interpretation is more detailed than the vision. In the case of others, however, this is not the explanation. Some, such as the heavenly Jerusalem, occur in Box' "interpolations" but others, such as the companions (v.52) and the showing of wonders (v.50) are in his "original" text. The common features which the interpretation has with the rest of the book have been dealt with in various sections above[352] while the special traits of the vision, the cosmic features and the outright military formulation of the Messianic figure in particular, both of which are toned down in the interpretation, are not found anywhere else in the book. Thus it may be concluded that the notion of the Messiah as formulated in the interpretation is substantially in accord with that of the Eagle vision while that of the vision, as far as can be determined is rather different. This supports the thesis proposed above that the vision represents an independent piece while the author of the book is responsible for the interpretation.

As in Vision V and opposed to 7:28ff. the activity of the Messiah commences before the beginning of his kingdom and he is active in the overthrow of evil. This is a traditional feature of the Messianic figure, one especially connected with the Messiah as warrior. The absence of the great opponent of the Messiah, the leader of the enemy host who was referred to in the "Four Empires" visions in IV Ezra 11-12 and in Ap. Bar. 39ff.[353] and who is mentioned in 5:6[354] may be imposed by the originally independent vision. The same reason could be argued for the activity of the Messiah before the end, but it seems safer to say that this is typical of the concept of the Messiah as warrior. In short, the Messiah presented by the author of Chapter 13 is largely in accord with the Messiah presented elsewhere in the book. The differences that are observed are explicable in terms of the variety of traditions which are available to the author.

5) 14:9

This is the only incidental reference to the Messiah in the book. The verse and its function in the thought of the

chapter were discussed above.[355] Here, the Messiah together
with the assumed righteous is preserved until the end of
times. The Messiah is called "my servant." No information
about his function and nature other than pre-existence, is
presented.

6) The Messiah in IV Ezra: Conclusions

In general, while few features of the Messianic figure
are found in all passages, most are found in a majority of
them and only few are completely contradictory.

The Messiah is pre-existent in all texts. Where information is provided he is expected to take care of the righteous
survivors.[356] Although his kingdom is only stated to have an
end in 7:28ff., 12:34 cf. 11:46, it is nowhere asserted to be
eternal. He is said to come with his company in 7:29, 13:52
and 14:9. This is not mentioned in Chapters 11-12 or in the
vision of Chapter 13. The term "survivors" is common to all
sources where the subject is raised except the vision of
Chapter 13. He is called "Messiah" in 7:26 and 12:32 and
"servant" in 7:29, 13:32,37,52 and 14:9. "Man" as a title
is found only in the vision of Chapter 13.

Although there is some multiplicity of tradition, the
common features of the concept of the Messiah stand out. This
is emphasized by certain other aspects of the materials.
Kingship nowhere figures in the concept of the Messiah in the
book and his rule is never described in these terms. He is
said to make the survivors rejoice (7:28ff., 12:34) or deliver

them (12:34 cf. 13:26), to defend them (13:49) or order them
(13:26). He never reigns over them. Thus the reference to
the Davidic descent of the Messiah in 12:32 should probably
be regarded as a traditional element and not at all central
to the concepts of the book.[357] Again, although the temporary
nature of the period of Messianic rule is made explicit only
in 7:28ff., 12:34 cf. 11:46, that rule is never found associated with the characteristic features of the day of judgement. It is found in the interpretation of Chapter 13, however, connected with the "survivors" and the "wonders" both
belonging to the same cycle of ideas, although there nothing
is said about its duration. Thus it seems that this should
be regarded as part of the cycle of ideas which we have called
the "Messianic kingdom" and on the whole, where this kingdom
is mentioned, it is temporary.

The paucity of information about the nature of the
Messianic age given in the two visions of Chapters 11-13 highlights their emphasis on the end of the present world order,
to the exclusion of any real interest in the nature of the
times of the Messiah. Conversely, in 7:28f. the Messianic
kingdom is only important as a stage towards the final day
of judgement which is the point of emphasis of 7:26-44. But
it is this passage which raises the main contradiction in the
views of the Messiah and the time of his appearance.[358] This
too may be a function of these differing emphases. There are
two distinct traditions, but they are not frequent enough in

occurrence for it to be established whether they stem from distinct associational patterns. The overall congruence of terminology and of the view of the Messiah is, however, adequate evidence for the substantial common authorship of these passages.[359]

The role of the Messiah in the total eschatological thought of IV Ezra is difficult to assess. He takes up the whole attention of Chapter 13 and plays a significant role in Chapters 11-12. It would seem, therefore, that he is of considerable importance. The Messiah, however, figures in few passages outside these two visions. He is mentioned only once in the first three visions with their detailed discussion of eschatological matters. This is the more significant when it is recalled that that single reference (7:28f.) is in the most comprehensive catalogue of eschatology. The reason for this may well be that the Messiah was not the answer to the questions that Ezra was asking. The final determination of the importance of the Messiah will depend on the total assessment of the thought of the book, and these questions must be borne in mind in making that evaluation.

I. The Company of the Messiah: "those who are with him" (v.28)

In 7:28 the Messiah is said to be revealed with those who are with him. 13:52 states that none can see the Messiah except those who are with him, until the fated day, while in 14:9 Ezra is told that he will be assumed to be with the Messiah and men like him until the end. "Those who are like

him" (the assumed) are referred to in 14:49. In 6:26, with
no mention made of the Messiah, it is said that the assumed
will appear after the end of this world.

The appearance of the assumed together with the Messiah
is a consistent feature of IV Ezra. A similar notion is the
concept of the Elect Ones seen with the Elect One in heaven
or before the Lord found in the Similitudes of Enoch.[360] Yet
there connection either with assumption or with the appearance
of the Messiah is absent. This concept is also connected
with the tradition of the eschatological prophet found at
Qumran[361] and elsewhere,[362] but in IV Ezra the term "prophet,"
typical of this tradition is not found. The idea of the
prophet is also related to the coming of Elijah before the
Messiah which is found in many sources,[363] but Elijah or any
one or two particular figures are not present in IV Ezra.

The closest parallel to our passage is to be found in 1
Thess. 3:13 which refers to the coming of Jesus with his holy
ones, but there the feature of assumption lacks. The concept
as it is formulated in IV Ezra, however, seems to refer to a
well known tradition. It may also draw on the angelic host
which is to accompany the Messiah.[364] Other assumption
passages in the Apocrypha and Pseudepigrapha do not show the
connection with other assumed men or with the Messiah.[365]

Thus IV Ezra presents a specific formulation of the
tradition of the company of the Messiah, identified with the
assumed and perhaps with the angelic host which is to

accompany him. This is connected with the Messiah in 7:29,
13:52 and 14:9 and it is justifiable, in this light to treat
6:25 as referring also to the Messianic kingdom. It is nevertheless significant for the evaluation of the place of
Messianism in IV Ezra's thought, that the Messiah is not
mentioned in that passage.[366]

J. The Limited Messianic Kingdom (vss. 28-30)

These verses contain, in addition to the matters discussed above, the elements of the rejoicing with the survivors,
the death of the Messiah and the end of the Messianic age.

1) Rejoicing with the Survivors

This term was discussed above. Joy is a general term
used for reward[367] and the phrase found here is typical of
the descriptions of the activity of the Messiah.[368]

2) The Death of the Messiah

The only similar tradition is Ap. Bar. 30:1. Most
sources, such as the Rabbinic materials, do not deal with
the specific fate of the Messiah. This is also true of IV
Ezra elsewhere.

3) The Limited Messianic Kingdom

Here we are presented with the idea of a limited Messianic
age to be followed by resurrection and judgement. This
touches directly on the "Two Eschatologies" theory. If IV
Ezra is to show two eschatologies, and not just varying complexes of tradition, then one of these must be the eternal
Messianic kingdom while the other is the new age. As long

as the eternity and finality of the Messianic kingdom are not
explicit in a given text, questions of context and purpose
become acute. If a passage mentions only the inception of
the Messianic kingdom and ignores everything subsequent, it
must be shown that its author is interested in describing the
succession of events before it can serve as proof that he
believed in an eternal Messianic kingdom. Conversely the
same consideration applies to descriptions of the day of
judgement which will be discussed below, and which do not
mention the Messianic kingdom.

In the discussion above the following points emerged
concerning the duration of the Messianic kingdom. This kingdom, ruled by the Messiah, is mentioned in three texts:
7:29-30, 11:46, 12:34 and 13:48. In none of these is it
described in any detail, nor is such a description the purpose of these passages. In 7:29-30 and 11:46, 12:34 the
Messianic kingdom is stated to be temporary while 13:48 is
non-committal. The Messianic kingdom is also thought to be
referred to in 6:7-10, 25-29 and 9:6-12. In none of these
is the Messiah himself mentioned, but other elements which
are typical of this complex of ideas are present. If Jacob
in 6:7-10 is indeed the eschatological kingdom of Israel,
then it must be noted that it is said to be the beginning of
the world to come, just as Esau, the Roman empire, is said
to be the end of this world. This might be an indication of
the limited nature of that kingdom.[369]

Both 6:25-29 and 9:6-12 occur in prophecies of the signs
of the end. The combination and sequence of Messianic kingdom
and judgement elements in 6:25-29 was dealt with above[370] and
a similar combination of such elements may be observed in
9:6-12. V.6 exhibits the wonders, vss. 7f. the survivors in
the land--clear Messianic kingdom ideas. Then in vss. 9-12
there is a discussion of torment after death. This is strange
to the Messianic kingdom concept found in vss. 6-8 and is
probably a reference to torment either at judgement or in
the intermediate state of the soul (cf. 7:79ff.).[371] Thus
it must be concluded that these verses do not present an
integrated Messianic kingdom eschatology. The superficial
nature of the description of the future state in both 6:25ff.
and 9:6ff. indicates that the intent of the passages is not
to provide a full and orderly recital of the eschatological
events, but just to evoke them. Therefore certain elements
of eschatology are introduced, drawn from differing cycles of
associated ideas and combined by the author in the same few
verses.

This weighs against the existence of the Messianic
kingdom and the world to come as equally valid independent
alternates in the mind of the author. Moreover, both passages
put the Messianic kingdom ideas before judgement ideas and
introduce the latter with "then" (6:26, 9:9). There may be
here a suggestion of a succession of Messianic kingdom and
judgement, but more than this cannot be said. It is clear,

however, that neither of these passages can be used as a basis for any argument about the eternity of the Messianic kingdom, either pro or con.

It was pointed out above that 4:26 and 5:41 both grew out of Messianic kingdom language. The juxtaposition of elements in the following verses, however, clearly indicates that the interest of these passages is not chronological or descriptive.[372]

The very attempt to determine the question before us highlights one of the outstanding features of IV Ezra to which there will be reason to return below. Nowhere in the book does the author give a detailed description of the Messianic kingdom similar to those found for example in Ap. Bar. 29:4-8 etc. This naturally makes the evaluation of the passages here under consideration the more difficult. From all this it is clear that the only passage in which there may be a basis for maintaining that the notion of an eternal Messianic kingdom is at home in IV Ezra is the interpretation of Chapter 13.[373] Since the description of the Messianic kingdom is sketchy and as has been shown, there is good reason to believe that this interpretation is the work of the author, the silence about the duration and nature of that kingdom should be understood as nothing more than a lack of interest by the author in that particular question at this point.

Outside IV Ezra, where the eternal Messianic kingdom is

proclaimed, it is usually specifically and emphatically eternal.[374] There are, however, some places where this is not the case. Ps. Sol. 17:23-50 does not indicate anything following the Messianic kingdom but perhaps v.39 suggests its eternity.[375] 1 Enoch 90:38 makes no mention of subsequent events. Indeed, it breaks off with the appearance of the Messiah and nothing is said of his rule. Sib. V:14-33 alone gives a detailed description of the activity of the Messiah and says nothing about the duration of his rule.

The temporary Messianic kingdom on the other hand is prevalent in the Apocalypse of Baruch.[376] Klausner points out both the distinction of the Messianic kingdom from the world to come in the Rabbinic writings and at the same time the tendency to confuse them.[377] Rabbinic literature preserves four versions of the answer to the question about the duration of the Messianic kingdom, dating from the early Tannaitic period.[378] All opinions limit the duration of this kingdom and one is that it will last for 400 years. This is attributed both to R. Eliezer[379] and R. Dosa[380] and is, of course, precisely the figure given in IV Ezra 7:28.

It may, in short, be observed that there seems to be relatively little basis for the eternal Messianic kingdom as one of the ideologies behind IV Ezra. The evidence for it within the book is far from convincing. Externally the occurrence of the idea in connection with ideologies which are not represented in IV Ezra, in the Similitudes of Enoch

and in the Testaments may be noted. Contemporary sources
such as the Apocalypse of Baruch and early Tannaitic traditions indicate the prevalence of the temporary Messianic
kingdom concept. This is not to deny the existence of this
eschatology; it is, however, to deny its occurrence in IV
Ezra. The Messianic kingdom in IV Ezra is not an independent
alternate to the new world. Below the question whether the
new world eschatology exists independently of the Messianic
kingdom will be examined.

6:25ff. and 9:6ff. should be noted as a remarkable combinations of language drawn from both the Messianic kingdom
and the new world cycles in passages whose purpose is not the
detailed exposition of the chronological order of the eschatological events. The absence of the Messiah from these passages
and from 6:7-10 emphasizes the general problem raised above
of the place of the Messiah in the scheme of events. It
suggests that the Messianic figure was not central to the
author's eschatological thought, for in these three passages
the same events are being discussed in much the same language
as in 7:29-30, 11:46, 12:34 and 13:48 where he is introduced.
While the introduction of the Messiah can well be explained
as the result of the force of traditional complexes of
thought and material employed by the author, a similar
explanation cannot be produced for his omission.

The views of most past scholars on the new world eschatology as opposed to the Messianic kingdom have been given above.

They see the limited Messianic kingdom as the author's attempt
to adjust these two views to one another, although this adjustment is not always deemed successful.[381] The historical question of whether the temporary Messianic kingdom is the result
of some combination of traditions in the time prior to the
writing of IV Ezra is beyond the realm of our interest
here.[382] Our concern is whether two such independent alternate eschatologies were employed by the author (or for that
matter by the redactor).[383] From the point of view of this
the question of the existence of the temporary Messianic
kingdom is asked and it must be answered in the negative.

K. Division of the Ages, the New Age (vss. 30-31)

These verses have been dealt with above.[384] Certain
further aspects will be dealt with in the sections to follow.

L. Resurrection (v.32)

There are five, perhaps six passages which mention
resurrection, one of which is 7:32. As with the other ideas,
it is as important to examine those contexts in which it is
introduced incidentally as those in which it plays a part in
an explicit exposition of the schema of eschatological events.

In 7:32 resurrection involves the rising of the body
from the dust and the return of the souls from their chambers.
It is subsequent to the reversion of the world to silence
and its new creation (vss. 30-31) and constitutes the prelude
to the day of judgement and the revelation of the great Judge
on his judgement seat (vss. 33ff. cf. v.37). The intimate

relation of resurrection with judgement and especially with
the reward of the righteous is supported in the other passages
dealing with this subject, cf. 4:33ff., 14:34f. 8:13 simply
refers to the fact that God is responsible for death and
resurrection.[385] The introduction of resurrection in 5:44 is
more an argumentative ploy than anything else. In none of
these passages does anything occur which suggests a contradiction of the place of resurrection in the scheme of Chapter
7.

The literary and notional function of resurrection as it
is used in the passages under consideration should be further
examined. In 4:37 and 14:35 the mention of resurrection
comes, as noted above, especially in connection with reward,
in both passages as evidence of the certainty of the recompense which is to come. In 4:37 it is part of the answer of
the angel Remiel to the souls of the righteous who are asking
when their reward will come. The reply is that they must be
patient for He will not arouse them until the measure of
times is full. It is interesting to note that resurrection
in the angelic answer (v.37) is evidently identical with
reward in the souls' question (v.35).[386]

In Chapter 14 resurrection is mentioned in the context
of a speech of encouragement which Ezra gives to the people.
The speech includes a historical prologue covering Exodus,
Sinai, the gift of the land and exile as a result of transgression (vss. 28-32). This is followed by a commandment to

observe faithfulness and a promise of reward (34), for judgement will come after death and resurrection and then the righteous and wicked will be made known. Although the introduction of resurrection, in a circumstantial clause, is incidental to the main line of thought which runs through the passage, it is present because it is connected with judgement and is naturally introduced in a context which deals with judgement.[387]

From these passages certain conclusions about the timetable and mechanics of resurrection may be drawn. This does not mean that the author has a tightly integrated picture of events and their ordering, but he doubtless has certain general ideas and was dependent on different traditions.

1) Resurrection is intimately connected with judgement and reward (4:35-37, 7:32ff., 14:35).

2) It precedes judgement (7:32ff., 14:35).

3) It involves the union of the soul which is preserved in the chambers with the body which had reverted to dust (7:32).

M. Soul and Body

1) Introduction

The third conclusion of the section on resurrection requires further attention. In 7:32 it is clear that the body is conceived of as being in the earth while the souls are in the chambers, and the reunion of these two elements is resurrection and reproduces man who is then placed before judgement. Soul and body will each be examined separately as they are understood by the author of IV Ezra.

2) The Soul

In the passage 7:75-98 are preserved interesting
materials about the fate of the soul after death, in the
intermediate state which precedes resurrection and judgement.
The main part of this material is not directly relevant to
the subject under discussion here, but in this passage occur
incidental references which are important for the understanding of the relation of soul and body.

The first point is that death is conceived of as the
separation of the soul from the body (7:78,88,101). According to 7:85,95 the souls of the righteous, but not of the
wicked, enter chambers or dwellings where they are guarded
by angels in silence.[388] The souls of the righteous with the
angel are also mentioned in 4:35. It is noteworthy that in
7:85,95 and in 4:35 only the souls of the righteous are in
chambers while 7:32 has no suggestion of any differentiation
between righteous and wicked souls in this respect. This
also seems to be the case in 7:101.

This difference may represent two traditions or two
differing interpretations of one and the same tradition, the
choice between them being conditioned by the question whether
the author's attention is centered specifically on the
righteous souls as in 7:85,95, 4:35 or on all souls in general
as in 7:32,101. That is to say that he clearly thought that
souls, between death and resurrection, were in chambers, and

in discussing the subject in general this was adequate. When
he wished to talk specifically of the righteous as opposed to
the wicked souls, then the righteous souls were in chambers
at rest, as in paradise in the future world, while the wicked
souls wandered in suffering.[389] There is, in strict logical
terms, a contradiction between the statement that all souls
are in chambers, and the statement that only righteous souls
are in chambers. This is a clear example of the problems
raised by the application of rules of consistency to a mode
of thought to which they do not apply.

In 4:41 the treasure-houses of unborn souls are mentioned,
while the wondrous divine providence which is evidenced by
the process of conception, pregnancy and birth is extolled
in 8:7-13. Here it is precisely the body and its function
which are seen as the great work of the Creator.[390] In discussing the creation of Adam (3:5) it is said that his body
was created from the dust and into it God blew the spirit of
life. It is possible that the spirit of life here is
identical with the soul elsewhere in the book. It is, however, most likely that the question of the relation of the
two did not occur to the author, for there is no indication
of its having been raised in his mind. Rather should the
formulation in this verse be seen as reflecting the Biblical
phrase describing the creation of man, while the passages
dealing with the souls draw on other cycles of ideas and
language.

3) <u>The Body</u>

The body is created from the earth (3:4) or the dust
(7:62) and it returns to the dust. The profound feeling of
the closeness of man to the earth is expressed in the imagery
and language of maternity and birth. The earth is the
mother's womb which brings forth man. This use, which may be
observed most clearly in Ezra's answer to the mourning woman
in 10:14, is a most prominent feature of the style of IV
Ezra.[391] It provided a bridge between two independent traditions which are combined by the author of IV Ezra in a novel
and striking fashion.

The tradition of the growing deterioration of the earth
as a result of the sins of men is well known and will be
examined in detail below. Quite independently of it there
existed a tradition of the deterioration of human bodily
prowess. This latter tradition is found in Jubilees, Philo
and Rabbinic literature. Stature, according to the Midrashic
sources, is reduced by sin and will return at the time of the
Messiah to its original proportions.[392] In the passage 5:50ff.
the angel points out (51-53) that the children of a woman's
youth are stronger than those of her old age. He continues:

> 54. Therefore you also consider how you are lesser in
> stature than those who were before you, 55. and those
> who follow you (will be likewise less) than you, for
> creation is growing old and is beyond the strength of
> youth.

Here these two traditions are combined with a sort of causal
relation between them and the catalyst and matrix which

enables this combination to be made is the language of maternity and birth used to describe the relation of man to the earth.

Not only the body, but even the mind[393] springs from the dust (7:62), and the body, the "corruptible vessel" (7:88) returns to the dust, from which in the end it is once again resurrected (8:13). Adam was created from the dust (7:116) as are his descendants. Above, the wondrous divine providence which is exhibited in the process of physical reproduction was noted. The fact that the body dies and that death, as will be seen below, is a highly negative concept for IV Ezra, does not result in a negative evaluation of the body. It is of note that in 5:50ff., the deterioration of the body is said to be a result of the aging of the earth, and not even as in Rabbinic literature, of contact with evil. The attitude to the whole material earth, which will be discussed in a following section, will be found to support the view that there is no negative moral evaluation of the material body, qua material. This is important for the understanding of the eschatology of the book.

N. The Earth and the World

The apparent contradiction between the arousal of a new world or age in 7:31 and the earth, subsequently to this, giving up the bodies which had, if one is to be consistent, been buried in the old world highlights the question of the meaning and implications of this terminology in the book. It

is most important to try to evaluate the meaning of this term
"world" so that it may be clear what Ezra means when he talks
of its passing away and so forth.

The central terms which will occupy us will be those
translated "earth," "world" and "age." It is necessary to
isolate the terminology for these general ideas in IV Ezra,
to see whether the Greek and ultimately the Hebrew originals
can be discovered. Only in this fashion can the real force
of these concepts in the mind of the author be established.
The implications of the words used in the extant versions,
and their various translations can only give an approximate
idea of the meaning of the original. It is particularly
pressing to discover the exact sense of the original, if this
proves feasible, since it is precisely in the realm denomin-
ated by this terminology that great confusions and disagree-
ments arise in the interpretation of the thought of the book.

The procedure employed is as follows. First the words
for these ideas were examined in three versions of IV Ezra,
Latin, Syriac, and Armenian. Latin and Syriac were chosen
because they are closer to one another than any other two
versions and this makes them good witnesses to each other.
Armenian was chosen because it is distant from the tradition
represented by the other two versions and thus provides a
necessary control. The distribution of words in these three
texts was examined to see whether there seemed to be any
consistent pattern. If such a pattern emerged it would be

possible to posit that the versions were employing more or less consistent translations for given Greek words.

Then the use of the terminology isolated in the versions was examined in the Latin, Syriac and Armenian Bibles. If a similar pattern was evident, then by consulting the LXX, the Greek originals for the terminology of the biblical versions, and thus most probably of the versions of IV Ezra could be discovered, this providing that the distribution patterns in Greek fitted those in the daughter versions. Since this latter part of the study was limited to Biblical books extant in Hebrew, it was then possible to investigate the question of the regularity of the Greek translations of Hebrew words, and to find out which Hebrew words most probably lay behind the terminology of the versions of IV Ezra. At this point the original meaning of IV Ezra's terminology could be established through Hebrew lexicographical considerations.

1

The Terminology of the Versions

of IV Ezra

The purpose of this section of the study is to try to establish whether there is enough agreement between the different translations of the lost Greek version of IV Ezra to establish a generally consistent pattern of translations.

A. Latin

This version, which is extant in the best critical text,

was chosen as a starting point. The terms saeculum, terra, orbis, and less crucially regio and mundus were found to be central to the terminology of the Latin. A survey of IV Ezra yielded the following frequency pattern:

Total occurrences:

Terra	56
Saeculum	51
Regio	11
Orbis	7
Mundus	1

Only those cases which had parallels in Syriac, Armenian or both were given further consideration.

Occurrences of Latin paralleled in Syriac and/or Armenian:

	Latin	Syriac	Armenian
Terra	56	52	34
Saeculum	51	50	20
Regio	11	9[394]	4
Orbis	7	7	4

B. Syriac

In Syriac the following situation prevails:

a) Every occurrence of saeculum in Latin was represented by the word ^{c}lm in definite, indefinite or suffixed form.[395]

b) Every occurrence of the word orbis was paralleled by the word tbyl.

c) 48 of 51 cases of terra were paralleled by 'r^c'.

d) 6 of 9 cases of regio revealed Syriac 'tr', three were 'r^c'.

From this it may be concluded tentatively that saeculum and
^{c}lm, orbis and tbyl, terra and 'r^c' and probably regio and
'tr' translate common Greek originals.[396]

C. Armenian

The Armenian gave the following results:

a) Every existing parallel to terra was երկիր.

b) Three of four existing parallels of orbis were երկիր.

c) Three of four existing parallels of regio were երկիր.

D. Saeculum and its Parallels

With saeculum, the most interesting and the most difficult of these terms, the situation is more complex and is
set forth in more detail:

a) Where Latin has saeculum = Syr. ^{c}lm (indef.) Arm. has (2
cases) յաւիտեան.

b) Where Latin has saeculum = Syr. ^{c}lm + suffix Arm. has (1
case) երկիր.

c) Where Latin has saeculum = Syr. ^{c}lm' (def.) Arm. has (13)
աշխարհ.

d) Where Latin has saeculum = Syr. ^{c}lm' (def.) Arm. has (4)
կեանք.

Syriac, like later Aramaic, differentiates in meaning
^{c}lm - "eternity" from ^{c}lm' or ^{c}lm + suffix = "world-Age,"
"time," "world," "people of the world."[397] Further, this
differentiation is precisely that which may be observed to
exist between cases a) and b), c), d) in Armenian. Thus it
is justifiable to conclude that the translators of the Syriac

and Armenian versions were conscious of the different meanings of these two uses. Since, however, Latin and Syriac
are both quite consistent in their use of the word <u>saeculum</u>
and the root ^{c}lm it can equally be concluded that they are
drawing on a text using one word in both these senses. This
interesting situation will be discussed further below.

E. Conclusions to Section 1

Thus it may be concluded that

1. <u>terra</u> = ʹr^{c}ʹ = երկիր.

2. <u>orbis</u> = <u>tbyl</u> = երկիր.

3. <u>saeculum</u> = rt. ^{c}lm = աշխարհ, կեանք, յաւիտեան.

4. <u>regio</u> = ʹtrʹ = երկիր, աշխարհ.

and that each of these complexes translates a common Greek
word.

F. Tables for Section 1

In these tables the relationship between the various
translation formulae is set out in detail.

	terra	saeculum	orbis	mundus	regio	TOTALS
ܐܪܥܐ	48				3	51
ܚܕܪ̈ܝ	1					1
ܬܒܠ	3	43		1		47
suffix + ܬܒܠ		4				4
ܥܠܡܐ		3				3
ܐܬܪܐ					6	6
ܠܥܠ			7			7
TOTALS	52	50	7	1	9	119

TABLE 1

Showing the relationship between and the frequency of
the Latin and Syriac terminology in the versions of
IV Ezra.

	terra	saeculum	orbis	mundus	regio	TOTALS
երկիր	34	1	3		3	41
կեանք		4				4
աշխարհ		13	1		1	15
յաւիտեան		2				2
TOTAL	34	20	4	0	4	62

TABLE 2

Showing the relationship between and the frequency of
the Latin and Armenian terminology in the versions of
IV Ezra.

	երկիր	կեանք	աշխարհ	յաւիտեան	TOTALS
terra – ܐܪܥܐ	33				33
terra – ܐܪܥܐ	1				1
terra – ܐܪܥܐ					0
saeculum – ܥܠܡܐ		4	13		17
saeculum – suff + ܥܠܡܐ	1				1
saeculum – ܥܠܡ				2	2
orbis – ܬܒܝܠ ܠ	3		1		4
mundus – ܥܠܡܐ					0
regio – ܐܬܪܐ	1				1
regio – ܐܬܪܘܬܐ	2		1		3
TOTALS	41	4	15	2	62

TABLE 3

Showing the relationship between and
the frequency of the Latin, Syriac
and Armenian terminology of IV Ezra.

2

The Terminology in the Latin,
Syriac and Armenian Bibles, in the Septuagint
and in the Hebrew Bible

It has been established that certain terms have common
distribution patterns in the Latin, Syriac and Armenian texts
of IV Ezra. The occurrence of these words will be examined
in the Syriac, Armenian and Latin versions of the Bible. If
it is clear that the same sort of correspondence exists as in
the IV Ezra texts, the Greek, and eventually the Hebrew Bibles
will be used to try to establish the originals which the terms
of the secondary versions are translating.

A. Terra, 'r^c' and երկիր

Since these words are far too frequent for an exhaustive
examination to be either practical or more convincing than a
partial study, the first six chapters of the book of Genesis
were taken as a test sample. The Old Latin (designated henceforth O.L.) was used as well as the Vulgate, although it
became evident in the course of the examination that, except
in instances where there is a divergence of reading between
M.T. and LXX, they showed almost no significant differences
in their treatment of the terms examined. The Peshitta and
Armenian were used in standard texts.

The examination showed that these terms are related to
one another in these versions in the same fashion as they are
in IV Ezra. In detail, the words coincided in the sections
of the four versions examined a total of 58 times. They were

157

also found in three of the four versions, with the fourth
version omitting an additional three times.[398] They occurred
three times in two versions with two omitting.[399] Thus there
is a total of 64 occasions in which there is agreement of the
extant texts in the treatment of these terms.

Furthermore there are a number of cases in which one
version alone gives a word varying from the normative readings noted above. The main version preserving such readings
is the Peshitta. It reads ddbr' parallel to terra and երկիր
in two cases,[400] and d'dmt' once.[401] In each of these cases
the other three versions are unanimous. The few remaining
cases where one or two versions have one of these words and
the others vary will be discussed below. Most are explicable
on textual grounds.

The above results are adequate, however, to establish
the fact that the same close relationship and the same
pattern of occurrence exists between these words in the
secondary versions of the Bible as was observed in the texts
of IV Ezra.

B. γῆ, ארץ and אדמה

An examination of the Septuagint reveals that in every
case quoted above except Gen. 1:25^2, which is not extant in
the LXX, these words translate Greek γῆ.

In addition to the above 66 cases where γῆ occurs with
parallels in two, three or four versions, there are three
cases in which γῆ occurs with somewhat different parallels.

These are Gen. 2:19 and 3:19 (twice). In 2:19 the text deals
with the creation of beasts from the earth and 3:19 is "for
you are dust and to dust you shall return." In 2:19 one O.L.
tradition and Vulgate read _humo_, while another O.L. text and
Syriac read _terra_ and 'r^c' respectively. In 3:19 the words
for _dust_ are read in all versions except the LXX and one O.L.
tradition. These three cases do not throw any doubt on the
conclusions drawn above. It may well be that the versions
in 3:19 reflect a variant Greek tradition, perhaps a result
of later revision of the Old Greek back to the Hebrew; see,
however, the discussion on p.174f. below.

The next step in this investigation, then, is to examine
the Hebrew words of which γῆ may be a translation. M.T. is
not extant for three of the cases mentioned above, exactly
those which are witnessed by the combination LXX + O.L. +
Armenian.[402] On the other hand it does have a reading in
1:25^2 which is not exhibited by the LXX although the secondary
versions read _terra_, 'r^c' and երկիր. The word translated by
Greek γῆ is Hebrew ארץ in 42 instances. To this may be added
1:25^2 for which a Greek γῆ should most probably be reconstructed, giving a total of 43 occasions. Further γῆ is a
translation of Hebrew אדמה 18 times and of Hebrew שדה 3 times.
One of this latter group is only in a variant tradition of
the LXX.[403] In short ארץ and אדמה are translated by no other
word than γῆ in the chapters examined.

The versions generally render this term in a consistent

fashion, but there are certain variations which were noted
above. הארץ is rendered by dbr' in the Syriac of 1:30[1], השדה
in the same way in 3:14 and אדמה as 'dmt' in 2:7. Vulgate
and one O.L. tradition render אדמה as humo in 2:19.

The word שדה is treated in a rather ambiguous fashion.
Of the 8 occasions on which it is found in Gen. 1-6 the translations of one (4:8) show no relationship, except in the O.L.
(agro), to any of the translations of שדה in the other
instances. As noted above, it is rendered γῆ by the LXX
three times (one only in cursives).[404] In the other places
it is rendered by ἀγρός.[405] In the secondary versions the
situation is more complex. Where it is rendered γῆ by the
LXX, the Latin versions have terra, Syriac ddbr' and Armenian
երկիր. In 2:20 where γῆ is only the secondary reading of the
LXX, the same situation exists in the versions as in 2:19
where the LXX has ἀγροῦ. In both cases Vulgate and one O.L.
tradition read terra, and another O.L. tradition, Syriac and
Armenian have agri, ddbr' and երկիր respectively. In the
other three instances of LXX ἀγρός, O.L. has agri, Syriac
ḥql', Armenian վայրի, but variation may be observed in the
Vulgate which translates differently on each occasion--2:5[1]
agri, 2:5[2] regio and 3:18 terrae.

The Hebrew עפר occurs three times in the section here
examined. Twice (3:19) it is translated by Greek γῆ, O.L.
(one text) terra; O.L. (other text), Vulgate pulvis, Syriac
ᶜpr', Armenian հող. In the third case (2:7) it is only

translated by words for dust, LXX χοός, Vulgate, O.L. humus,
Syriac ^cpr', Armenian ᏚᎥᎥ.

C. Methodological Note

It should be noted that in sections A and B above, the
basis of study has been the ancient versions of the Old Testament. Certain problems of the interrelation of these versions,
and of their complexity should be mentioned. The Vulgate is
a translation from the Hebrew. However, as has been noted
above, Jerome draws on a vocabulary stock similar to that
used by the translators of the Old Latin versions. Indeed
his first attempts at translation were revisions of Old Latin,
and it seems that in his later work he used the language
familiar to him from that version. The Old Latin itself is
not a single translation, but rather a series of different
translations. This, of course, makes the evidence from it
the more impressive, for the consistency of usage seems thus
to run through Latin Christian translations. Little work has
been done on the translation techniques of the Armenian or
Syriac. Of the Armenian it is known that, on the whole, it
is remarkably true to its Greek original.

The Greek translations of the Bible present a complicated
series of revisions or recensions of an Old Greek version to
a developing Hebrew text or texts. Again in spite of this,
the singular regularity of the Greek equivalents examined
strengthens the view that the technique used here does establish the regular translation equivalation in these versions.

A historical assessment of the versions might help clear up
variations of grammatical usage, but in the terms examined
the statistical correspondence between the versions is such
that no serious doubt can be thrown on the fact that they
were the normative translations of the Hebrew words mentioned.
Appreciation of the situation of the versions may help clear
up some of the variations and exceptional readings, but the
case is made here precisely on the basis of those readings
which are not exceptional.

D. Conclusions from Sections A and B

From the evidence assembled above the following conclusions may be drawn:

1) Latin <u>terra</u> + Syriac '<u>r</u>^c' + Armenian երկիր translate
Greek γῆ.

2) Latin <u>terra</u> + Syriac '<u>r</u>^c' + Armenian երկիր + Greek γῆ
translate Hebrew ארץ or somewhat less frequently אדמה.

3) Latin <u>terra</u> + Greek γῆ + Armenian երկիր + Syriac <u>dbr'</u> do
not necessarily indicate Hebrew שדה (cf. 1:30[1]) but   may do
so (cf. 3:1, 14).

4) Greek γῆ does not translate ^c<u>pr</u> of the Hebrew unless the
other versions indicate that this is the case.

It should be noted that the only occasion on which the Armenian
varies significantly from extant Greek traditions is in its
rendering of 3:19.[406]   The interesting combination of V.L. +
Armenian + Greek against Vulgate + Peshitta + M.T. is discussed below

E. Tables

VULGATE \ OLD LATIN	terra	ager	limus	humus	pulvis	campus	TOTALS
terra	62	3					65
ager		1				1	2
regio		1					1
limus			1				1
humus	1			1			2
pulvis	2				2		4
TOTALS	65	5	1	1	2	1	75

TABLE   4

Illustrating the use of terminology in the Old
Latin and Vulgate versions of Gen. 1-6. This
table shows the versions only where both of them
are extant together. Alternate traditions of
the Old Latin have been counted as separate
readings.

VULGATE – OLD LATIN	SYRIAC ܐܪܥܐ	ܐܦܪ	ܚܩܠ	ܥܦܪ	ܐܕܡܬܐ	TOTAL
V.-O.L. terra	55	4			1	60
V.-O.L. ager			1			1
V. terra-O.L. ager		2	1			3
V. ager-O.L. campus						0
V. regio-O.L. ager			1			1
V.-O.L. limus				1		1
V.-O.L. humus	1					1
V. humus-O.L. terra	1					1
V.-O.L. pulvis				2		2
V. pulvis-O.L. terra				2		2
TOTAL	57	6	3	5	1	72

TABLE   5

Showing the terminology of Vulgate, Old Latin
and Syriac versions of Gen. 1-6. Readings are
shown only when all three versions are extant.
Alternate traditions of the Old Latin are
treated as separate readings.

a.

	Greek γῆ	Vulgate terra	Old Latin terra	Syriac	Syriac	Armenian երկիր	TOTAL Hebrew
ארץ	42	42	43	42	1	44	44
TOTALS of each term	67	62	70	60	5	66	

b.

	Greek γῆ	Vulgate terra	Vulgate humus	Old Latin terra	Old Latin humus (one tradition)	Syriac	Syriac	Armenian երկիր	TOTAL Hebrew
אדמה	18	15	1	18	1	17	1	17	18
TOTALS of each term	67	62	1	70	1	60	1	66	

TABLES 6 a. and b.

Illustrating the Hebrew words ארץ and אדמה and their
rendering in the various versions of Gen. 1-6.
Divergences in the totals are explained either by
omissions of certain cases or by special readings
discussed in the text.

F. Saeculum and its Syriac and Armenian Parallels

In this case rather than taking a sample of text, the word saeculum was examined as it occurs in the Vulgate[407] and a total of 104 cases were found.[408] The Peshitta and the Armenian were examined in the same passages and the following observations were made:

1) In the Peshitta 99 parallels were found.[409] In 97 of these the parallels were formed from the word ^clm in one form or another. The exceptions were Syriac Ps. 48:14, 102:28. Syr. Ps. 74:12 will be discussed in detail below.

2) Armenian translates 103 of the 104 cases in the Vulgate.[410] Of these 98 are forms of the word յաւիտեան (eternity), three of աշխարհ (Ps. 72:12, 80:16, Isa. 9:6) and one կեանք (Ps. 89:8). Once inexplicably, it offers its regular translation of Hebrew דור ודור, յազգէ մինչեւ յազգ (Ps. 17:51).

The Vulgate uses the word in a limited number of grammatical contexts which will be of interest to us, and they are:

1) Saeculum, singular or plural, including repetitive uses such as saeculum saeculi, saecula saeculorum, with the prepositions usque in, in, a, ante: 90 uses

2) The phrases semita saeculi, semitae saeculorum: 2 uses

3) The phrase dies saeculi: 3 uses

4) Other uses in the genitive with adjectival force:[411]   4 uses

5) Use in the genitive case with temporal force: 1 use

6) Use in accusative case (Ps. 89:8 (90:8)):   1 use

7) Other:[412]   <u>3 uses</u>
                104 uses

The distribution of uses is also of some interest. The vast majority of occurrences are in Psalms (74) followed by Isaiah (12), Jeremiah (6) and Daniel (5). The other uses are distributed between Genesis (1), Exodus (1), II Chronicles (1), Job (1), Habakkuk (1) and Malachi (1). The text of Psalms used is the Gallic Psalter--Jerome's second revision, but still based on the LXX.[413] Further, of all the uses in Psalms, only two occur without a preposition (Ps. 144 (145):13, 89 (90):8). Of those uses which are unique, or occur few times, the majority are found in Isaiah.

The situation in the Syriac text is here set out:

1) Uses of ^{c}lm indefinite, in singular or plural, including repetitive expressions: 94 uses

2) Uses of ^{c}lm' (definite):[414]   <u>4 uses</u>
                98 uses

Jenni's distinction of the definite and indefinite uses of the Syriac word, enables the fixing of a temporal meaning for ^{c}lm (indefinite).[415] The other cases will be discussed in detail below.

The Armenian is of considerable interest. As noted above the vast majority of cases read յաւիտեան - "eternal," "eternity." It is instructive to set out the Armenian cases which read աշխարհ - "world" or կեանք - "life" with their Syriac and Latin parallels.

Armenian		Syriac		Latin
Ps. 72:12 աշխարհի	Ps. 73:11 ܠܥܠܡ	Ps. 72:12	in saeculo
Ps. 80:16 յաշխարհի	Ps. 81:15 ܠܥܠܡ	Ps. 80:16	in saeculo
Isa. 9:6 աշխարհի	ܥܠܡܐ		saeculi
Ps. 89:8 զկեանս	Ps. 90:8 ܥܠܡܢ·	Ps. 89:8	saeculum nostrum

It will be noted that in the first and third cases it is in
precisely those instances where the Syriac has ᶜlm' (world)
that Armenian employs the word աշխարհ. Further if the meaning "span of time" for ᶜlm had developed, then the reading
կեանք - "life," "lifetime" as used as the equivalent of
saeculum nostrum in the fourth instance is highly appropriate.

G. The Greek and Hebrew

A check of the readings of the Greek Bible in these
places shows that in 96 places the above series is represented
by some form of the word αἰών and in a further six cases by
the forms of the related adjective αἰώνιος. Of the two
omissions, one is found in the Theodotion text of Daniel,
which is closer to the Massoretic tradition (Dn. 2:20^2), and
one is problematic (Hab. 3:6). Further the reading in Isa.
9:5 (9:6) is represented only in some uncial traditions
(A.S^s, Luc.) and is under the asterisk in some Hexaplaric
MSS.[416] This suppletory reading is, however, αἰῶνος.

Of those cases in which αἰώνιος occurs, five are "adjectival genitive" uses of the Latin.[417] The remaining occurrence
is Isa. 61:4.

This leads to the conclusion that the combination of
Latin <u>saeculum</u> + Syriac ^clm (^clm') + Armenian յաւիտեան, աշխարհ ‹
and perhaps կեանք represent αἰών or some derivative in the
Greek. Further it may be concluded that the "adjectival
genitive" use in Latin may represent αἰώνιος, especially if
it is paralleled by the adjectival form յաւիտենական in
Armenian, as is the case here in Job 22:15 and Isa. 60:15.[418]

When the Hebrew is examined for these same cases a
quite consistent picture appears. In all these instances
the Greek αἰων, αἰώνιος translates only Hebrew עולם or עד .
The only outright exception to this is in Ps. 74:12 where
Hebrew מקדם is translated by LXX πρὸ αἰῶνος. This is the
only case in which this expression was found in the materials
examined. Latin and Armenian expressions which are similarly
unique among those examined were also encountered as translations in this verse, they read <u>ante saecula</u> and յառաջ քան
յաւիտեանս respectively. Syriac reads (exactly as Hebrew)
<u>mn qdym</u>. In two cases LXX reads the consonantal text of the
Hebrew otherwise than the Massoretic tradition. Thus Ps.
84:5 (LXX 83:5) M.T. reads עוד, LXX and versions ἀπὸ τὸν
αἰῶνα τοῦ αἰωνος reading עד, Ps. 89:8 (M.T. 90:8) M.T. has
עֲלֻמֵנוּ (correctly), LXX + versions ὁ αἰὼν ἡμῶν reading עלמנו.
In Ps. 102:28 (LXX 101:29) inexplicably M.T. + Syriac read
לפניך while LXX + Vulgate + Armenian have εἰς τὸν αἰῶνα.[419]

In 97 of the total cases examined there is a sure Hebrew
alongside a sure Greek. The reading of Ps. 84:5 discussed

above cannot be considered, for it is not certain enough.
The reconstruction of the reading of Ps. 89:8 (M.T. 90:8)
is definite enough, however, to justify using it for evidence
of the Greek translator's treatment of the word עולמנו. This
reading is of especial interest since no affixed forms occur
among the examples taken, and further the word seems to have
been understood by the secondary versions in a sense not
regularly employed in the Bible. The reading of Ps. 102:28
is of interest because it shows the affinity of the Gallic
Psalter which is closer to LXX in this case than to M.T.
Since twelve of the phrases considered above as single units
are repetitive, the number of actual occurrence of the words
עולם and עד is 110. It is necessary, nevertheless, to consider these double phrases as idiomatic unities. Of the 95
examples found 5 are in the Aramaic section of Daniel and
are not included in the following table. They are Dn. 2:20
(twice), 6:27, 7:18 (twice).

	ἀπ᾽ αἰῶνος	ἀπὸ τοῦ αἰῶνος	εἰς αἰῶνα	εἰς τὸν αἰῶνα	εἰς τοὺς αἰῶνας	εἰς τὸν αἰῶνα	εἰς τὸν αἰῶνα τοῦ αἰῶνος	ἕως αἰῶνος	εἰς τὸν αἰῶνα χρόνον	ἕως τοῦ αἰῶνος	αἰώνιος	αἰῶνα	αἰῶνος ἐξ	ἐν τοῖς αἰῶσιν	TOTALS
מעולם	3	4													7
למן עולם	1												1		2
עד עולם								3		6					9
עד העולם										1					1
לעולם			1	25	1	1	1		1						30
עולם		1		1							6	3*			11
עולמים					1							2*			3
לעולמים														1	1
עולמנו												1**			1
עד יעד						1	2			1					4
לעד						4	6								10
ועד							4								4
לעולם ועד						1	3								4
עולם ועד					1	1	2								4
ועד עולם							1								1
עד עולמי עד											1				1
TOTALS	4	5	1	26	3	8	19	3	1	9	6	6	1	1	93

* Genitive case   ** Nominative case

TABLE   7

Illustrating the use of the terminology for <u>saeculum</u> in the
Greek and Hebrew Bibles.

H. Conclusions

From the above chart it is clear that:

1) עולם / עולמים on its own or with a preposition is translated by αἰῶν (once):   57 times

2) עולם with a preposition is translated by
αἰῶν αἰῶνος: 2

3) עולם on its own is translated by αἰώνιος: 6

4) עד on its own or with a preposition is trans-
lated by αἰῶν αἰῶνος: 17

5) עד on its own or with a preposition is trans-
lated by αἰῶν: 1

6) Combinations of עד and עולם are translated
by αἰῶν: 2

7) Combinations of עד and עולם are translated
by αἰῶν αἰῶνος: 8

From this it may be concluded that αἰῶν (once) is a regular
translation of עולם; αἰώνιος a regular translation of עולם
with adjectival force and αἰων αἰῶνος of עד and of combinations of עד and עולם.

Thus there remains no doubt that the combination of
saeculum + ᶜlm + յաւիտեան in the daughter versions of the
Old Testament presupposes Greek αἰῶν, and that these with
Greek αἰῶν reflect Hebrew עולם and עד according to the considerations set out above.

I. Orbis, tbyl etc.

The word orbis was checked in a number of sample cases

following the same procedure employed in the previous sections. In all cases of the sample where the Vulgate reads
<u>orbis</u> and LXX has οἰκουμένη Syriac reads ܐܪܥ or ܬܒܝܠ.[420]
Armenian in these cases has either տիեզերք (universe) or
աշխարհ (world).[421] In all these cases Hebrew was תבל . A
check of תבל then showed that it is translated by οἰκουμένη
in the LXX 24 times in instances in which the LXX and M.T.
are both extant. In all of these Latin reads <u>orbis</u>. תבל is
translated 5 times by γῆ in four of which Latin reads <u>orbis</u>.[422]
συμπᾶσα and τῆς ὑπ'οὐρανῶν are found once each and are
rendered by Latin <u>orbis</u>, Syriac ܬܒܝܠ. Armenian translates
the first by երկիր and the second is a literal translation
of Greek.[423]

In Gen. 41:45, 47:13 Latin alone reads <u>orbis</u>, Hebrew has
ארץ Greek γῆ, Syriac 'rᶜ' etc. Certain cases occur such as
I Sam. 2:8, Jer. 51:15, Job 34:13 where M.T., Vulgate and
Syriac read תבל, <u>orbis</u> and ܐܪܥ respectively and no reading occurs in the LXX. In Job 18:18 M.T. + Syriac read
while Vulgate + LXX omit. In every case where M.T. has תבל,
LXX has συμπᾶσα, τῆς ὑπ'οὐρανῶν, οἰκουμένη Latin has <u>orbis</u>
and Syriac ܬܒܝܠ or ܐܪܥ. Thus it may be concluded that
any of these combinations represents an original תבל . Vulgate
has <u>orbis</u> idiomatically in a number of verses where this
usage is reflected in neither LXX nor versions.[424]

3

While it seems that in general the identification of the
terms in IV Ezra is thus established, there are some significant differences, especially in the use of the ^cōlām- αἰών -
saeculum-^clm' complex which must be assessed. The word ^cōlām
was discussed in some detail as it occurs in Biblical and
extra-Biblical sources by E. Jenni. His major conclusions
are that in Biblical Hebrew, except for Qoh. 1:10 and 3:11,
it is not used as an independent noun, but always adverbially
or with a preposition, and further that in all instances in
Biblical Hebrew except those two mentioned above it means
"most distant time" (past or future). In these two latter
instances it means "age" or "time."[425]

He also established "most distant time" as the primary
meaning of the word in extra-Biblical North West Semitic
documents. He sees a development, perhaps under the influence
of Greek αἰών which is found as the translation of this word
not only in the Greek Bible, but also in Palmyrene bi-lingual
inscriptions[426]--to a meaning "period of time" becoming "age,"
"time" and eventually "world." The earliest occurrence of
עולם meaning "world" he discovers in a Palmyrene inscription
of the year 134 C.E. In all later dialects of Aramaic there
is a distinction between the absolute form meaning "eternity,"
"most distant time" and the definite meaning "world." In
this connection it is necessary carefully to evaluate the
instances of this word in IV Ezra and try to discern which

of these meanings may be found there.

As was noticed by Jenni, one of the characteristics of
the Biblical Hebrew use of the word is the fact that it is
not used as an independent noun, but is generally employed
in an adverbial sense, most often with a preposition. In the
sample readings examined in the Bible this was, of course,
found to be precisely the case. In the Greek Bible the only
case of the word in the nominative case was the misreading
in Ps. 90:8 (αἰῶν ἡμῶν).

In the Syriac for these examples it was observed that 90
of the cases had the indefinite form while only 4 had the
definite. This more or less reflects the situation in the
Hebrew and Greek, but the four examples of the definite use
should be examined more closely. Of these, Isa. 9:5 is a
translation of עַד in a verse which caused difficulties in all
the versions and is too problematic to serve as more than
supporting evidence in this discussion. Two of the remaining
examples, Job 22:15 and Isa. 63:9 are possessive in form and
neither of them is one of the recurring adverbial or adjectival phrases. Beyond this, however, it is difficult to pin-
point any internal reason for the Syriac reading in these
cases. Ps. 73:11 has in common with Job 22:15 that the
Hebrew עוֹלָם is a nomen rectum used with adjectival force.

A number of the readings mentioned above suggest that
Peshitta is dependent on a tradition close to the Massoretic
Hebrew. In Gen. 1:12^2, 1:14., 1:28^2 readings were found to

be common to LXX + O.L. + Armenian against the evidence of
M.T. + Vulg. + Peshitta. In Ps. 102:28 Syriac renders q̱dmyk
where M.T. has lpnyk while the LXX, Gallic Psalter and
Armenian all read εἰς τὸν αἰῶνα and its regular parallels.
In Job 18:18 M.T. + Syriac read tbl while Vulgate and LXX
omit. Even where LXX translates M.T. tbl as γῆ (e.g. Isa.
26:9), Syriac renders ܐܪܥܐ although in 42 of the 44 test
cases of 'rṣ examined it translates ܐܪܥ where the LXX renders
γῆ. Of the two exceptions, one is ܬܒܪ! and one lacks. ܐܪܥܐ
is never found.

Thus it might be suggested, on the basis of this evidence
alone, that Syriac is directly familiar with the Hebrew
expressions and is interpreting עולם in them in the sense of
world. It is, therefore, of no little interest to observe
that it is precisely in Ps. 73:11, treated by LXX as it
treats the commonest phrase of them all (לעולם-25 occurrences),
that Armenian, which is usually close to LXX, translates
աշխարհ i.e. "world." In this case, as evidently in Isa.
9:5 (6) (cf. p.166f.), a common tradition of interpretation
is known to Armenian and Syriac. It is surely more than mere
co-incidence that two of the four exceptional readings of
each Armenian and Syriac are identical. This indicates that,
whether there is a common tradition of interpretation of the
LXX known to both Armenian and Syriac, or whether Armenian
is influenced by Syriac, the possibility, indeed the existence
of at least two distinct meanings of Hebrew עולם as "eternity"

or "world" was clearly known to the Syriac and Armenian translators. These were apprehended by the versions either directly, or through its LXX rendering αἰών and are reflected in their translations.

When the uses of ܥܠܡ in the Syriac of IV Ezra are examined, a picture very different to the Peshitta emerges. In the Peshitta four definite uses were observed as against 90 indefinite. In IV Ezra on the other hand, 43 occasions were observed with ܥܠܡܐ (definite), and only three indefinite were found, in addition to four suffixed forms. Further, the three indefinite forms which do occur are all with preposi- tions and clearly show the sense "most distant time"-- ܠܥܠܡ twice (8:20, 9:31) and ܥܕ ܥܠܡ (9:8). Likewise, the Armenian reads overwhelmingly յաւիտեան in the Bible (98 of 103 cases). In IV Ezra, however, յաւիտեան occurs only twice, in 8:20 and 9:8, precisely two of the three cases in which Syriac has the indefinite form ܥܠܡ. Armenian has no reading in 9:31.

Thus an understanding of the meanings of this semantic complex common to Syriac and Armenian, such as has already been remarked to exist in the Armenian and Syriac Biblical translations, seems to be present in IV Ezra, although the frequency of occurrence of these various uses in IV Ezra is quite different to that observed in the Bible. The change reflected by the versions in their usage is consonant with the sort of development outlined by Jenni. This conclusion is also borne out by the Latin usage. Of the three cases of

the status absolutus in Syriac, the meaning of a saeculo in
9:8 is clearly "of old" (two Latin MSS, M and N, even read
ab initio). Similarly in 9:31 the sense is "for ever"--Latin
per saeculum. 8:20 reads in Latin Domine qui inhabitas
saeculum. Syriac reads ܥܠܡ, Armenian յաւիտեան, Ethiopic
"for ever," la^c̄alam. Perhaps the Syriac, Ethiopic and
Armenian reflect an original Hebrew יושב (ל)עולם and Latin
(?+Ar²) reads this as "dwelling in the saeculum (world?),"
while the Syriac, Ethiopic and Armenian seem to preserve the
original force of the text. The fact that Latin could read
in this fashion is a further indication of the change of
meaning of this word.

The many uses of saeculum in the nominative, accusative
and genitive cases further reflect its new role as an independent substantive. Instances of saeculum with prepositions,
but without that adverbial, temporal meaning which the
identical grammatical form has in the Bible strengthen this
case even more. Thus 13:20 speaks of those who pass as a
cloud a saeculo, meaning clearly here "from the saeculum" and
not "of old" which is expressed by exactly the same phrase in
9:8, cf. Gen. 6:4 (Heb. מעולם, Syriac ܡܢ ܥܠܡ), Ps. 92:2 (93:2),
118:52 (119:52) et. al. The new meaning of this word is
strongly enough established for it to be used in the same
grammatical construction as the set phrase used with the older
meaning.

The problem, then, is to identify the meaning or meanings

of עולם in the overwhelming number of occasions on which it occurs in IV Ezra. The lexicographical considerations, including the major shift in usage, have been set out above. The word may occur meaning "time," "world-age" or "world." This latter meaning is first discovered by Jenni in the inscription of 134 C.E. and IV Ezra must in all probability be dated to the end of the first century C.E. The difference between "world" and "age" is often difficult to discern in any given text. The only version which seems to make any sort of distinction is Armenian which uses կեանք in cases evidently considered to mean "age, span (of life)."[427]

The only further external indication is the interesting fact that while in the Biblical samples the Syriac never used ܐܪܥܐ as the equivalent of the Latin terra and Armenian երկիր it is found as such in IV Ezra 3:35, 5:1 and 8:17 (Armenian omits 5:1 and 8:17). The Syriac translator evidently felt a close relationship to exist between these terms, even to the extent of interchangeability. The meaning "world" is primary in Rabbinic Hebrew.[428] A further check of the Qumran materials produced only one reading with the possible significance "world" (1QH iii:35). This one example cannot stand alone, and thus the phrase אושי עולם is best translated "eternal foundations." It is clearly possible, nonetheless, that the widespread later meaning was developing in Hebrew towards the end of the first century C.E., and it is not surprising that it is found in IV Ezra.

The uses of the saeculum-^{c}lm' complex in IV Ezra were
examined in context, in the attempt to determine its major
meanings. Special attention was paid to the words used
parallel to it, and to the overall meaning of the passages
involved. It is often difficult or impossible to decide
whether in a given passage the meaning "world" or "world age,"
"aeon" is involved. Certain uses, however, were observed,
whose meaning it was felt was sufficiently unambiguous to
serve as evidence.[429]

The word seems definitely to mean "age," "world age" in
11:44, 14:10,11.[430] It is possible it has this meaning in a
further four cases.[431] The meaning "world" was found definitely to be present in 5:49, 6:1, 6:59 (twice), 7:30,70,
8:50, 9:20, 11:40 and 13:20.[432] A further nine instances
were located where this is the probable meaning[433] and eight
additional cases where it is possible.[434] Twelve cases were
found where the meaning is either "world age" or "world," but
the context in these cases was judged to be such that no
definite decision could be made between them.[435]

From the above discussion it is clear that by the time
that IV Ezra was being written, the shift to the meaning
"world" had already taken place and that this was well on the
way to becoming the major meaning of the word עולם. It is
further evident, and this is most important, that the meaning
"age" cannot be used to establish an immaterial view of the
future for the author of IV Ezra, even though he speaks of a

new _saeculum_. The word had a semantic content which enabled
it to develop from the temporal "most distant time" to the
spatial "world." Its meaning as "age" must have lain closer
to "world age." Had the author wished to stress the non-
material nature of the coming age, one suspects that he would
have used a less polysemantic term, at least one whose range
of meaning did not include the idea of world, which presumably
would be an anathema to a man teaching of a "spiritual, non-
material" future state.

Thus it seems that the word עולם reflects, as it is used
in IV Ezra, a later state of development than that found in
the Hebrew Bible, or in the sectarian documents from Qumran,
and it is moving close to the situation in Rabbinic Hebrew.
Thus for the eschatology these considerations must be brought
into account, insofar as these terms are involved.

O. The Earth

From the preceding it is evident that in discussing IV
Ezra's concept of the earth the ארץ and תבל complexes will
be the main subject of our investigation and in particular
those uses which reflect ארץ in the sense of "the earth"
rather than "land" or "soil."[436]

The earth is created by God (3:4, 6:1ff.,38) and it in
turn brings forth created beings. Thus man (5:48, 6:54), his
mind (7:62), Adam (7:116) and cattle (6:53) are all brought
forth by the earth. Above, the special language of birth
used in connection with the creation of man was noted. The

corollary of this is that the earth mourns the death of man
as a mother mourns for her child ($10:9,12,13^2,14$). It also
brings forth minerals and ores ($7:55f$; $8:2f.$). Men are
called the inhabitants of earth,[437] and also may be spoken of
as "those upon the earth"[438] and those created on it.[439] In
fact these are by far the most frequent uses of the word.

The old idea of the precariousness of the earthly creation and its tendency to quake and shake at epiphanies and
other supernatural happenings is also clearly present. Thus
the earth quakes at Sinai ($3:18$) and its foundations shake
at the end ($6:15$). It quakes too at the cry of the mourning
woman as she is transmuted into the heavenly Jerusalem
($10:26$) and is terrified at the time of the disappearance of
the eagle ($12:3$).[440]

It is the earth that after the end of days will deliver
up the bodies of the dead for resurrection ($7:32$). The earth,
and more generally the world, are those which deteriorate as
time goes on. The concept of the deterioration of the earth
was mentioned above. It is of great interest to examine it
as it occurs in IV Ezra. The idea is applied to the world or
the world age as well as the earth,[441] and although the precise meaning of עולם cannot always be established, nonetheless
the fact that this concept is applied to it, as well as to
the creatura and parallels, which latter reflect the Hebrew
בריאה and thus the created world, makes these uses not incompatible. It also clearly indicates that the meaning world-age

sometimes implies the world too.

The question which this raises is that of the moral evaluation of the earth. Is the material earth considered bad, or the cause of evil? 7:32 seems to indicate that the earth will continue to exist in the new age. The earth, through the idea of deterioration, however, is seen sometimes, as in 14:16, as responsible for the troubles of the end-time. 5:50ff. makes the old age of the earth the cause of the lesser stature of men. Now this idea stems from the concept of the fixed measure of the times, found on a number of occasions.[442] The revelation of the end of times or the secret of the ages likewise implies their predestination.[443] It is of note that this idea serves as the answer to questions about the tarrying of the end or is employed in prophecies about the end.[444]

Keulers thinks that the passing away of the world is a direct result of the sins of men.[445] He points to 7:11f. which associate the toils and distresses of life on this world with the transgression of Adam, which raises the complicated ideas involved in the sin of Adam and its effects. Thus, as well as the linking of the troubles of this world to Adam's sins in 7:11f. they are said to be removed at the end. Equally in 9:19f. the statement is found that the corruption of man has brought troubles to the world. Adam's transgression is, in 7:117, considered responsible for the troubles of human existence. All these verses occur in quite

different contexts to those dealing with troubles stemming
from the deterioration of the earth.

In 8:50 the Messianic woes are said to come as punishment for man's sinfulness. Thus this verse also attributes
troubles to human action and not to the age of the earth.
Either the deterioration of the earth or human action may be
seen as the cause of troubles depending on the purpose and
context of the particular passage. Nonetheless, it does seem
that Keulers goes too far when he says:

> Wenn Esra es auch nicht ausdrücklich spricht, der
> Weltuntergang am Ende der Zeiten . . . ist für ihn
> die Folge der Sünder der Menschen. (p. 145).

This may be implied by 9:20, yet the predestinarian view of
the times, the precreation of eschatological things in general
(6:6) and of judgement in particular (7:70) weigh against
this, for judgement we are told, was made before Adam and
before the world. Ezra can even suggest, in 4:38, that the
end is being delayed by human sins.

There is thus tension and unclarity on this point. Both
the almost mechanistic view of the deterioration of the earth,
and that giving human action as the cause of the troubles of
the end of the age seem to occur or to be implied. In all of
this, however, there is no hint that the material as such is
the cause of sin. The opposition of material and spiritual
is not present in any form in the discussion of the earth any
more than it was found to be present in passages contrasting
the two ages.

In the Apocalypse of Baruch the sin of Adam is held responsible for physical death.[446] 17:13 seems to hint that a decline in human years was also a result of this, and this is even more explicit in 54:15, 56:6. That the general decline of the human state is attributable to sin is taught in 56:6. The troubles of this life are listed in considerable detail in 73:2-5 but they are said to be the cause of the toilsomeness of human life while no reason is offered for their existence. The reasons for the weariness of this world are likewise not discussed in 15:8.[447]

The only occurrence of the terminology of the advanced age of the world is in 85:10, where the youth of the age is said to be past, but this is only a sign of the imminent end. Neither there nor elsewhere in the book does this idea occur with the association of deterioration.[448] Thus too the fixedness of the times is far less prominent a theme than it is in IV Ezra.[449]

In short, in the Apocalypse of Baruch the idea of the deterioration of the earth as the cause of troubles is absent. Insofar as the toilsomeness of human life is attributed a cause it is caused by human action. This highlights the special features of IV Ezra. An explicit statement that sin is the cause of the end of this world lacks in Baruch just as it lacks in IV Ezra.[450]

P. The Concept of Death

To complete the study of these elements, death must also

be added. It is implied, but not explicit in our text. IV
Ezra uses the language of death in two major fashions. The
first is of physical death. This, he says, was a result of
the sin of Adam (3:11) and there are those who were excepted
from it, "who were taken, who did not taste death from their
birth" (6:26). Indeed, in 14:9 Ezra himself is told to pre-
pare for such a fate. Thus he is instructed:

> Renounce now the corruptible life,
>   Remove from yourself mortal thoughts,[451]
> Cast away from yourself human burdens,[452]
>   Put off now the infirm nature
> And place on one side the thoughts which distress you,
>   And hurry to move from these times.[453]   (14:13d-14)

In this interesting passage it appears that the corruptible,
mortal element in human life, from which he is to remove himself, is the end of life through death. This supposition is
further strengthened when in 7:15f., in a context having
nothing whatsoever to do with Ezra's assumption, the angel
asks him why he is disturbed by his corruptible and mortal
nature, and admonishes him to think of what is to come, not
of what is present. Again the parallelism of mortal and
corruptible, and the general sense of the passage support
the view that mortal and corruptible are virtually synonymous.[454]   A similar consciousness of man's mortality may be
observed in 4:11. In 8:53f. the text tells how in the world
to come death and Sheol will be hidden away and immortality
made manifest.

A somewhat different context illustrating the use of the

word death for "ordinary" physical death is found in 7:78.
The passage, discussing the intermediate state of the soul,
immediately after death and before resurrection, describes
death as the separation of the soul from the body in accordance with a divine decree. God's direct responsibility for
death is also mentioned in 8:13. The fact that judgement
and punishment or reward follow after death is discussed in
8:38, 9:12 and 14:35 while in 7:29 the Messianic kingdom is
said to conclude with the death of the Messiah and of all men.

Thus it may be observed that in one series of passages,
physical death is considered highly undesirable. It is the
same as corruptibility. It will be, above all, that which
will be removed in the future world. This view of death is
not connected with a negative evaluation of the body although
it is clear in e.g. 7:78ff. that the body is the part of man
which dies. The fact that the body is, evidently, not considered evil is significant, for such an outlook could
easily have arisen given the other views here outlined. In
the other series of passages, however, death is seen simply
as a stage in the total life of man, and after it punishment
and reward will come. In these passages there appears to be
no evaluation of death as either good or evil, desirable or
undesirable.

The second major use of this notion is more general,
less precisely defined. In it death appears as the equivalent
of perdition or damnation and in opposition not just to life

but to eternal life. Thus 7:48 tells us that the "evil heart"
has made known "ways of death . . . and removed us far from
life" and 7:92 expresses the same idea. 7:119 opposes death
to the immortale tempus and in 8:31 it is just the equivalent
of eternal punishment. Clearly, too, in 7:137f. life means
salvation and 8:60 says that it was prepared by God for man.
Two versions in 9:13 translate "live" as "be saved."

It appears that this usage is a natural development from
the negative evaluation of physical death observed above. It
most clearly stems from cases like 7:48f. In this passage,
too, the connection with the evil heart is of great interest.
The evil heart is directly linked to Adam, as the cause of
his transgression (3:21ff;), and is said in 7:92 to bring men
to death. From context and sense it is proper to understand
14:48f. as representing an example of the second usage of
death with the meaning "damnation" or the like, although it
is the same evil heart which brought physical death to Adam,
and through him to his descendants, which here is the cause
of damnation, eternal death. This once again illustrates the
complex implications of this term and the interrelatedness of
its various uses.

Q. Judgement

In 7:33-44 there is a long description of judgement and
of the day of judgement. The features which characterize
this material will be dealt with as they occur here and elsewhere in IV Ezra. The most detailed treatment is that of

Keulers[455] based, to some extent, on that of Vagany.[456] He has, however, introduced new and illuminating insights. In this study those features which others have treated adequately will only be touched upon and we shall concentrate on those points at which new information is available.

"Judgement" may refer to two major types of divine activity, to God's historical actions in general[457] and towards Israel in particular[458] or most frequently to his eschatological judgement. Above, the tendency of certain of the versions, most notably the Ethiopic, to read "judgement" where others have "tortures" or the like was noted.[459] This is an indication of the close relationship which exists between eschatological judgement and reward and punishment.[460]

In IV Ezra there is no suggestion of Divine Warrior in any of the passages dealing with judgement. Its legal aspect is overwhelming.[461] Thus the legal form of the rebuke in 7:37 and of the language of 7:115 drawn from the law-courts is clear, cf. also 7:73.[462] The judgement seat or throne in v.33 is likewise a specific legal feature. It is known in the Hebrew Bible[463] and the occurrences there indicate that it is intimately connected with the king's judicial function. It is found in the New Testament[463a] and the divine judgement seat is pre-created according to Rabbinic sources.[464] In Daniel 7:9 the divine Judge sits on a throne and the throne of judgement occurs elsewhere in the apocalyptic literature.[465]

In 8:61 Ezra is told that judgement is close and the

urgency which he felt about the time of reward has already
been observed. Like many other eschatological things, it is
said to be pre-ordained and pre-created.[466] According to
7:26-44 judgement is to come after the Messianic kingdom,
similarly 12:34 cf. 11:46. 7:113 says that it will be the
end of this age but has no indication of its place in the
eschatological scheme while 14:35 simply says that it comes
after death.

1) The Nature of Judgement

In 5:42 it is clearly stated that judgement is equal
for all and 7:66 makes it equally apparent that it is only
for men. Its primary characteristics are its decisive and
ultimate nature combined with the full revelation of truth.
7:33-35 describe this event in abstract terms. The withdrawal
of mercy and longsuffering serves to emphasize its absolute
and decisive nature. The strongest statement of this is in
7:104 when it says:

> The day of judgement is decisive[467] showing[468] to all
> the seal of truth.

This and the interesting passage 7:112ff. also emphasizing
the same facets of judgement both occur in a discussion dealing with the inapplicability of intercession to the day of
judgement (7:102-115). This is, of course, precisely the
point made in 7:33.

Box suggests that this is specifically directed against
the Rabbinic concept of the merits of the fathers which avail

the sons in judgement.[469] Schechter pointed out, however,
that in Rabbinic circles the relevance of the merit of the
fathers in the question of individual moral responsibility
at the time of judgement was negligible.[470] Some Rabbis even
held that the merit had ceased to have any effect, and a
variety of points of time are offered for this cessation,
all within the period of the first temple.[471] This again
makes evident the danger of characterizing Rabbinic views by
use of a single statement or group of statements.

The absence of any possibility of intercession should
not be seen primarily as serving to emphasize the unremitting
fate of the sinners as Gunkel thinks.[472] The fate of the
sinners and a sense of vengeance are absent from all the
contexts in which the denial of intercession is found. As
has been stated, the contexts lead to the conclusion that
the withdrawal of intercession is to be seen as a function
of the full revelation of truth which is to characterize
final judgement.

The intimate relationship between truth and judgement is
witnessed in a number of places in Rabbinic thought as well
as in IV Ezra. Thus, for example in Mek. to Ex. 14:29 of the
Judgement of God it says: הכל באמת והכל בדין.[473] It is this
view of judgement which finds its expression in the rejection
of intercession in 7:102ff. and in the ingathering of grace
and mercy and the appearance of faithfulness and truth in
7:36ff. This too is the unspoken link in the logic of 5:41ff.[474]

Truth is said to stand, to be established (7:34). The seal
of truth in 7:104 is interpreted by Gunkel as the judge's
seal on the documents.[475] It is of interest that in Yoma 69b
God's seal is said to be truth.[476] This is another legal
feature of the representation of judgement. The decisive
character of the day of judgement is also emphasized in
7:112ff. The complete revelation of divine glory seems to
be connected with this, and the full declaration of truth
features in the description in 14:35 cf. Ap. Bar. 83:2-3.

2. 7:33-35 Literary Form

6:27-28	7:33-35	8:52f.
Then evil will be blotted out,	And mercy will pass away,	For you paradise is opened,
Deceit will be extinguished;	Grace be made distant,	The tree of life is planted,
But faith shall flower,	Longsuffering be gathered up;	The future world is prepared,
And corruption will be overcome,	But judgement alone will remain,	Delight is prepared,
And truth which for so long was fruitless shall be evident.	And truth will be established,	The city is built,
	And faith will increase,	Rest is appointed,
7:114	And reward will follow,	Goodness is established,
In which corruption will pass away,	And recompense will appear,	Wisdom (pre-) constituted.
Weakness is abolished,	And justice will awaken,	The root is sealed up from you,
Faithlessness is cut off;	And injustice will not sleep.	Infirmity is blotted out before you,

7:114	14:17	8:52f.
But justice springs up,	For truth draws farther off,	And death is hidden,
Truth grows forth.	Falsehood approaches.	Sheol has fled,
		Corruption is forgotten,
		Distresses pass away,
		And in the end the treasurehouse of life appears.

All these passages are descriptions of the future state except 14:17 which refers to the troubles preceding the eschaton. They all occur as angelic prophecies: 6:27f. and 8:52f. are prophecies of the end while 7:33ff., 114 are descriptions of the day of judgement. The theme of judgement is specific to 7:33ff., 7:114 and both of these are concerned with intercession. These five passages form a distinct literary type. They are characterized by short sentences composed of a (predominantly) abstract noun and a verb. They show parallelistic structure and seem to be formed generally of groups of two lines each of two hemistychs. Thus 6:27f. 2 + 2 (+1), 8:52 2 + 2, 2 + 2, 2 + 2 + 2 (+1). 7:114f. shows 3 + 2 and 7:33f. 3 + 3 and then the predominating 2 + 2 structure.

Further, they are closely related in language. Five basic terms together with their opposites characterize these verses and the most dominant of these are truth and deceit,[477]

corruption and weakness.[478] The other three main concepts
involved are faith and faithlessness,[479] evil and goodness[480]
and justice and injustice.[481] There is also considerable
coincidence of verbal usage. The negative qualities are
said to "pass away,"[482] "be blotted out,"[483] or the like
while good qualities "flower" or "spring up,"[484] "are evident" or "established."[485]

In spite of the similarity between these passages it is
clear that they cannot be either parts of one original piece
or secondary forms of one original composition. The contents
of each are conditioned to a considerable extent by the context in which it is found. The emphasis on the absolute
nature of judgement and the absence of intercession in 7:33
is not found in 7:114 where it is not required, for this has
been the subject of the whole section in which this verse
occurs. The list of rewards in 8:52 is not reflected in the
other verses. This verse is a promise of reward to Ezra
and so these elements are appropriate.

In spite of this variation, the substantial common function, literary structure and vocabulary combine to suggest
strongly that here we are dealing with a distinct literary
form. While poetic descriptions of the eschata, especially
in prophetic passages, are frequent[486] this particular form,
as here described, seems peculiar in its full-blown development to IV Ezra. The Hebrew Bible has a number of examples
of sentences with an abstract quality as subject. Thus Hos.

‏פרח משפט‎ 10:4, Ps. 85:12 ‏אמת מארץ תצמח‎ . In Deutero-Isaiah we find more sustained examples, thus 59:14 ‏והסג אחור משפט וצדקה‎ ‏על כן רחק משפט ממנו‎ cf. 59:9 ‏מרחוק תעמוד כי כשלה ברחוב אמת‎ ‏ולא תשיגנו צדקה‎ . These are however still rather removed from the sort of passage presented in IV Ezra. A similar sentence structure, but lacking the abstract elements, may be observed in Song 7:14. ‏אז פרחה הגפן, פתח הסמדר הנצו הרמונים‎ . Similar language may also be observed in Isa. 35:11 and parallel in Isa. 51:11.

Although similar individual phrases are found in I En. 69:29, only in Ap. Bar. does a close resemblance occur. The two closest passages are 44:8 and 73:1f. cf. also 57:2.

> 44:9 For everything which is corruptible will pass away,
> And everything that dies will depart,
> Nor will there be any remembrance of the present time which is filled with evils.

> 73:1f. Joy will then be revealed,
> And rest will appear,
> And healing will then descend in dew,
> And disease will withdraw,
> Anxiety and anguish and lamentation will pass from among men,
> And gladness will proceed through the whole earth.

These too are in a context of eschatological prophecy and seem to reflect the same poetic form as the IV Ezra passages, although the latter are more complete and polished.[487]

These lists bear a certain similarity to the ethical lists, Haustafeln best known from the New Testament.[488] They differ from these, however, not only in that they lack the participial formulation and other features which seem to be

typical of them[489] but also in both content and form. The
lists of vices and virtues in the Dead Sea Scrolls (e.g. 1QS
iv:9-11) have been discerned to bear some relation to the New
Testament materials,[490] but these too are not similar to IV
Ezra. It should be noted that neither in content nor in use
can the passages in IV Ezra be considered to have a primarily
didactic purpose. Indeed, if anything, they are parallel in
function to the difficult passage in 1QS iv:19f. In none of
the above-mentioned lists may a poetic form be discerned.
Likewise the Adam lists isolated by Otzen show almost no
similarities with the materials in IV Ezra.[490a]

Thus it can be concluded that these poems play a significant part in the description of the future world. They seem
to draw, in language and image on older materials, biblical
and extra-biblical. The function which they play in the
description here is played by largely similar elements in
other apocalypses[491] but the distinctive poetic and literary
form is unique to IV Ezra and to Ap. Bar.

The language in 7:33-35 and 7:114 is so specifically
connected with the central features of IV Ezra's concept of
judgement that it is difficult to divorce 6:27ff. from this
same complex of ideas. The elements of truth and faithfulness, however, lack in 8:52f. which, as noted above, fulfils
a rather different function to the other passages.[492]

3) Paradise and Gehenna

The next step in the process of judgement, the appearance

of paradise and Gehenna, is described in 7:36. Gehenna is the place of damnation and it is described as a fiery pit. The word Gehenna occurs only here in IV Ezra, which generally employs Latin _infernum_.[493] The various features of Gehenna and of the place of punishment have been described by past scholars and the concept in IV Ezra is in basic accord with that found elsewhere in contemporary writings.[494]

Keulers suggests that the language of "annihilation" (_Vernichtung_), used of the fate of the wicked, comes from the national eschatology where the enemies are annihilated and that in IV Ezra it is transferred to the individual escha-tology.[495] In his listing of annihilation terms he includes the word _perditio_. This noun probably reflects ἀπωλεία which is the LXX equivalent of Hebrew אבדון . In the Hebrew Bible this is a name for the underworld,[496] parallel to Sheol or Māwet.[497] Its technical status is confirmed by its trans-literation into Greek in the New Testament and its use at Qumran.[498] Thus this term does not imply annihilation and it may well be that the concept of death, which means the loss of salvation, is behind much of this language.[499]

Gehenna is found here in close connection with judgement. While there are many references to the general fate of the ungodly, this and 8:53 are the only specific references to Gehenna or _infernum_ in eschatological contexts. To these 10:10 must be added as the clearest use of _perditio_ = אבדון It may well be the case, however, that Sheol in 8:53 is being

used as an equivalent for death to which it is parallel as is
the case e.g. in Isa. 28:15, Prov. 5:5 cf. Ap. Jn. 6:8 etc.
The other references to the fate of the wicked in the book do
not speak of the place of punishment. In 7:36ff. the position
of Gehenna in connection with final judgement and the new age
is clear.[500]

In Ap. Bar. Sheol appears as the place of the dead, thus
23:5, 48:16, 52:2, 56:6.[501] In 1 En. Gehenna is found in
specific connection with the judgement and punishment of the
wicked in 27:1 and 90:26f. It occurs in conjunction with
the wrathful divine destruction of the wicked in Ass. M. 10:10.
As the place of punishment it figures in Rabbinic sources,
e.g. Avot 1:5, 5:19,20.[502] Thus the connection of Gehenna as
the place of punishment with the judgement, reward and punishment ideas seems clear although the occurrences in the
Apocrypha and Pseudepigrapha are sparse.

One main problem which arises in connection with paradise
or the Garden of Eden in IV Ezra is the precise connotation
of this term. On the one hand "paradise" or "paradise of
delight" is the translation employed by the Greek and daughter
versions for "Garden of Eden" in Gen. 2 etc. Paradise was
eschatologized, however, and it became the place of reward.
It also became elevated to the heavenly sphere.

In 3:6 paradise signifies the Garden of Eden in which
Adam was placed. It was created before the world, an idea
also found in 6:2 where before "the foundation of paradise"

is an expression for the remotest antiquity. The same notion
is found in Rabbinic sources, there specifically based on the
interpretation of Gen. 2:8.[503] Although this is in connection with Adam Pseudo-Jonathan reads   גינוניתא מעדן לצדיקיא
showing the working of eschatologization.

In 7:36f. and 7:123 paradise is clearly eschatological.
It is connected in 7:36f. with judgement, reward and punishment. It is reward, too, that characterizes the use in 7:123
where it is clear that paradise is for the end. Reward is
also the theme of 8:52 where it might be suggested, however,
that a heavenly paradise to be entered by the assumed Ezra is
referred to. A careful examination of the passage reveals
that at the most this can be considered as the use of eschatological features to describe Ezra's reward.[504]

The most interesting occurrence is perhaps that of
4:7-8[505] where paradise is one of the objects of super-human
knowledge. Box pointed out that Rabbinic sources always use
the expression גן עדן except for the famous passage in Hag.
14b, the story of "four who entered paradise (פרדס)." The
place of this story within the Jewish mystic tradition was
clearly established by Scholem.[506] He also showed its relationship to II Cor. 12:2-4. Most interesting is his point
that:

> the biblical word pardes was, in fact, used as a
> technical term for the heavenly paradise in the oldest
> Jewish esoteric writings. . . . (p. 16)

He draws attention to the use of the expression prds qwšt' in the Qumran Enoch fragments referred to above.[507] The expression "entered paradise" in 4:8 must be seen in the tradition of פרדס as the heavenly paradise and an object of theosophical knowledge, although the point of the passage is the rejection of such knowledge.

The language used for paradise is here set forth.

V.	Lat.	Eth.	Syriac	Armenian
3:6	paradisum	ganat	prds	դրախտին փափկութեան
4:7	paradisi	ganat	prds	դրախտին
4:8	---	ganat	---	դրախտին
6:2	paradisi	ganat	prds'	դրախտին
7:36	iocundatis p.	g. tefšeḥt	prds dbwsm'	ճշմարիտ դրախտին փափկութեան
7:123	paradisus	ganat	prds	եկնաւոր դրախտին
8:52	paradisus	ganat	prds	ճշմարիտ դրախտին

Note also:

7:123	saturitas	tefšeḥt	pwnq'	փափկութիւն
8:52	habundantia	tefšeḥt	pwnq'	փափկութեան

Of note is the fact that Armenian reads in 8:52 ճշմարիտ դրախտին "true paradise" and in 7:36 ճշմարիտ դրախտին փափկութեան "true paradise of delight." It is, of course, not sure that these unique readings do reflect prds qwšt', but the closeness is

undeniable. In any case it must be admitted that the origins
of this reading are unknown; perhaps it reflects an acquaint-
ance of the translator with the "paradise of righteousness"
of other books. The Hebrew ^{c}dn is doubtless reflected in
the parallel phrases in 7:123 and 8:52 and these probably
provide evidence for a Hebrew original gn ^{c}dn. This is
equally clear in 7:36 where "paradise of delight" occurs in
all versions. Armenian also reads thus in 3:6. No suggestion of this reading can be found in 4:7f. and 6:2, but it is
dangerous to speculate on the original of these.[508]

Little information is available about the nature of paradise. Eden in 3:6 was planted by God (cf. Gen. 2:8). According to 6:2 it has flowers. 7:123 speaks of its incorruptible
fruit while 8:52 says that it contains the Tree of Life.[509]

Scholars have evinced two major concerns with respect
to the nature of paradise in IV Ezra. The first is the relation of the earthly to the heavenly.[510] The other, connected
problem is the question of the spiritualisation of the concept of paradise, its "transcendence" and how the trees and
flowers and so forth relate to this. It seems clear that
insofar as the terms "paradise" or "Garden of Eden" are used
they imply features of a garden. Even where paradise became
a terminus technicus for a heavenly object of mystic knowledge, the language used of it was still formed by the idea
of a garden.[511]

Second, unless a good reason for doubt arises, if the

author speaks of the Tree of Life as in 8:53 or of fruit or
flowers as in 7:123, 6:2 he should be taken to mean what he
says. The secondary question of the importance of this or
that notion in his thought as a whole may arise, but this
is independent of the clear meaning of the text. Keulers
connects the paradise of 4:7f. with 7:123 and 8:52 and sees
in them all the heavenly, transcendent paradise, the place
of the saved.[512] He goes further and suggests that paradise,
Tree of Life and the like in 8:52 are all really only graphic
expressions for the future, eternal, transcendent state of
the righteous.[513]

The argument which Box invokes for the transcendence
and heavenly nature of paradise is that it is pre-created.[514]
It may be observed, however, that this is precisely a feature of the Rabbinic notions about Adam's garden mentioned
above. Keulers' argument for the purely symbolic nature of
paradise in 8:52ff. is the transcendence of the heavenly
paradise. This transcendence implies for Keulers that Ezra
"hat . . . mit dem himmlischen Paradies nicht mehr die
plastische Vorstellung eines wirklichen, wenn auch wunderbar,
Gartens verbunden" (p. 186). It seems to this writer that
this conclusion in all its ramifications is far from obvious.
Admittedly for a mode of thought opposing material and
spiritual this may be so, but there is every reason to think
that the apocalyptic authors attributed at least the same
physical reality to the heavenly realm as they did to the

earthly. It may be more marvellous, but it is as real and
the book gives us no reason to think otherwise. Keulers
rightly senses that 8:52 cannot be treated as an integrated
description of the future age (p.187). It is, however, not
therefore necessary to regard each element mentioned there as
a pictorial expression of the same transcendent, future state.

8:52f. occurs in the context of the promise of reward
to the righteous which it opposes to the afflictions of the
wicked in the last generation. The emphasis of v.52 is on
the fact that the reward is already prepared and of v.53 on
the removal of death and infirmity. In this context v.52 is
best understood as a list of various elements associated with
reward. The list contains certain ideas not found elsewhere
in the book such as the Tree of Life,[515] and a similar listing of features of reward may be observed in 7:119-125.
There is no reason to think of either of these as implying
more than this.

Therefore not only is paradise at least one element of
the joyous future state, but it is to be understood literally
as far as it is described, although not many details are
given. Views of paradise in other sources are quite explicit
and have been very adequately treated as they relate to IV
Ezra by past scholarship.[516]

This same "transcendence" has forced Box to a complex
reconstruction of the view of paradise supposedly held by IV
Ezra. He says:

> Paradise is essentially transcendental in character. . . .
> It was prepared by God before the creation of the world
> and was Adam's first abode (3:6); but after Adam's sin
> it was withdrawn from contact with the earth, and
> remains in heaven, reserved by God for the righteous."
> (p.197)

The pre-creation motif has already been discussed, it
was part of the Rabbinic ideas about Adam's garden. Thus it
cannot serve as evidence for "transcendence." The only
passage which speaks clearly of a heavenly paradise is
4:7f. which, as has been seen, draws on a very specific
tradition in which paradise was a terminus technicus and
must be treated independently. 7:38 gives no hint of
heavenly venue nor does 8:52 or for that matter 7:123. In
fact no information whatsoever is given about the location
of paradise. Moreover there is no hint of its withdrawal to
heaven in 3:6 nor of its descent from heaven elsewhere. Its
position is similar in many ways to the new Jerusalem which
was found to be heavenly but to appear on earth. Most of
this construction then comes from the use of the expression
"transcendent," taken by Box as the equivalent of "heavenly"
and the opposite of "earthly."[517]

As with other concepts, it is best to treat the paradise
tradition in IV Ezra in terms of its use, not to try to
construct an integrated theory, especially one based on
philosophical presuppositions which there is no reason to
think that the author held. The use in 4:7f. must be distinguished from the others. 3:6 and 6:4 are similar and

seem to refer to the paradise of Adam. 7:38, 123 and 8:52
all occur in the context of future reward. They speak of
the eschatologized paradise which is pre-existent and prepared and will be revealed at the fitting time--all features
of most eschatological figures and events. It evidently contains the Tree of Life (8:52) and the fruit of this tree is
doubtless referred to in 7:123. There is no reason to doubt
the literal meaning of these statements. The creation story
provided the typology for many of the features of the
eschatological tendency which has been called here the "new
age" and paradise is one of them. No hint of its transfer
into the heavenly realm may be observed in eschatological
contexts. The lack of detailed description is in agreement
with the general trend of the book which gives no detail
about the eschatological state.

4) Reward and Punishment

Certain of the traditions concerning reward and punishment have not yet been discussed in detail.[518] The language
of joy or delight and torment prevalent in phrases contrasting eschatological reward and punishment was remarked upon
above.[519] Spaciousness is found twice as a description of
reward, in 7:96 and 7:18 cf. 7:13. This may stem from uses
such as Ps. 31:9 and similar occurrences may be observed in
1QH v:34, vi:31, ix:27f.[520]

The element of seeing occurs here in three contexts. In
v.37 seeing God brings full understanding of the enormity of

sin against him. In his address to the aroused peoples in v.38 God calls on them to look at paradise and Gehenna, reward and punishment while in v.42 we are told that the earth is illumined by the glory of the brightness of the Most High by which all will see that which is established, presumably the decree of the divine court.

The seeing of the Most High and its effect on the wicked are described in the seventh of the ways of punishment of wicked souls in the intermediate state (7:87). Conversely the righteous souls rejoice when they see the glory of the Most High (7:91,98). This joy or distress is enhanced, the texts say, by the souls' knowledge of their future judgement. Eternal seeing is reward in I En. 102:8.

This sort of sight is analogous to the concept of recompense through seeing the fate of the other group which seems to lie behind the pointing out of paradise and Gehenna in 7:38. It likewise figures in the suffering and joy of the souls in the intermediate state (7:83-86,93-94). The same notion occurs in Ap. Bar. 51:5 where the wicked are said to waste away at the sight of the glorious righteous and then depart for torment. The limited period of contemplation of the fate of the other seems to correspond to the seven days allowed the souls in IV Ezra 7:100f.

The most interesting of these features is the evident relationship between the revelation of the glory of God and the manifestation of true judgement. In 7:42 the established

decree is seen by the light of the glory of the brightness of
God. As an explanation of the existence of intercession in
this world Ezra is told in 7:112 that the imperfect nature
of this world results in an incomplete revelation of glory
in it. That this incomplete revelation of glory means an
imperfect judgement is made explicit in 7:113 where the day
of judgement is said to be the end of this world. Therefore,
by implication, the divine glory will be fully revealed on
that day and thus on it true judgement is manifest. For
this reason there is no intercession on the day of judgement.[521] Glory and its full revelation must be connected
with the revelation of true judgement. This is confirmed by
Ap. Bar. 55:8 where the revelation of glory is said to cause
both conviction and rejoicing. The rejoicing of the righteous
and the distress of the wicked at the sight of divine glory
are thus the complement of the intimate connection between
the revelation of glory and the establishment of true judgement. The brightness of divine glory in the future world
is also connected with the idea of its illumination by the
glory of God.[522] The close relationship of divine glory and
truth is also attested in the Qumran texts.[523]

5) Shining Faces

7:97, referring to final reward, says that the face of
the righteous will shine like the sun and that they will be
like the light of the stars, henceforth incorruptible. In
7:125 the faces of the abstinent are said to shine above

the stars. This may be connected with the glory which is
said to await the righteous in 7:95,98, 8:49, cf. 9:31. Glory
may, in 8:51, be a term for reward in general. The shining
of the faces of the righteous is, however, a widespread
tradition, and may be part of the broader idea of the light
of the saved.

In both statements in IV Ezra it should be noted that
specifically the face is mentioned. Gunkel suggested that
the comparison with the stars suggests the origin of this
feature is astral religion.[524] It will be seen below that
this feature does have ramifications,[525] but that the explanation offered by Gunkel is not totally satisfactory[526] for the
sun features at least as prominently as the stars in these
passages. It is impossible here to enter into all the implications of this tradition but some of its main lines of
development should be traced.

The earliest mention of the shining of the righteous at
the end is Dan. 12:3 והמשכלים יזהרו כזהר הרקיע ומצדיקי הרבים
ככוכבים לעולם ועד . The face is not mentioned, but a prayer
attributed to R. Ḥannina in Ber. 17a, using language drawn
from Daniel, expresses the wish פניך יזהרו כזהר הרקיע . The
face is introduced in this later formulation. In Sifre Deut.
10 (67a) and parallel in Lev. R. 20:2 we read that the faces
of the righteous in the future will be like seven things, the
sun, the moon, the firmament, the stars, the lightning, roses
and the Temple candelabrum. In a text called Maᶜaseh Abraham

it is recorded that on his birth the face of Abraham shone
like the sun.[527]

In Ap. Jn. 1:16 the face of the "one like a Son of Man"
is said to shine like the sun. In II En. 1:5, 19:1 it is the
faces of angels which shine like the sun while in I En. 71:1
the angels' countenances shine like the snow. Thus the faces
of both angels and righteous shine and the major element with
which they are compared is the sun. This is the situation
in IV Ez. 7:97a. In 7:125, however, they are said to shine
above the stars while 7:97b says that they are as the light
of the stars.

There is another series of passages which deals with
shining faces introducing no element of comparison. The
background may lie in such biblical uses as Qoh. 8:1.[528]
1QH iii:3, iv:5 seem similar to these. The shining of faces
in an eschatological context may be observed in Ap. Bar.
51:3 as part of the beauty of the resurrected body of the
righteous. In I En. 51:4f. the righteous are said to become
as angels and their faces will be lighted up with joy. In
I En. 38:4, in the Similitudes, it says that the Lord of
spirits caused his light to appear on the face of the holy,
righteous and elect. The same brightness of face may be
observed in I En. 14:21, 89:22 and San. 100a. The brightness
of Moses' face when he descended from Mount Sinai is attested
in Targ. Ex. 34:29-35 and this idea is used in II Cor.
3:7-18 where the connection with "glory" is made explicit.

An interesting series of passages in Rabbinic sources
concerns the brightness of the face of Adam which was
removed from him when he was expelled from the Garden.[529]
This seems perhaps to have been connected with the creation
in the image of God.[530] As Ginzberg points out[531] this originally distinct tradition became combined with the idea
of the wondrous light created on the first day and hidden
when Adam sinned.[532] This material serves to confirm the
distinct tradition of the shining of the face of the
righteous. Above, however, the use of this attribute for
both righteous men and angels was observed and the stars were
not found. This leads to a brief examination of comparisons
with heavenly bodies in which general brightness rather than
the shining countenance is mentioned.

In Dan. 12:3, as already observed, the righteous are as
bright as the זהר הרקיע and as the stars. This latter idea
is found in IV Ez. 7:97, 123, and I En. 104:2. In similar
contexts the sun is also found, thus Ad. Ev. 29:9 cf. Sifre
to Deut. 6:5, ch.32 (73b), Sanh. 101a, Arm. IV Ez. 6:25.
There are, in contrast to these passages, a number of places
in which, although the elements of brightness and of face
lack, the righteous are said to be like stars or intimately
connected with the stars. Thus in IV Macc. 17:5 the seven
sons are said to be "star-like, with God" and in Ass. M.
10:9 Israel is said to be exalted by God and caused to
approach the stars in their place of habitation. As in Jer.

51:9, Isa. 14:13 so also Ps. Sol 1:5 describes the overween-
ing pride of the wicked as the attempt to reach the stars.
In light of this the versions of Isa. 14:13 are most interesting. M.T. and Syriac read השמים אעלה ממעל לכוכבי אל ארים כסאי
LXX and Armenian "stars of heaven." In Targ. we find עמיה
דאלהה. This suggests a direct correlation between the
righteous and the stars. In Ap. Bar. 51:10 a further combination of elements may be observed. There the righteous are
said to be made like angels and equal to stars.

This introduces us to another group of passages in which
the blessed righteous are associated with angels. In I En.
104:2 the righteous are said to shine like stars while in
v.6 of that chapter they are said to be companions of the
host of heaven perhaps angelic. Ap. Bar. 51:5 sees them as
transformed into the splendour of angels and I En. 51:4 says
that they are like angels in heaven. It was noted above
that the brightness of faces is a feature both of the
righteous and of angels.[533] The stars as the host of
heaven are well documented in the Hebrew Bible.[534] The most
interesting of all the verses in Job. 38:7 where the stars
are parallel to the angels. In addition to I En. 104:6,
stars are used symbolically of angels in I En. 86:1,3, 90:21
etc. They are equally the symbol of the righteous in I En.
46:7 cf. 43:1-4 cf. Dan. 8:10f. The striking aspect of the
usage in post-biblical materials is that there the stars and
angels share their characteristics with the blessed righteous.

This may, in some cases, go so far as an identification.

Now some such view may well be the source of the language of IV Ezra 7:97b. The question must be raised, however, of the place of this sort of view in the total concept of the fate of the righteous in the book. The tradition of the bright faces, although applied both to angels and men, seems to be somewhat independent of the traditions of the righteous as similar to angels or stars. This is so because the main feature of comparison is not the stars but the sun. The main force of this tradition is the bright face as a sign of holiness. The lack of any references to the relationship of the righteous to stars or angels elsewhere in the book weighs against seeing this as more than the use of language drawn from a tradition which did not play any major role in the thought of the author.

R. The Future State

Most of the outstanding features of reward were dealt with in the preceding sections, and in the nature of the case they constitute a description of the future state. 7:26-44 does not take the order of events beyond the end of the day of judgement, but major features of the fate of the righteous were dealt with in this connection. It is of greatest signifi-cance to note that the future age is nowhere described in any detail.

Some elements are preserved in 7:13 and these were dis-cussed above.[534a] The closest approach to a description of the future age is contained in 7:117-125. There the features of "immortal time, without death" (119),[535] "imperishable hope" (120), "habitations of health and safety" (121), protection by the glory of the Most High (122), paradise (123), and shining faces (125) are mentioned. This may be compared with 8:52ff. where many of the same elements occur. In both of these lists certain themes are persistent. Above all the removal of death and infirmity characterize the future world.[536] The only features which here give any idea of the nature of that world as distinct from the nature of the reward of the righteous in it are paradise and the habitations of health and safety. To these may be added delight, rest and the city of 8:52, the broad, safe ways of 7:13 and the spacious liberty of 7:96. This is not an adequate basis on which to formulate the view of the nature of the coming world. The very lack of information is the more significant when it is recalled that in the case of the Messianic kingdom a similar vagueness was observed. This provides final confirmation of IV Ezra's interest in describing not the future state, but the mode of its coming.

Keulers maintains that the transcendence of the new age resulted in the lack of material descriptions and this is the reason for the use of such general terms as glory, life and so forth to describe it.[537] Yet, the removal of infirmity and death and the receiving of delight and joy may have been understood in a quite material fashion. After all, the

removal of weaknesses of the body is a physical benefit.
Admittedly, this is a more "elevated" notion than other
concepts of the future life which could be adduced, but
Keulers draws the contrasts more strongly than is warranted.
This is the more so when it is recalled that at least some
of the terminology of this description is also that used of
the Messianic kingdom. Indeed nothing more than the joyous
existence of the survivors is asserted about that kingdom
either. In neither case is any detail given. In addition,
no view maintaining a disembodied, non-material future state
can be detected in the book, nor is a heavenly future age
asserted. It appears, as has been suggested above,[538] that
the differences between this age and the age to come were
conceived of as differences of world order rather than arising from material-spiritual opposition.

Box thinks that in the so-called S document there is no
resurrection of the body, that the author is obsessed by the
material-spiritual conflict.[539] This supposed absence of
resurrection is flatly contradicted by 5:44 which must reflect
Hebrew hyw (D or H form) and could only make sense in terms of
resurrection. The same is true of the implication of 4:37ff.
when put alongside 7:32. Both 5:44 and 4:37ff. are within
Box' S document. It might be added that the removal of death
at the end only makes sense in conjunction with the resurrection of the body for the soul evidently did not die cf. 7:75
etc. It is of note that terra and equivalents is never said

to pass away. Taken in addition to the other considerations
urged above, it can be thus concluded that no evidence of a
material-spiritual opposition between the ages can be discerned.

S. The New Age: an Independent Eschatology?

Complementary to the question raised in Section J 3)
above whether the Messianic kingdom occurs as an independent
eschatology is that of the independence of the resurrection,
judgement and new age materials. Does this complex of ideas
occur, in a passage relating the chronology of events,
immediately following the last generation? The ideas of
judgement, reward and punishment are central to IV Ezra and
he mentions them very often, but rarely in contexts giving
any indication of their place in the eschatological scheme of
events.

It is clear in 7:26-44, 11:46, 12:34 that the Messianic
kingdom precedes judgement. This is probably also the implication of the term beginning in 6:7-10. The combination of
elements in 6:25, 9:6-12 and the features of 5:41ff., 4:26ff.
have been dealt with at length above. It was concluded no
chronological information can be drawn with assurance from
these passages, but that, if anything, they add a little
support to the evidence for an intermediate kingdom. The same
is true of 7:112f. discussed above.[540]

No other passage occurs which gives a view of chronological
sequence. Very often, however, judgement rather than the

Messianic kingdom is invoked as the solution to problems which
Ezra raises. In the questions about theodicy and human sinfulness which make up the body of the important third vision,
for example, it is always judgement and final recompense
which are invoked as solutions and never the Messianic kingdom. This may be observed, for example, in 7:60, 66-69, cf.
7:73, 7:104ff. and elsewhere and is a function of the decisive and final nature of judgement and recompense. This
phenomenon is in part the explanation of the lack of
chronologically sequential contexts within which judgement
may be placed. Where such are found it follows the Messianic
kingdom.

Thus, although there are many mentions of the judgement-
new age materials alone, it is not justifiable to conclude on
this basis that an eschatological sequence last generation,
judgement and new age occurs, for where a sequence is given,
at least some hint of the Messianic kingdom is found. There
does not seem to be a basis therefore, for regarding this
complex as an alternate, in IV Ezra, to the Messianic kingdom
materials. It is a more significant and central idea in the
book than that complex, but it does not seem that it is an
independent eschatology, where eschatological schemes are the
subject of discussion.

Chapter III

CONCLUSIONS

The basic contention of this thesis is that a new examination indicates that previous understanding of the mode of
thought of IV Ezra has been inadequate. It is further maintained that the new formulation of that mode of thought
attempted here demands changes in the methodology of analysis.
At the heart of these lie the abandonment of the attempt to
describe his thought on the covert or overt presumption that
logical consistency between the author's statements, implied
or explicit, exists or should exist and a willingness to
search elsewhere for elements giving that thought its
coherence. This carries with it the introduction of new
criteria of analysis such as the considerations of context,
purpose and association. At the level of the study of
textual and literary phenomena this has minor importance,
but in the exegesis of particular passages or groups of
passages and in the reconstruction of the ideas of the author
it is central. In these areas the application of such considerations has proved fruitful and has enabled us to reach
new insights about particular passages and more satisfactory
views of general concepts. Thus, the results of the research
fall into a number of classes dependent on the type of

material examined, be it a particular text or a more general
concept.

1. New Exegetical Solutions

The first stage of the examination was text critical and
the results of this may be found in the footnotes to the
second chapter. In the task of exegesis of the text thus
established a number of new suggestions arose, some with
respect to highly significant passages. The most important
of these are listed here.

1. 7:12f. There is no doubt that "ways" is the translation
of the problematic term here (p.55).

2. 6:7-10. The new Rabbinic parallels which were adduced
establish beyond any reasonable doubt that Esau signifies
Rome and Jacob, Israel. This disposes finally of attempts
to make identifications with specific historical figures.
Even more significant is that it seems decisive against the
Kabisch-Box hypothesis according to which Jacob is the
incorruptible age to come and Esau, this corruptible age
(pp.48f.).

3. 4:26-32. Careful exegesis leads to the conclusion that
this passage falls into two parts and that the crucial vss.
28-32 must refer to the change of hearts and not to the
passing away of the earth. This is most important in view
of the supposed rejection of the material which scholars
have found in this passage. Such an interpretation is no
longer tenable (p.65ff., cf. p.89f.).

4. 8:52-54 is best understood, not as a sequential description of a specific view of the eschatological state, but as
a list of elements intended to evoke the idea of reward.
This conclusion is based on the factors of context and purpose (pp.79f., 202, 212f.).

5. 5:41ff. This passage is neither a description of the
order of eschatological events nor a rejection of the Messianic
kingdom idea. It is concerned with problems of reward and
it receives its coherence from this concern (p.86f., 106).

6. 6:25-29 and 9:6-12 are not intended to be detailed and
full expositions of the author's scheme of the events of the
end-time. This is supported by the considerations of purpose
and association and is confirmed by the sequence of both
Messianic kingdom and new age elements in these passages
combined with a remarkable lack of descriptive detail. (pp.
79f., 137).

7. 4:7f. The view of paradise in this passage must be
connected with the concepts and terminology of the esoteric
tradition and thus viewed to some extent independently of
the paradise traditions reflected elsewhere in the book
(pp.198f.).

8. 7:26. "Hidden land" most probably refers to the land of
Israel (pp.102f.).

9. 11:46 clearly speaks of final judgement to follow the
Messianic kingdom (pp.110-113).

10. 8:20 should be read "enthroned for ever" or the like
(p.177).

11. 10:10. Latin perditio should be seen as a translation
of ἀπωλεία going back to אנדון, a technical term for Gehenna.
(p.196).

2. New Definitions of Eschatological Events and Concepts

The second group of conclusions has to do with two
classes of individual elements of the eschatological scheme.
A. The first type is what may be called "rubric" concepts.
These are general concepts whose specific content may vary
within certain fairly broad limits. The determining elements
with respect to content were found to be contextual and
associational.

1. The Two Ages. This idea has as its primary terminology
the expressions העולם הזה and העולם הבא (pp.63, 75, 81). It
does not seem to be limited to any specific eschatological
scheme and may be found of the Messianic kingdom, of the
future age or of an undefined future state (pp.64f., 76).
The idea of "the world/age to come" was found often in the
context of hope or promise of reward (pp.64, 76). In general,
the differences of the two ages were found to be differences
of world order and not based on "material"--"spiritual"
oppositions or the like.

2. The End. The terminology is Latin finis, Syriac šwlm'
etc. (p.84). The term indicates the decisive turning point
of history viewed from an eschatological orientation (pp.91f.).
It may be the start of the Messianic kingdom or of the day of
judgement or an undefined future point (pp.84-91). The choice

between these is determined by contextual and associational factors (pp.91-97).

B. The second type is composed of specific concepts or events whose content does not vary and which often have a fixed technical terminology and close associations with other such concepts or events.

1. The Messianic Woes. They are called "signs" (p.100) or "visitation" (p.84 and Ch.2, n.180), terms specifically used of the events of the last generation. The woes are intimately connected with the anti-christ materials (p.100). They are associated with the survivors (p.103), the wonders (p.105), and the Messianic kingdom (p.102).

2. Heavenly Jerusalem is called "the city" or "Zion" (p.102). It is pre-created and will appear on earth at the end. It is connected with the Messianic kingdom (pp.101f.).

3. The idea of the "survivors" or "those who remain" (p.103) results from the eschatologization of the doctrine of the righteous remnant. It is applied to the righteous of the last generation who survive the Messianic woes or the eschatological battle. It is intimately associated, there-fore, with the woes, the Messianic kingdom and the wonders (pp.103f.).

4. The survivors are said to "see wonders" or "salvation." These expressions are associated with the survivors, the Messiah and the Messianic kingdom (pp.105f.).

5. The Messiah is called "servant" or "Messiah." He is

associated with the survivors, the final overthrow of evil
and the assumed (pp.106-133).

6. The Company of the Messiah or "those who are with him" are
identical with the assumed. They are to appear with the
Messiah at the beginning of the Messianic kingdom (pp.133ff.).

7. The reuniting of soul and body constitutes resurrection
which will take place before final judgement. It is found
in closest connection with judgement, reward and punishment
(pp.141ff.).

8. Judgement is equal and decisive for all. It is clearly
legal in nature and is characterized by the full revelation
of truth, the correlative of which is the withdrawal of
intercession. It is connected with reward and punishment
and with resurrection (pp.187-191).

9. Gehenna is also called _infernum_ or אבדון . It is a fiery
pit and is most closely associated with judgement, paradise
and punishment (pp.195ff.).

10. "Paradise" or עדן גן appears in three aspects, as Adam's
garden, as the eschatological paradise of the blessed
righteous and as the heavenly object of theosophical knowledge. It is found especially associated with Adam, Gehenna,
judgement and final reward (pp.197-204).

11. Reward and Punishment. There are a number of terms
found for these, "joy and torture" (pp.76f.), "spaciousness"
(p.204), "salvation and perdition" (Ch.2, n.519).

12. Shining Faces. Found connected with final reward (pp.
206ff.).

3. The Associational Complexes and the Two Eschatology Theory

Thus it may be observed that there are two major groupings of associated eschatological ideas. The one centers
around the last generation and the increase of evil until its
consummation which is to be followed by the Messianic kingdom.
The other is made up of the elements of resurrection, judgement, reward and punishment. It was discovered, however,
that these two associational groupings do not occur as independent, alternate eschatologies. One indication of this is
that they occur together in certain passages such as 6:26ff.,
9:6ff. Further, in 5:41ff., 4:26ff. the author moves easily
from one to the other. Again it was noted that where the
author gives his only detailed eschatological chronology, in
7:26-44, these two groups are considered subsequent to one
another. The same sequence of elements was also observed in
6:26ff., 9:6ff., 11:46, 12:34.

As far as IV Ezra is concerned, therefore a "two eschatology theory" cannot be maintained. The question of the
difference between these two groupings and their supposed
conflict with one another has been largely aroused by the
attempt to contrast the "materialism" of the "national"
eschatology with the "spiritualism" of the "universal." In
fact, it was seen that there is little information given
about the nature of the eschatological state as viewed by
either of these. What evidence there is tends to weigh
against a material-spiritual contrast between them (pp.213ff.).

This question of the material-spiritual opposition has been
so central in past scholarship that some further observations
should be made about it.

In the examination of passages contrasting the two ages
which can be presumed to contain IV Ezra's statements about
things he considered crucial to the difference between them,
no assertion of the passing away of the material could be
found.[1] The future age is to be characterized fundamentally
by a change of world order, above all by the passing away of
death or corruption.[2] Yet it is precisely in connection with
death that once again the absence of any view of the material
as evil is starkly evident. It was observed that although
the body is that which dies (7:75 etc.) and although death
is considered highly undesirable, no implicit or explicit
negative evaluation of the body can be found, indeed the contrary is the case.[3] Similarly, in the treatment of the
earth, nothing indicated that it was regarded as evil.[4] In
fact, 7:32 seems to imply that it will continue to exist in
the new age. The resurrection of the body also weighs against
this view. Were the body considered evil, the promise of
the return of the soul to it could be scarcely regarded as
a desired for surety of reward.[5] In light of all this,
above all in view of that fact that nowhere does IV Ezra
state the body or the earth or the material to be evil, it
is justifiable to deny the relevance of the spiritual-material
opposition to his thought. The introduction of this opposition

has been the justification for many of the supposed contrasts
drawn between the "two eschatologies," yet such a dualism
cannot even be discerned to exist between the two ages,[6] not
to speak of two different views of the future world.

The question of the origin of these two associational
complexes lies beyond the limits of this investigation. It
is important, however, to distinguish between the existence
of associational complexes and the existence of consciously
formulated eschatological theories. The existence of the
groups of associated ideas which have been discerned may arise
from their common origin or from a common focus around a
given theme or various other factors. It in no way implies
an exclusivity in the thought of the author: the utilization
of one such group does not mean the rejection of all others.
On the other hand, the acceptance of one formulated and
express eschatology must of necessity imply the abandonment
of other incompatible eschatological ideologies. It is for
this reason that the question of the adequacy and reality of
the scheme which Keulers and other have maintained and which
was raised in the Preamble to Chapter 2 must be answered in
the negative. These two views did not exist for the author
as independent ideologies which he tried to reconcile in his
book. The various elements existed in associational groupings which were part of the range of ideas which the author
brought to bear on the various problems which faced him.
That these concepts were not conceived of as integrated

schemes is clear from the mixing of features from both of
them in the author's responses to certain sorts of problems.
This mixing is neither synthesis nor conscious eclecticism.
It is the result of the response of propositionally non-
consistent thought heavily dependent on traditional ideas to
questions which are raised. Both synthesis and conscious
eclecticism would produce neater, more consistent statements,
for both imply recognition of schematic consistency.

It seems that at least one of the focuses of these
associational complexes was typological. Some features of
the Messianic kingdom complex seem reminiscent of the Exodus.
Thus we may observe the four hundred year period of the
Messianic kingdom alongside the four hundred years slavery
in Egypt,[7] the splitting of the river before the Ten Tribes
alongside the splitting of the Reed Sea and the Jordan before
the Israelites, both of which are called "wonders."[8] There
are, of course, other elements involved such as the survivors
and the Messiah which are drawn from quite other tradition
complexes. On the other hand, the inauguration of the new
age is called a "renewal of creation"[9] and it is preceded by
seven days' silence in which no men exist. Paradise will
again appear to men (7:33f.) and perhaps even the shining
faces hearken back to the traditions about Adam.[10] These
typologies may well have played a part in the crystallization
of these different complexes of ideas.

4. Other Eschatological Matters

In addition to the features of the eschatological ideas
of the book which are involved in the complexes of thought
described above, there are a number of new facets of other
eschatological ideas which came to light.

1. The book, as has been remarked, shows very little interest
in the future state as such. A careful reading of Visions V
and VI revealed almost no details about it. Only the most
general information was observed in Visions I-III and even
the detailed passage, 7:26-44 has but a very sketchy description of the Messianic kingdom and no information at all about
what is to follow the day of judgement.[11] The interest
throughout in the nature, mechanics and time of the end is
one of the most striking characteristics of the book and it
serves to emphasize the author's use of eschatological ideas
as solutions to his questions rather than his interest in
them as such. This seems to be in tune with his rejection
of those areas of special knowledge which have no bearing on
these problems.[12]

2. In this context the ambiguous position of the Messianic
figure is best understood. The Messiah, although the subject
of much of the latter part of the book, is scarcely mentioned
in the first four visions. This leads to the conclusion that
the Messiah did not serve as a solution to the questions
which IV Ezra was asking in these visions.[13] His absence
from 6:25 adds further weight to this conclusion. From this

point of view, the place of the Messiah in the author's
eschatological scheme cannot be doubted, yet it is misleading
to see him as the center of his aspriations.

3. It is significant to note that for the author of IV Ezra
the figure of the Man seems to have had little or no importance. The vision of Chapter 13 should be regarded as an
independent piece employed by the author who is responsible
for its interpretation. While the Man is central in the
vision, the figure is treated in the interpretation in the
same fashion in which the author treats each of the other
symbols in the vision. The special features of the vision
are played down or ignored.[14]

4. The Messiah's activity was not described in any great
detail. In the materials that were available, however, it
was found that neither the function nor the language of kingship were ascribed to him. This was so in spite of the
Davidic title given him in 12:32. His activity was described
in legal language, but it was seen that this was the result
of the legalization of the eschatological battle. Behind
the legal language lay a military function. None of the
features of the final judgement were found ascribed to the
activity of the Messiah.[15]

5. On the other hand, in the descriptions of divine activity,
no hint of God as Warrior could be discerned (p.188). The
final judgement was thoroughly legal in form and language.
This contrasted with the situation of the Messiah where the

military functions were clearly in evidence which tends to
indicate a separation of the old features of God as Warrior
and Judge, perhaps in two directions. Not only did the
eschatological war come to be spoken of in legal terms, but
parallel with this there came a separation of these two functions, with the Messiah taking over the function of Warrior.[16]

6. The particular formulation of the idea of the companions
of the Messiah which was observed in IV Ezra was not
paralleled elsewhere. The identification with the assumed
righteous of those who are to come with the Messiah and the
occurrence of these as his companions in heaven were found to
be unique in this book.[17]

7. By the comparison of IV Ezra 11-12 with Ap. Bar. 39ff.
certain common elements were isolated which may have constituted a "Four Empires Vision Complex," probably directly
dependent on a tradition of re-interpretation of Daniel 2 and
7. The basic features of this complex, beyond the four
empires theory itself, may well have been the symbolic vision
form and the military-legal functions of the Messiah. Other
common features were also observed.[18]

8. The passages 6:27-28, 7:33-35,114, 8:52f., 14:17 were
found to be characterized by common features of style,
literary form and to have a substantially common function.
Although paralleled only in Ap. Bar. 44:8, 73:1f. these
materials are so distinctive that they have to be regarded
as an independent literary type. The passages in IV Ezra

are more polished and elaborate than those in Ap. Bar.[19]

9. Significantly absent from Ap. Bar. were two features of IV Ezra, the term "survivors" (pp.103f.) and the idea of the deterioration of the earth through old age (p.184).

FOOTNOTES

Chapter I

[1]The older literature is discussed by J.A. Fabricius, Codicis Pseudepigraphi Veteris Testamentis (Hamburg: Felginer), 1722, II, 174-192 in his introduction to IV Ezra.

[2]Clement, Stromateis, 3:16 from IV Ezra 5:35.

[3]So already F. Lücke, Versuch einer vollständigen Einleitung in die Offenbarung des Johannes und in die apokalyptische Litteratur überhaupt (2 ed.; Bonn: Weber, 1848), 151, M.R. James, "Introduction" in R. Bensly, The Fourth Book of Ezra (Cambridge: Cambridge University Press, 1895), xxix, whose views are accepted by Bruno Violet, Die Ezra-Apokalypse (Leipzig: Hinrichs', 1910), I, "Die Überlieferungen," xlviii-1. Violet also throws doubt on other suggested uses of IV Ezra in earliest Christian literature, for example, Hermas, I,4,2 (IV Ez. 10:33) and other first and second century sources (Apoc. Paul, Ass. Mos., Sib. III). Compare also G.H. Box, The Ezra-Apocalypse (London: Pitman, 1912), xii.

[4]E. Schürer, Geschichte des jüdischen Volkes im Zeitalter Jesu Christi (3 ed.; Leipzig: Hinrichs', 1898), III, 236-239.

[5]A. Hilgenfeld, Die jüdische Apokalyptik in ihrer geschichtlichen Entwickelung (Jenna: Mauke, 1857), 190 n. Die Propheten Esra und Daniel und ihre neusten Bearbeitungen (Halle: Pfeffer, 1863), 9f.

[6]Schürer, III, 239. The destruction of Jerusalem and the Temple and the exile and humiliation of the people are referred to on many occasions. Thus 3:2, 4:23, 5:17, 6:57-59, 8:16f. (?). The destruction is central to all of vision IV, thus specifically 10:6,20,39,48 and also 12:44,48. In addition to these explicit references, it is basic to the argument of visions I and II in general.

[7]Thus Richard Kabisch, Das vierte Buch Esra auf seine Quellen untersucht (Göttingen: Vandenhoeck und Ruprecht, 1889), 85, 132, Wilhelm Baldensperger, Das Selbstbewusstsein Jesu im Licht der messianischen Hoffnungen seiner Zeit, erste Hälfte "Die messianisch-apokalyptischen Hoffnungen des Judentums" (3 ed. rev.; Strassburg: Heitz und Mundel, 1903), 52 and n.2, Box, Ezra Apocalypse, xxxviii f., A. Kahana, "עזרא חזון" in הספרים החיצונים (Tel Aviv: Masada, 1956), I, 609, Joseph Keulers, "Die eschatologische Lehre des vierten Esrabuches," Biblische Studien, 20, Nos. 2-3 (1922), 119, L. Gry, Les dires prophétiques d'Esdras (Paris: Geuthner, 1938), I, xcviii f.

[8]This view is maintained by H. Gunkel, "Das vierte Buch Esra" in Die Apokryphen und Pseudepigraphen des Alten Testaments ed. E. Kautzsch (Tübingen: Mohr, 1900), II, 352 and n.c and in Der Prophet Esra (Tübingen: Mohr, 1900), xxxii and by F.C. Porter, The Messages of the Apocalyptical Writers (New York: Scribners, 1905), 334.

[9]Thus Lücke, 194 f., n. 2, Hilgenfeld, Jüdische Apokalyptik, 190, n.3, Esra und Daniel, 10f., L. Vagany, Le problème eschatologique dans le IVe livre d'Esdras (Paris: Picard et Fils, 1906), 15. G. Volkmar, Handbuch der Einleitung in die Apokryphen, Part 2 "Das vierte Buch Esrae" (Tübingen: Fues, 1863), 360 sees 30 as a number portending the rebuilding of the Temple.

[10]Thus Kabisch, 85, 132, Box, Ezra Apocalypse, xxxviii f., see it as the date of the authorship of the so-called S document (Salathiel Apocalypse). E. de Faye, Les apocalypses juives (Paris: Fischbacher, 1892), 103, Kabisch and Box all use this date as a "type" date and thus as part of their demonstration of the independence of the S document.

[11]Baldensperger, 52 and n.2, Keulers, 119, Gry, I, xcviii f. use this date as support for interpreting the end of the Eagle vision (Chapters 11-12) as in the time of Trajan, while Kahana sees 3:1,29 as the time of the composition of the first vision.

[12]The suggestion of the relation to Ezekiel 1:1 was already made by Lücke, 154. It was taken up by those who maintained that the date indicated a general period of time, in part, evidently, as a justification for their own lack of specificity. Thus it was used by Gunkel, Apokryphen, 352, Der Prophet Esra, 69. In addition it was used by those who totally rejected the importance of this date, in order to explain its presence in the text. Thus, Lücke, 154, Hilgenfeld, Esra und Daniel, 10f., Jüdische Apokalyptik, 190, n.3, Vagany, 15.

[13]A. von Gudschmit, "Die Apokalypse des Esra und ihre spätern Bearbeitungen," Zeitschrift für wissenschaftliche Theologie, 3 (1860), 78.

[14]Kabisch, 154, de Faye on the basis of their source division. Earlier A. Hilgenfeld, Jüdische Apokalyptik, 237.

[15]For example, Clemen, "Die Zusammensetzung des Buch Henoch, Ap. Baruch und IV Ezra," Theologische Studien und Kritiken 71 (1898), 237-246, especially 239.

[16]Thus Vagany, 76, Box, Ezra Apocalypse, xxxi and

commentary ad loc., Bruno Violet, Die Apokalypsen des Esra
und des Baruch in Deutscher Gestalt (Leipzig: Hinrichs',
1924), (referred to henceforth as Violet, II) ad loc.

[17]P. 64. He compares with Sib. IV:135f., V:33f., 214-
227. Violet, II, 23 sees this passage as based on a
Sibylline oracle. Compare, however, comments on this in P.B.
Rigaux, L'Antéchrist et l'opposition au royaume messianique
dans l'Ancien et le Nouveau Testament (Paris: Gabalda, 1932),
184.

[18]180 ff.

[19]See E. Boehmer, "Zur Lehre von Antichrist, nach
Schneckenburger," Jahrbücher für deutsche Theologie, 4
(1859), 405-467, especially 413-415, Wilhelm Bousset, The
Antichrist Legend, tr. A.H. Keane, (London: Hutchinson,
1896), 191-195, Rigaux, 184.

[20]Compare the brief treatment of the evil ruler here
with that in Dan. 7:7-14.

[21]J. Wellhausen, Skizzen und Vorarbeiten (Berlin: Reimer,
1899), VI, 247, Box, Ezra Apocalypse, xxxi.

[22]Antiq. xv:5.2. Thus de Faye, 44f.

[23]One outstanding passage is in Mic. 1:3f. which
describes the splitting open of valleys before Yahweh.
Zech. 14:4 mentions similar phenomena in the context of
eschatological battle. Compare also the chaotic place in
I En. 21:7.

[24]Jüdische Apokalyptik, 222, n.2. He also sees in 5:4f.
a description of the civil war in Rome, ibid., 236.

[25]Ibid., 195, 236, Esra und Daniel, 22f., Volkmar,
Einleitung, II, 361.

[26]III, 236f.

[27]Kabisch, 50f., Box, Ezra Apocalypse, 67. This is
conditioned by the source division theory and the supposed
eschatological peculiarities of the S document, see especially
Box, 68-70. For a critique of this position see Keulers, 47f.
and below.

[28]So Gunkel, Apokryphen, 337, 365n. He points out the
mysterious form and compares with Gal. 4:21-31. Also see
Schürer, III, 236f., Vagany, 41, Keulers, 41,47f., 107.

[29]Chapters 11-12.

[30]12:11.

[31]Schürer, III, 236-239.

[32]See Richard Laurence, Primi Ezrae Libri, Versio Aethiopica (Oxford: University Press, 1820), "General Remarks," 312-315. On p. 319 he definitely proposes a pre-Christian dating. Thus also C.J. van der Vlis, Disputatio Critica de Ezrae Libro Apocrypho Vulgo Quarto Dicto (Amsterdam: Müller, 1839), 167-189, Lücke, 205-206. All these scholars identify the little wings and wings with rulers of monarchical and republican Rome. Hilgenfeld's earlier view, as expressed in Jüdische Apokalyptik, 218ff. identifies the wings (11:1,3) with the Ptolemies and the heads with Caesar, Anthony and Octavian, thus placing IV Ezra and the end of the Jewish apocalyptic before the beginning of Christianity. His later view in Zeitschrift für wissenschaftliche Theologie, 3 (1860), 335-358, retains this terminal dating and identification of the heads, but identifies the wings and little wings with the Selucids.

[33]Gudschmit, Zeitschrift für wissenschaftliche Theologie, 1860, 48, 68 ff.

[34]A.M. Le Hir, "Du IVe livre d'Esdras" in Etudes Bibliques par M. l'abbé Le Hir (Paris: Albanel, 1869), 139-250. The vision is treated on pp. 176-192.

[35]Thus Gudschmit reckons Commodus as the third little wing, while Le Hir is not sure whether to combine him with M. Aurelius or to omit one of the preceding emperors and make him an independent twelfth wing. Le Hir introduces Clodius Albinus as the sixth little wing while he is given no place in Gudschmit's scheme. Neither of them includes Galba, Otho and Vitellius, while Titus and Nerva are the two first little wings.

[36]Especially in view of its sevenfold nature pointed out by Gunkel, Apokryphen, 350f. This observation was further investigated in the area of groups of seven objects (and somewhat less probably) of seven lines in poetic sections by Keulers, 21. The purported sevenfold internal structure of some of the visions is suggested by Gry, I xcvii, n.74.

[37]Some of these difficulties are avoided by Vagany who regards the vision as an original piece of the time of Domitian reworked in 218 C.E., thus pp. 21-23. All references to the little wings are, on this theory, secondary. The

interpolator added 11:3,10-11,22-30, 12:1-3,17-21,29-31a, retouched 12:14 (but forgot to fix 11:21) and 12:27-28. For similar views see A. Dillmann, Sitzungsberichte der Berliner Akademie, (1888), 215-237, Clemen, 242, Gry, I, xcviii ff. This is desiderated by the view which would take the wings as "originally" in pairs, which view is clearly contradicted by 12:12,14-16, cf. 11:1,13,18.

[38]Thus Volkmar, Einleitung, II, 157-158 and n., Dillmann, Sitzungsberichte, 1888, 215-237, Wellhausen, Skizzen, VI, 241f. Wellhausen also considers that the last pair of little wings is an addition after the time of Domitian. C. Sigwalt, "Die Chronologie des 4 Buches Esdras," Biblische Zeitschrift, 9 (1911), 147 accepts all wings and little wings as original but takes them in pairs. Box, Ezra Apocalypse, 265 also accepts this hypothesis for his "original form" of the vision as far as the wings are concerned, but in light of 11:24-28 he is forced to accept the little wings as single and not in pairs. The only reason that he can adduce for this differentiation is the greater importance of the wings. The reworking, c. 120 C.E., by R he says was then made on the basis of one wing = one emperor. Thus R is responsible for phrases in 11:12,19,20,32 and especially in 12:14.

[40]Thus A. Gfrörer, "Das Jahrhundert des Heils," Part I of Geschichte des Urchristentums (Stuttgart: Schweizerbart, 1838), 82ff., A. Dillmann, art. "Pseudepigrapha" in Real-Encyklopädie für protestantische Theologie und Kirche, ed. Herzog (1 ed.; Gotha: Besser, 1860), XII, 312, K. Wieseler, "Das vierte Buch Esra nach Inhalt und Alter untersucht," Theologische Studien und Kritiken, 43 (1870), 270f., Gunkel, Apokryphen, 345, Der Prophet Ezra, xxv-xxvi, Schürer, III, 242f.

[41]Gfrörer, 88f., Wieseler, Theologische Studien und Kritiken, 1870, 272f. take them as Herodians; Kabisch, 163 takes them as various rulers of Palestine, but thinks that in any case they are probably interpolated.

[42]Dillmann, Real-Encyclopädie, XII, 312 suggests that they may be generals or pretenders, but thinks that they are interpolated. The former view is supported by Gunkel, Apokryphen, 345, Der Prophet Ezra, xxvi who thinks that the two little wings which fell with Vespasian were Mucianus and Tiberius Alexander, the rulers of Syria and Palestine. He suggests that in the case of the little wings the author is drawing on detailed information about minor usurpers and pretenders not preserved in the extant sources. This is also the view of Schürer, III, 243.

[43]See ibid., 241f. where the major arguments to which nothing of substance has since been added are summarized.

[44]See below, pp.148-180 for references for and demonstrations of these statements.

[45]For documentation and argument see p.54.

[46]The most analogous use is in phrases like קיצין מבני in Talmudic literature, e.g. Sanh. 97b. In these cases, however, קץ means "end," not "period of time."

[47]See above, n.7.

[48]Review of Kabisch in Theologische Literaturzeitung, 16 No.1 (1891), 5-11.

[49]Ibid., 9f.

[50]See especially ibid., 10, his remarks on the treatment of 3:7f. and 7:32.

[51]Ibid., 11.

[52]Ibid., 7. This approach is even more explicit in his introduction to IV Ezra in Apokryphen, 335-348.

[53]Der Prophet Esra, xxvii ff.

[54]Apokryphen, 343.

[55]Ibid., 348.

[56]Thus, for example, 12:34, cf. Gunkel, Apokryphen, 348.

[57]Ezra Apocalypse, xxi-xxxiii, cf. also xxxiv-lxviii.

[58]Keulers, 36-41.

[59]Ibid., 44.

[60]Ibid., 45.

[61]Ibid., 46-54.

[62]Ezra Apocalypse, especially xxi, xxiii f.

[63]Keulers, 47-51.

[64]IV Ez. Chapters 11-14.

[65]Keulers, 52.

[66]Ibid., 52 f.

[67] Ibid., cf. above p. 8 and n.36.

[68] Cf. R.H. Charles' introduction to II Baruch (Ap. Bar.) in The Apocrypha and Pseudepigrapha of the Old Testament (Oxford: Oxford University Press, 1913), II, 474-476, The Apocalypse of Baruch (London: Black, 1896), liii-lxvii.

[69] Frank Moore Cross Jr., The Ancient Library of Qumran and Modern Biblical Studies (rev. ed.; New York: Anchor Books, 1961), 199.

[70] Cf. B.J., II, 124f.

[71] See, for example, the material collected by י. אבן-שמואל, מדרשי גאולה (Tel Aviv: Bialik Institute, 1943).

[72] Y. Kaufmann, תולדות האמונה הישראלית מימי קדם עד סוף בית שני (Jerusalem: Bialik Institute, 1956), VIII, 485-487 emphasizes this first point but ignores the equally important development of the apocalyptic.

[73] See n.56 above.

[74] See pp.45f. and notes there.

[75] H. and H.A. Frankfort and others, Before Philosophy: The Intellectual Adventure of Ancient Man (Harmondsworth: Penguin, 1963), 14-16.

[76] Ibid., 28,29.

[77] Ibid., 51.

[78] Cross, Ancient Library, 78n.

[79] The Theology of Seder Eliahu (New York: Bloch, 1932), 17-32. In the text we have drawn mainly on his short analysis in this book. He develops his concepts further in Organic Thinking (New York: Jewish Theological Seminary, 1938). Especially relevant are Chapter 1, Section I, pp. 1-3, Sections III-IV, pp. 6-12 and Chapter 4, pp. 179-261. In this latter he investigates some of the implications of "organic thought," among others the idea that logic may be used to a limited extent within the organic whole, ". . . though organic thinking may be the framework for logical thinking, it is thinking of another order different from the latter" (260). These matters are touched upon in his The Rabbinic Mind, (New York: Jewish Theological Seminary, 1952), especially Ch.2, pp.11-34.

[80] Theology, 21-29.

[81]Ibid., 29.

[82]I. Heinemann, דרכי האגדה(Jerusalem: Magnes Press, 1954), 168.

[83]30,32.

[84]William F. Albright, History, Archaeology and Christian Humanism (New York: McGraw Hill, 1964), 51-56.

[85]Gunkel, Apokryphen, 347 f., Keulers, 53 and n.67 above.

[86]Thus 4:12-21,40-43,48-50, 5:41,46-49 etc. Ezra also speaks in these terms, for example, 5:50 ff. etc.

[87]Thus, for example, 5:41-6:11 cf. pp.27f. below.

[88]For example, II En. 3 ff.

[89]Gershom G. Scholem, Major Trends in Jewish Mysticism (3ed. rev.; New York: Schocken, 1954), Jewish Gnosticism, Merkabah Mysticism and Talmudic Tradition (New York: Jewish Theological Seminary, 5720-1960). This latter work is almost totally devoted to the recovery of aspects of the earliest stages of the mystic tradition in Israel.

[90]Thus 4:12,23f., 5:28-30 etc.

[91]Apokryphen, 335-339.

[91a]The point at which the literary unity of a document must be denied may be determined in a number of ways. We have already observed that the normal methods of the historical critical study of literary documents are in no way to be rejected. It is clear that such methods of study may lead to the conclusion that a given document is not a literary unity. A similar result may also be reached by other means, for example through a knowledge of its literary history. The methodology being suggested here is seen as an addition to the techniques developed by past scholarship. If a book is judged on the basis of language, style, literary structure and so forth to be a unity, then it is not clear to this writer just what sorts of problems would have to arise in the analysis of the thought for such unity to be denied. One suspects that if a work is composite, then this would be evident in these former areas.

[92]Violet, I, xiii-lxii, II, xiii-lv.

[93]"The Georgian Version of Fourth Esras from the Jerusalem Manuscript," Harvard Theological Review, 19 (1926),

299-320, "The Georgian Text of Fourth Esras from the Athos Manuscript," idem, 22 (1929), 57-105.

[94] Harvard Theological Review, 1926, 309.

[95] Ibid., 313.

[96] Ibid., 317 f.

[97] Joshua Bloch, "Was there a Greek Version of the Apocalypse of Ezra?" Jewish Quarterly Review, N.S. 46 (1956), 309-320.

[98] Wellhausen, Skizzen, VI, 240, Violet, I, xiii f., II, xxix-xxxi, Box, Ezra Apocalypse, xi-xiii etc.

[99] Jewish Quarterly Review, 1956, 311-312.

[100] In addition to the material cited by Violet, I, xiii f., II, xxix-xxxi and Box, Ezra Apocalypse, xi-xiii, Gry, I, xviii f. see below, Chapter 2, nn. 64, 213, 227, 234, 255, 339. See also Violet, II on 5:41, 7:116 etc., Box on 7:124 cf. 8:31 etc., Hilgenfeld on 9:5. Compare Box and Violet on 13:26, both building on the suggestion of Wellhausen, Skizzen, VI, 236.

[101] I, xxiii.

[102] See below on the Armenian version.

[103] See Gry, I, lix and n. on 13:32.

[104] I, lxxvi f.

[105] I, lxxvi, 2).

[106] For further considerations for a Hebrew original see A. Kaminka, Beiträge zur Erklärung der Esra Apokalypse und zur Rekonstruktion ihres hebräisches Urtextes (Breslau: Marcus, 1934). He perhaps goes too far, but taken in conjunction with the considerations urged by other scholars, his work adds more weight to the theory of a Hebrew original.

[107] Apokryphen, 333.

[108] See Violet, II ad loc.

[109] Berliner Philologischer Wochenschrift, 18 (1913), 547-551.

[110] Personal communication to Violet quoted Violet, II, xxiv f.

[111] Gry, I, lxxxvi-xciii.

[112] Treatment of some of the features of this text may be found in M. Stone, "Contradictions of Translation as Revealed in the Apocrypha" to appear shortly in Proceedings of the International Conference on the Armenian Language.

[113] Similar problems arise in connection with the Armenian versions of the Testaments of the XII Patriarchs and of Song of Songs.

[114] See Chapter 2, n. 152 below.

[115] See pp.198ff. and notes there.

[116] See pp.71ff. below.

[117] Further special readings are treated in my forthcoming "Contradictions of Translation."

Chapter II

[1] Keulers, 143. The translation is our own.

[2] Thus Kabisch, 67-70, 75 et passim, Porter, 52, 336, Gunkel, Theologische Literaturzeitung, 1891, 10, Lagrange, "Notes sur le Messianisme au temps de Jesus," Revue Biblique, N.S.2 (1905), 500, de Faye, 10ff., H.H. Rowley, The Relevance of Apocalyptic (new rev. ed.; New York: Association Press, 1964), 116-118, Baldensperger, 102,113f., Vagany, 82f., Keulers, 6-10,36,143 etc.

[3] Thus Kabisch, for example, 96f., 67ff. This view was attacked by Gunkel, Theologische Literaturzeitung, 1891, 10. See also, de Faye, 10f., Box, Ezra Apocalypse, xxii-lvii largely refuted by Keulers, 46ff.

[4] 10f.

[5] For instance, 7:26ff., 12:34.

[6] Revue Biblique, 1905, 500.

[7] 162.

[8] 53f., 336.

[9] 337f.

[10] 82f.

[11] 6-10, 36.

[12] Thus Porter, 52,336, Kabisch, 96f. 67f. Gunkel, Theologische Literaturzeitung, 1891, 10. Box, Ezra Apocalypse, xlvii ff.

[13] Porter, 52, Keulers, 7f. On pp. 46-49 he clearly recognizes that some of the oppositions set up by Box are not as stark as Box would have them. See also Box, Ezra Apocalypse, xxxvii, xlvii.

[14] These verses are missing in the Armenian version.

[15] Note Latin temporum, cf. 4:26, saeculum.

[16] Syriac, "first world . . . second . . ." (^{c}lm' qdmy' . . . tnyn' . . .), Ethiopic, "first . . . second world . . . ," Arabic[1] is periphrastic, Arabic[2] as Ethiopic.

[17] Ethiopic, Arabic[2] MS B, Isaac, Arabic[1] "the generation

of Abraham and his family." The readings of Ethiopic and Arabic[2] are evidently secondary and interpretative. Syriac and Arabic[1] (implicitly) support Latin.

[18]Ethiopic omits to the end of the verse.

[19]Violet, II suggests that Latin and Arabic I represent Greek ἀπ'ἄκρου and reconstructs an original Greek ἄκρου from Hebrew ראש meaning "extremity." It seems reasonable, however, to assume that "heel" itself is an adequate expression of extremity and the reading of Latin and Arabic[1] should thus be accepted. This best fits the interpretation of vss. 9f.-- at the beginning, directly on their birth it was so and thus it will be in the end.

[20-20]Thus Latin and the part of the verse preserved in Ethiopic. Violet, II, Gunkel, Apokryphen, and Box, Ezra Apocalypse read partly with Syriac, "the heel of the first age . . . , the hand of the second . . . ."

[21]Ibid., 67-70, F. Rosenthal, Vier Apokryphische Bücher aus der Zeit und Schule R. Akiba's (Leipzig: Schulze, 1885), 59 n., considers IV Ezra 6:8-9 a quote from R. Gamliel. That this is not the case is evident from the other Rabbinic traditions adduced here.

[22]Translation from G. Friedlander, Pirqê de Rabbi Eliezer (London: Kegan Paul, 1916), 235, cf. Pes. de R. K. 23a.

[23]Midrash Haggadol, ed. S. Schechter (Cambridge: C.U.P., 1902), "Genesis," Toledoth, 25:26, cf. Pes. de R. K. 23b.

[23a]M. Jastrow, A Dictionary of the Targumim, the Talmud Babli and Yerushalmi, and the Midrashic Literature (New York: Pardes, 1950), s.v. Edom. cf. Ab. Zar. 10b etc.

[24]The major views were also mentioned above p.6.

[25]This is the view of Hilgenfeld, Jüdische Apokalyptik, 195, 237, Esra und Daniel, 22f., Volkmar, Einleitung, II, 361.

[26]Kabisch, 50f., Box, Ezra Apocalypse, 67-70.

[27]See references above, Ch. I, n.28, see further Schürer, III, 236.

[28]Gunkel, Apokryphen, 364, n.5.

[29]Perhaps as A. Hilgenfeld, Messias Judaeorum (Lipsiae: Reisland, 1869) suggests ἀπὸ τοῦ Ἀβρααμ ἕως τοῦ Ἀβρααμ but what Hebrew could this reflect?

[30]See Arabic[2] of v. 10 which seems to be based on precisely some such word play.

[31]See the passage from Midrash Haggadol quoted above.

[32]This interpretation implies the reading of Latin and
Ethiopic accepted in v.9, see n. 20 above.

[33]See K. Stendahl, The School of St. Matthew (Uppsala:
1954), 190-194. The present view of the Biblical texts is
rather different from that held by Stendahl in 1954, largely
due to the discovery of new manuscripts. His discussion of
the nature of the pešer mode is, however, highly illuminating.

[34]Latin vana, Syriac byšt', similarly Ethiopic. The
Arabic versions are problematic and Armenian omits the whole
verse. Cf. 7:14.

[35-35]The versions are difficult. The text here is read
according to Syriac which has the clearest rendering. Latin
has ut non properes. Box, following Gunkel suggests a play
of words אל הבן . . . תבהל פן in Greek μὴ σπουδάσῃς . . .
ἵνα μὴ σπεύσῃς. This would explain Latin, Syriac and
Ethiopic.

[36]All versions: 7:84, 12:25, 11:9, 12:23, 28, 13:20(Syr.
šwlmhwn dzbn'), 12:9 (Armenian կատարած), 10:59 (Ethiopic
varies), 7:73,77. Armenian alone omits: 5:42, 13:46, 8:50,
63, 14:22, 13:18, 6:34, 7:87. Armenian and Ethiopic omit:
7:95.

[37]Thus for example Syriac, Greek, Hebrew, Latin,
Armenian in Gen. 49:1, Deut. 4:30, Jer. 30:24. Armenian
uses synonymous եղիս with all other versions parallel in
Isa. 2:2, Jer. 23:20, Ezek. 38:16, Mic. 4:1, Prov. 31:25, Dan.
2:28. Similarly it employs կատարած in Hos. 3:5. Armenian
is problematic in Isa. 30:8, Prov. 23:18, Neh. 8:18 where
the other versions agree. Syriac is completely consistent
in all cases examined. Latin has an exceptional reading in
Deut. 31:29, in extremo tempore.

[38]Thus, for example 13:46, 6:34, 7:73,77. Once it reads
cdn' (12:9).

[39]12:9, 7:77.

[40]12:9, 6:34, 7:73,77, 13:46. The phrase is fixed in
Ethiopic and occurs, for example, where Latin reads novissimus
alone, thus 7:84, 8:50,63, 12:23,25, 13:20.

[41] See E. Hatch and H. Redpath, A Concordance to the Septuagint (Oxford: Clarendon Press, 1897), s.v. καιρός.

[42] The expression in diebus novissimis or the like, a standard phrase, is not discussed. It occurs in Gen. 49:1, Isa. 2:2, Neh. 8:18 and many other places, also IV Ezra 10:59, 13:18.

[43] Similarly Deut. 31:29.

[44] Cf. tempus alone, Ezek. 7:7 (קץ --πέρας), 7:12 (עת-- καιρός) also מועד in Ps. 102:14 and עת in Ps. 119:126.

[45] 1QS iv:16-17, 1Q$_p$Hab vii:7,12. These latter two are in contexts dealing with eschatological mysteries.

[46] The use of אחרונים as in CD xx:9 seems to lie behind IV Ezra 5:42 which has the plural in Latin and Syriac. The cases of עת such as 1QS ix:13f., CD xvi:3 and מועד in 1QS iii:18, iv:18f., 25f., 1QM i:8, iii:7f. etc. are interesting but the combination with אחרון or the like is not found.

[47] See Ch. 1, n.46.

[48] "Entrances," thus Latin; Syriac, Armenian, Ethiopic and Arabic read "ways." The same variation is to be observed in v.13 except in Armenian which omits that verse. Perhaps Hebrew מבוי see below n.53.

[49] Cf. v.11 above. Perhaps = העולם הזה .

[50] The order of attributes varies somewhat in the different versions. Latin is followed here. Latin, Syriac, and Ethiopic have seven attributes, Arabic[1] and Armenian have eight and Arabic[2] one.

[51] Thus Syriac. Latin has maioris saeculi, Ethiopic "that world," Arabic[1] "the world to come."

[52] See below n.435 and pp.62,63.

[53] See especially vss. 4,7. In Rabbinic Hebrew, however, מבוא or מבוי means also "way," "lane" or "passage," cf. Lev. R. 9:2. This would explain the usage here.

[54] See p. 182 below.

[55] See vss. 15f. and discussion pages 185f.

[56] The late Professor Y. Gutman drew my attention to the

passage in Hesiod, Works, 290-292:

> Goodness . . . : long and steep is the path that leads
> to her and it is rough at first; but when a man has
> reached the top, then indeed she is easy, though other-
> wise hard to reach.

. . . μακρὸς δὲ καὶ ὄρθιος οἶμος ἐς αὐτὴν
τρηχὺς τὸ πρῶτον· ἐπὴν δ'εἰς ἄκρον ἵκηται
ῥηιδίη δὴ ἔπειτα πέλει, χαλέπη περ ἐοῦσα.

Text and translation in Hesiod, the Homeric Hymns and
Homerica, ed. E. Evelyn-White (London: Heinemann, 1915).
This text is quoted in Xenophon, Memorabilia, II, 1, 20 and
is followed there by a legend quoted in the name of Prodicus
which makes use of the idea of two women representing the
way of vice and the way of virtue. This latter woman
describes her way to Heracles the hero of this legend by
saying that the rewards and joys of following the path of
virtue come only after great toil and labour. I. Heinemann
pointed out the influence of the Prodicus story on LXX Prov.
2:16,"האליגוריסטיקה של היהודים ההלניסטים פרט לפילון" in
Commentationes Iudaico-Hellenisticae in Memoriam Iohannis
Lewy, edd. M. Schwabe and I. Gutman (Jerusalem: Magnes Press,
1949), p.48. This formulation of the idea of the way bears
a certain similarity to that which may be observed here, but
the origins of IV Ezra's concept should be sought in the
materials cited below.

[57]Yalq. Shim., II, 919.

[58]See, for example, Ps. 1:6, II Sam. 22:22, 1QH iv:4.
See also the materials collected in W. R. Morfill and R. H.
Charles, The Book of the Secrets of Enoch (Oxford: O.U.P.,
1896), 42 n. With the elements of danger mentioned in v.3
compare Ps. 66:12.

[59]Cf. for example, 1QS iii:13-iv:26.

[60]F.M. Braun, "L'arrière-fond judaïque du quartrième
évangile et la Communauté de l'Alliance," Revue Biblique, 62
(1955), 5 n.4, 24-26.

[61]J.-P. Audet, "Affinités litteraires et doctrinales du
'Manuel de Discipline,'" Revue Biblique, 59 (1952), especially
226f., idem, 60 (1953), 41-82.

[62]See also Cross, Ancient Library, 201.

[63]Latin annos is original. The reading also occurs in
the Syriac as published by Ceriani and, although it lacks in
the translation of the Syriac published in Violet, I, it is
mentioned in the commentary in Violet, II. It is missing
from the Ethiopic. The whole verse is omitted by Arabic[1],
Arabic[2] and Armenian, probably for dogmatic reasons.

[64]Thus Ethiopic. Latin reads _filius meus Christus_.
Filius perhaps represents παῖς as a translation of עבד. That
a Christian translator, in this context, should render παῖς
as "son" is clearly possible while it is far less likely
that he render ὑιος as "servant." See also Violet, II,
ad loc., J. Drummond, _The Jewish Messiah_ (London: Longmans,
Green & Co., 1877), 285f. See below pp.71ff.

[65]Latin reads _adsumetur_ on dogmatic grounds, cf. Gunkel,
Apokryphen, 370, n.1, followed by Violet and Box.

[66]Reflected in Syriac, Ethiopic and Arabic[1].

[67]Arabic[2], "as on that seventh day."

[68]Ethiopic and Arabic[1] omit. This is a Hebrew idiom
and there is no reason to doubt its originality, especially
since it is attested by both Latin and Syriac.

[69]Latin _corruptum_ (sc. _saeculum_), thus Ethiopic. The
Syriac ḥbl' can be construed either as a noun "corruption"
or an adjective "corrupt." Arabic[1] and Georgian "corruption."

[70]See p.182 below.

[71]See p.144 and n.388 below. Box, perhaps correctly,
understands this as a reference to prayer, _Ezra Apocalypse_,
84n. See Ap. Bar. 3:7.

[72]See 7:12-13 and exegesis pp.55ff., and also p.185.

[73]The Messiah and his company will be revealed, although
they are presently hidden, 13:52.

[74]Violet, II, 81n.

[75-75]The versions vary here. Syriac reads "the world
has an end," Ethiopic "the end of the world has not yet
been," Arabic[2] "the being of this world does not end." See
the discussion of the texts in Violet, II, _ad loc_. The major
readings seem to be either as in our text following Syriac
and Arabic[2] or as Latin "is not the end." The reading
accepted here suits v.113 better.

[76]Thus Latin. See discussion in the exegesis of this
verse.

[77]Restored in Latin by Bensly.

[78]Arabic[2] "day of resurrection." Note this interesting
equivalation.

[79] Latin temporis, Syriac ^{c}lm', Ethiopic ^{c}alam, Arabic[1] dahr, Arabic[2] ^{c}alam, Armenian աշխարհ^c. Here read "world (age)" as Syriac, Ethiopic, Arabic[2], Armenian.

[80] Latin omits.

[81] Thus Latin and Syriac. Violet, II reads with Arabic[1] "the living will not die" following "world" #2 this then constituting the first of six hemistychs which follow. This suggestion is quite plausible.

[82] See Violet, II, 97 n. who considers Latin best but compare n.75 above.

[84] Violet, II, ad loc.

[85] 183 f.

[86] G. Scholem, Major Trends, 46 and n.16 on page 358, cf. 66, Jewish Gnosticism, 37.

[87] Thus, for example, Ex. 33:18, Ezek. 1:28, 10:4 etc.

[88] Thus 7:95,98, 8:51.

[89] See p.55 and n.52.

[90] Thus Syriac, Ethiopic.

[91] Saeculum etc.

[92] On "world to come" see below p.63 etc.

[93] Armenian has a long additional section introduced at this point.

[94] Syriac, Armenian "he answered and said to me," Ethiopic "he answered me and said to me," Arabic[1] "he answered," Arabic[2] "he said to me."

[95] Thus Latin, Syriac. Ethiopic reads zentu $^c\bar{a}$lam = "this world" . .. zeketu ^{c}alam = "that world," similarly Arabic[1]. Arabic[2] is corrupt and Armenian omits. It is difficult to reach a decision between a reading with "world" and one without; both may reflect genuine traditions.

[96] Plural--Syriac, Latin.

[97] See p.55, n.52 above.

[98] Verse 47 makes this even more explicit.

[99] See pp.49-52 above.

[100] 48, 107.

[101] "This world," thus Arabic[1], Arabic[2] and Armenian, cf. v.27.

[102] The phrase is omitted by Syriac, Ethiopic and both Arabic versions. It is implied in Armenian "not being able to bear the evil of its time." The interpretation of this passage in the Armenian is different to that in the other versions.

[103] Armenian adds "men of." V.28 is omitted by this version, although it may be vestigially represented in v.29a.

[104-104] The words are omitted in Ethiopic. Arabic[1] has 29b and c only in periphrastic form.

[105-105] Omitted by Arabic[1] perhaps on dogmatic grounds.

[106] Lacks in Latin but represented one way or another in Syriac, Ethiopic and Arabic.

[107] Ethiopic and Arabic[2] read "harvest." See pp.66f. #3 below.

[108] incipiant reflects μέλλειν cf. 7:42.

[109] See p.182f. below.

[110] 3:4-34, especially vss.20 ff.

[111] Latin incipiet, Syriac ^{c}tyd = Greek μέλλειν, cf. n.108 above.

[112] Ethiopic yemṣa' "will come." This same alternation may be observed in 7:33 and there Arabic[1] also reads as Ethiopic.

[113] Syriac ^{c}tyd = μέλλειν.

[114] 6:5, 7:104, 10:23.

[115] 6:5 speaks of the sealing up of those who gather the treasures of faith, referring evidently to the fixing of their predestined number or perhaps to their being marked out, cf. Ezek. 9:4 etc. In 10:23 this language is evidently applied to the decisive nature of the destruction of Zion. 7:104 is discussed below.

[116]Thus Syriac, Ethiopic, Arabic[1]: Arabic[2] is abbreviated and Armenian is quite different.

[117]Thus Latin, Ethiopic.

[118]Arabic[1] reads "the conclusion of the end of this world-age." Armenian has "and after the completion of these signs, books will be opened and at that time my glory will appear."

[119]Thus 7:27, 9:8, 13:19-23. Perhaps 14:15f. should also be seen in this light, although that passage seems to draw on the tradition of the deterioration of the earth, see pp.181f. below.

[120]Thus, for example, 4:26, 7:27.

[121]It may be seen, for example, in 5:41, 6:25, 7:27, 9:8.

[122]See above, #4, p.65.

[123]Such are 7:33-35,114, 8:52f., 14:17. These passages will be discussed below.

[124]Cf. also 14:9,49.

[125]See p.65 above.

[126]Latin residuum = τὸ λοιπον (Volkmar).

[127]See pp.71-75 below.

[128]This is suggested by the readings of Ethiopic "the world is ended," Arabic[1] "the times of the world are ended," Arabic[2] "the end of the world."

[129]See pp.53f. above.

[130]See pp. 65, 70 above.

[131]Drummond, 285f.

[132]A. Dillmann, Lexicon Linguae Aethiopicae (Reprint; New York: Unger, 1955), s.v. ፈለጸ.

[133]Ezra Apocalypse, lvi. Lagrange also sees Ps. 2 as the basis of Vision VI, but this is not as obvious as he thinks.

[134]The much debated reading of 1QSa ii:11 cannot be considered as firm evidence. See F. M. Cross, "Qumran Cave I,"

Journal of Biblical Literature, 75 (1956), 124, n.8 and based
on new photographs, Ancient Library, 87, n.67. While the
text clearly reads ywlȳd, the context is very difficult and
judgement should be suspended until all the Essene material
is published. Cross suggested an emendation to ywly<k>,
ibid. For another view see Yigal Yadin, "A Crucial Emendation in the Dead Sea Scrolls," Journal of Biblical Literature,
78 (1959), 238-241. A reading "I and my son" occurs in I
En. 105:2 but this is too isolated to be of any help. No
suggestion of any connection with Ps. 2 can be observed
there. A text recently published by J. Starcky, "Un texte
messianique araméen de la grotte 4 de Qumran," in Mémorial
du Cinquantenaire de l'Ecole des langues orientales anciens
de l'Institut Catholique à Paris (Paris: Blond et Gay, 1964),
51-66 also seems to represent the Messiah as son of God (cf.
1. 10).

[135]Syriac "coming world" ᶜlm' d't', thus Ethiopic,
Arabic[1]; Armenian "that world" is a technical term for the
world to come. Arabic[2] omits.

[136]Latin pertinebit. Bensly suggests μέλλησει which
certainly seems to lie behind Syriac hw ᶜtyd . . . dnᶜbd.

[137]Ethiopic yetkʷēnanu = "will be judged." This is a
common substitution, see n.151 below.

[138]See p.55 and references in n.52 above, cf. n.135.

[139]Thus it is found in connection with paradise in
7:36,38,123 and less directly 8:52. It is necessary to distinguish 7:36,38 which have the exact phrase "paradise of
delight" and probably are just translations of Hebrew עדן גן
from cases like 7:123, 8:52 where the joy is said to occur
in paradise. These latter cases, nevertheless serve to highlight the intimate connection between this interpretation
of עדן גן and the wider use of the concept of joy.

[140]7:28, 12:34.

[141]7:95; 7:131 speaks of the joy over salvation of the
righteous.

[142]8:59, 9:9,12.

[143]7:36,38.

[144]7:75,76,80,84,86,99.

[145]Ethiopic "I answered him and I said to him," Arabic[1]
"said to him," Arabic[2] "said," Armenian "answered and said
to the angel of the Lord."

[146]Syriac "Lord, Lord." Ethiopic and Arabic omit. Here read as Latin and Armenian.

[147]Thus Latin and Syriac. Arabic[1] is somewhat freer, Arabic[2] omits. Armenian omits "now."

[148]Latin and Syriac preserve reflexes of Hebrew infinitive absolute + finite verb.

[149]Arabic[1] "place of rest," see n.388 below.

[150]Greek μέλλεις cf. 7:42,88,122, 4:32, 13:29 etc.

[151]Ethiopic 'eska yebaseh ^{c}edemehu 'ama yaqawem dayeno "until the time comes when he will establish his judgement," Armenian մինչեւ զօր դատաստանի "until the day of judgement." The tendency of Ethiopic to use "judgement" where the other versions have different eschatological terms may be observed, for example, in 7:36 for "tortures." Armenian in 7:70 has "delight and torture" where the other versions read "judgement." In light of this it is not clear how far independence can be attributed to the readings of these two texts. They do, however, indicate a freedom of substitution of eschatological terms which may well throw light on the concept of the eschatological events held by the translators. In general, compare the situation in 8:38 and its parallels in 8:39, cf. 7:113, 9:13.

[152]Armenian reads "shall we enter into the place of torture or shall we be at rest until the day of judgement or henceforth shall we enter into tortures." This last phrase is true to the text witnessed by the other versions but does not sit well with the first part of the verse as it is found in Armenian. The first part of the verse has been remodeled as was the wont of the Armenian translator or of his source text. Furthermore it lacks in one Armenian MS (see Violet, I, ad loc.). This may well be a scribal error or it may be one of the rare instances of a real difference of textual tradition within the Armenian version.

[153]See pp.56f. above.

[154]For example, II Chr. 24:4,12 of the Temple.

[155]Lam. 5:21 "restore our days as of old." This may also be the meaning in Ps. 104:30, 51:12.

[156]1QS iv:25 "a new making" referring evidently to a new ordering of the relation between the two spirits. See also 1QH xi:13.

[157]Ab. Zar. 3:7.

[158]Kel. 13:7, cf. Yadayim 4:3.

[159]Sanh. 92b. Note also Hagig. 12b where the rising and setting of the sun is said to מחדש בכל יום תמיד מעשה בראשית, cf. Sot. 11a. In Sanh. 97b the separation of the Messianic age from the world to come is explicit and of the latter it is said that God מחדש עולמו.

[160]In general compare Ap. Bar. 32:6, 57:2. The relation of Urzeit to Endzeit is discussed by H. Gunkel, Schöpfung und Chaos in Urzeit und Endzeit (Göttingen: Vandenhoeck und Ruprecht, 1895), especially 367ff.

[161]Plural in Latin, Syriac, Ethiopic; singular in Armenian.

[162]Armenian "true paradise." Is this related to the term פרדס קושטא which occurs as a name of paradise in the Enoch fragments from Qumran published by J. Milik, Revue Biblique, 65 (1958), 71,76? See the notes on this in Scholem, Jewish Gnosticism, 16, n.10 on 17. He refers to Ap. Mos. 13, 37. How the term could have entered the Armenian text remains a mystery. See also below pp.198 ff.

[163]Armenian "the tree of true paradise is planted."

[164]Latin tempus, Syriac ʿlmʾ, Ethiopic ʿālam.

[165]Thus Syriac, Ethiopic and Armenian. Latin has habundantia. The Hebrew was probably ʿdn.

[166]Latin only.

[167]On Ethiopic which reads "the root of wisdom is torn up" see Violet, II, n. ad loc.

[168]The text is doubtful. This is the reading of Latin and Syriac. Ethiopic and Armenian, however, the other two extant versions, read "infirmity is sealed up." We have noted that in v. 52 Ethiopic reads "root," but in a context which arouses suspicion. Thus Latin and Syriac should be followed here. The meaning of the phrase is not very clear.

[169]Syriac, Latin.

[170]Armenian "driven from you." The verb lacks in Latin.

[171]Singular in Ethiopic and Armenian.

[172]This only Latin, Syriac.

[173]Armenian, appropriately, "immortality."

[174]Cf. 8:55ff.

[175]See p. 57, n.72, p.55, n.55 and p. 185.

[176]The terminology of 8:52-54 will be discussed below.

[177]No attempt is made here to deal exhaustively with the materials in 8:52-54.

[178]See above pp.53f., from which it is clear that this is the sense of the _novissimus_ terminology.

[179]For example, 5:41, 6:15 etc.

[180]The expression _visitare_, Syriac _pqd_ occurs only three more times in the book, 5:56, 6:18 (lacking in Syriac), 9:2. It probably reflects Hebrew _pqd_, see Violet, II, 43n. In 6:18 and 9:2 the word introduces the Messianic woes and refers to them. In the Apocalypse of Baruch, as Charles notes (35n.) the word always refers to God's penal visitation. It is generally used, he observes, in a good sense in the New Testament and may be either good or bad in the Hebrew Bible. It occurs in Ass. M. 1:18 in a good sense cf. Wisd. Sol. 3:7. At Qumran _pqwdh_ does not imply troubles in 1QS iii:18, iv:26 and evidently applies to reward in iv:6. In 1QS iii:14, iv:11, 18f., however, and probably in 1QH 1:18f. it is specifically used of punishment. The verb _pqd_ is used of punishment in CD vii:9, viii:2f. Most other uses are not of eschatological significance, thus 1QS vi:21, v:22,24, CD i:7, xiii:11, 1QM xii:4 etc. Thus the major eschatological use in the Dead Sea Scrolls is also of punishment. In light of all this the use here may be taken to refer to punishment.

[181]Latin omits the rest of the verse and reads it in 6:6. It might be original there and lost in the other versions by haplography of 'ḥr . . . 'ḥr or ετερου . . . ετερου. Box, _Ezra Apocalypse, ad loc._ thinks that it is original in 6:6 and was omitted by the Oriental versions on dogmatic grounds. This would not explain its being read in all versions except Latin in 6:1. In view of this there is no doubt that it is original in 6:1 where, incidentally, it makes better sense. See also Violet, II, _ad loc._

[182]Syriac _byd_, Ethiopic _ba-_, Georgian "on account of."

[183]Syriac _br 'nš_, Ethiopic _bawaleda 'eg^wāla 'emaḥeyāw_. These

may both reflect Greek υἱος ἀνθρώπου, Hebrew אדם‎ בן‎. This is not Messianic, as Box thinks, cf. Arabic, Georgian "man." Violet suggests a reading "+not+ through man." Gressmann in Violet, II notes that the verse might refer to the Assyrians or the like. See below for our interpretation.

[184] Thus Syriac.

[185] See nn. 181, 183.

[186] Similarly 8:54 is not technical. The use there may be compared with לסוף‎ in Sot 3:5, 8:1 bis.

[187] For example, 12:21ff.

[188] Latin finis dies iudicii, Syriac šwlm' dym' ddyn', Armenian "the end of judgement" կատարած դատաստանի, Ethiopic "the day of judgement," Arabic[1] "the fulfilment of judgement," Arabic[2] "⟨the end (Gildermeister)⟩ of judgement." "End," "day" and ‘judgement" must all be original and there are two possibilities, "the end, the day of judgement" (Latin) or "the end of the day of judgement" (Syriac). The former makes far better sense in context. Violet, II suggests +die Entscheidung+ des Gerichtstag, based on ὅρος = גזר‎. This would presuppose a Hebrew יום‎ הדין‎ גזר‎ which is most unlikely for the word גזר‎ only occurs in the fixed expression גזר‎ דין‎.

[189] Cf. 6:20.

[190] See 5:41, 12:34 et al. and p. 70, n.121 above, pp.103f. below.

[191] Cf. 14:9 and p. 71, n.124 above, pp. 133ff. below.

[192] On the possibility that vss. 27f. are a description of the world to come see above p. 70.

[193] See above pp. 51f.

[194] This passage has been most often compared to I Thess. 4:13-18. which speaks explicitly of a resurrection of the dead and the continued life of the last generation, both immediately following the end of the world. This is also a possible interpretation of this passage and is accepted by Gunkel, Der Prophet, n. ad loc., Kabisch, 45f. Kabisch compares with 4:26f. which will be dealt with below. The question in 5:41 could only arise out of the concept of the Messianic kingdom. As remarked above, had this concept been rejected and not just considered irrelevant to the problem of final reward, then in all probability such a rejection would have been made explicit. The idea was too widespread

for one opposed to it to cloak his opposition in as obscure
a form as 5:42. Here the author is simply not concerned
either with the Messianic kingdom or with eschatological
chronology, he is concerned with reward. In I Thess. 4:13ff.
there are two groups involved, the survivors and the
resurrected and this is made explicit, while the resurrection
referred to here in v.45 is of all men. This adds further
weight to the argument being put forward. It is difficult
to give any real meaning to v.41 in the context in which it
stands if this text is said to reflect a view of resurrection immediately following the last generation. I
Thessalonians, where this view is being taught, makes it
most unmistakable.

[195]Similarly the question in v.45 which seems valid in
logical terms, is not really answered by vss. 46ff. Ezra
asks what seems to be a theoretical question about the
physical capacity of the earth, but he is not really interested in this theoretical question and is not answered in
terms of it. He is really enquiring about the time of the
coming of reward and expressing his desire that it come as
quickly as possible. It is this that is responded to in
vss. 46ff.

[196]See above p. 71.

[197]The Latin temporum novissima and Syriac 'ḥrthwn d^c dn'
only occur once more in those versions, in 14:5. Ethiopic
has "the end of the days of the world," Arabic[1] "the last
of the ages," Armenian "the completion of the times." Here
the reading is as Syriac and Arabic[1] and, perhaps as implied
in Latin.

[198]Compare also Kabisch, 101.

[199]Pp. 65ff.

[200]See p. 70, nn. 120, 121, pp. 103f., 105f.

[201]Keulers, 35-41.

[202]The occurrence in 6:15 is not identifiable and the
end is best taken there as referring to the eschatological
events in general. It signifies, perhaps, the whole of the
following prophecy, thus covering a conglomeration of various
eschatological ideas. 12:21 and 12:30 say that the destruction of the eagle, and in particular of its last two little
wings immediately precedes the lion and that they are "for
the end." In 12:21 it is not clear whether the end of the
eagle or the end of times is intended, probably in light of
v.30 the latter is the case. These two occurrences are too
unclear to serve as evidence.

[203] See Section B 3) and 4), pp. 64f., Section D 4), p. 76 and p. 81 above.

[204] Keulers, 47, 107.

[205] See above pp. 86ff.

[206] Cf. 7:102,104. The legal nature of the language of v.115 was pointed out by Violet, II, ad loc.

[207] Ezra Apocalypse, 274, n.z.

[208] For further discussion of this, see pp. 110ff. below.

[209] Cf. 14:9 etc.

[210] See above, pp. 86ff.

[211] See above pp. 48ff.

[212] Thus Latin, Arabic, Armenian, also Violet, II. Syriac and Ethiopic are evidently influenced by 5:1, 6:18 and read "behold days are coming." The Greek behind tempus is evidently καιρός.

[213] Thus Arabic[1], Armenian. Latin sponsa, Syriac klt' reflect an inner-Greek corruption νῦν μὴ φαινομένη, by a process of dittography and correction producing νύμφη φαινομένη. So Volkmar, II, Violet, I, II, Box, Ezra Apocalypse, ad loc. Volkmar thinks that the Latin and Syriac may have been influenced by Ap. Jn. 21:2.

[214] Armenian բարձրելոյն "of the Most High." On the change in person in Armenian see above p. 73.

[215] "My son," Arabic[1]: see Violet, ad loc.

[216] See "Excursus: Messiah as the Son of God," above pp. 71ff.

[217] Thus Latin and Syriac. Ethiopic "raised up," "elevated" la'ella tanse-'u. Violet, II suggests that this may reflect an inner-Greek corruption ἀνελείφθησαν or -θεντες to ἀνελήφθησαν or -θεντες. It may, however, reflect a Hebrew variant showing in two Greek traditions, הנשאים and הנשים. For the readings of Arabic[1] and Armenian see Violet, II, ad loc.

[218]
[2] Latin 400 (MS A, 300), Syriac 30, Arabic[1] 400, Arabic[2] 1000, Ethiopic and Armenian give no figure. Violet suggests that 1000 and 30 represent a confusion of ‚A = 1000 and Λ' = 30. 400 would then be represented by Υ'. Latin MS

A is probably inner-Latin (CCC for CCCC). There are thus two traditions, 30/1000 and 400.

[219] See above, n.63.

[220] See above, pp. 71ff. and n.64.

[221] See above, n.65.

[222] See above, n.66.

[223] See above, n.67.

[224] See above, n.68.

[225] See above, n.69 and p. 57.

[226] Some such verb is reflected in Syriac, Ethiopic and Arabic[2]. Perhaps Latin omits for stylistic reasons.

[227] One Latin MS and the Arabic read "his throne . . . ." Ethiopic is emended by Dillmann from zafaṭara "which he created" to zafeteḥ "of judgement" and it is suggested that this may reflect a Greek corruption of κρίσεως to κτίσεως.

[228] The text of the beginning of the verse in Arabic[2] and Armenian appears to be contaminated by v.31. Armenian adds "and the life which is not revealed will come." This may give some support to the Syriac expansion wn't' šwlm'.

[229-229] The criticism of the whole verse is difficult due to great variation between the versions. The phrase is present in all versions, but Ethiopic and Arabic[1] read it with opposite meaning to the others. Thus Arabic[1] has the verb 'ty and Ethiopic mṣ', both meaning "to come." Similar variation is noted in 6:20. See also Violet, II, ad loc.

[230-230] Latin, Arabic[2] omit. Syriac is best, supported by implication in Arabic[1]. Armenian is problematic.

[231] Thus all versions. Ethiopic tetgāba' is wrongly taken in Violet, I but see retraction in Violet, II, ad loc. Armenian shows an expanded text, introducing an additional clause before "longsuffering."

[232] Perhaps "my judgement," Syriac and implied Arabic[1].

[233] The Syriac trwn is discussed by Box and Violet, II. See also Brockelmann, Lexicon Syriacum (2 ed. rev.; Gottingen: Niemeyer, 1923). The readings of the other versions may represent Hebrew from stem פרה (Violet, II) or equally from אמצ.

[234] Latin _opus_. Wellhausen suggests Greek ἔργον (ἔργα) reflecting Hebrew פֹּעַל or פְּעֻלָה "work" or "reward," cf. LXX Ps. 108 (109): 20, Isa. 40:10. The phrase is missing in Arabic[2]. Armenian and Arabic[1] basing themselves on Greek ἔργον meaning "work," misinterpret the parallelism here. Thus, for example, Armenian translates "and after works come their rewards," thus combining the first two members of the verse into one sentence.

[235] Latin MSS of Ψ type (cf. Violet, II, "Introduction," xxii) omit, perhaps due to re-interpretation. This may also be the reason for the lack of negative in Arabic[2] and the omission in Armenian.

[236] Armenian shows the same basic text as Latin with re-arrangement of the phrases. This seems to be based on the combination of all phrases dealing with one subject into a single, consecutive sentence which results in a disturbance of the originally contrasting parallelism, cf. 6:28 and also n.234 above. No textual basis for these changes can be discerned. A similar treatment of the first and third members of this verse may be observed in Arabic[2]. Armenian also has the curious addition "the deathless worm which is prepared for the wicked and the lawless."

[237] Following Bensly's suggested readings of Latin (A reads _locus_) and Syriac, where he emends from ܠ ܒ ‍ ‍ ‍‍ cwb' which makes no sense here, to ܒ ‍‍‍ ‍ gwb' "pit." Thus Ethiopic, Arabic[1].

[238] Singular only in Latin and Arabic[2]. Ethiopic has "judgement," see nn. 137, 151 above.

[239-239] The versions vary in their treatment of this phrase. Latin and Arabic[1] alone have the verb.

[240] Thus Latin, cf. Syriac, Ethiopic, Arabic[1].

[241] Gehenna as a fiery place: Arabic[1], Arabic[2], Armenian.

[242] Arabic[2] "sinners." Armenian has an enlarged text including a speech to the righteous before the address to the sinners found in all the other versions.

[243] The order of these clauses is reversed in Armenian.

[244] Latin _videte contra et in contra_. Omit _contra_ # 1 as a dittography (Box, Violet, II).

[245] Thus Syriac, Ethiopic and perhaps Armenian.

[246] Armenian "delight prepared for (you) righteous ones,"

Arabic[2] "grace and joy which I have prepared for my faithful ones." The idea of Eden as prepared is found here only in these two versions. It occurs elsewhere and is especially common in special readings of the Armenian, such as the addition to the first part of 7:37 cf. 5:43,44, 7:14. Armenian and Arabic[2] have common special readings elsewhere, such as 3:5.

[247] Armenian, Syriac, Ethiopic and one Latin MS.

[248] There is some support for light as a fourth element in this list, cf. Armenian, Arabic[1].

[249] Armenian has a longer text introducing an adjectival attribute after most of the elements in the following list, for example, "nor the lightgiving sun."

[250] Thus Latin, Arabic[2]. "Lightning" precedes "thunder" in Syriac, Ethiopic. It is omitted in Armenian.

[251] "Rain," Arabic[2].

[252] Arabic[2] omits. Armenian ՀՈՂՄՆ is used as a translation of both "wind" and "air" in this verse, but a differentiation is made through the attributes.

[253-253] Thus Latin, Syriac, Ethiopic, Arabic[1]. This text also lies behind Armenian where the third element is աՇՈՂՈՒԹԻՆ "prosperity." This clearly refers to morning in view of the glosses of the Armenian which describe the activities carried out at different times of day.

[254] Perhaps "summer," see Violet, II and Box, *Ezra Apocalypse*, *ad loc.*

[255] Latin aestum has the same meaning as aestatum, here translated "summer." The texts of the other versions are complicated and they are evidently translating a Greek word which could have a number of meanings. Syriac reads ryš šnt' "new year" or "beginning of year." Ethiopic mā'rar which means "time of harvest" evidently refers to the late spring-early summer or to autumn. See Dillmann, *Lexicon*, s.v. ՄԸՀՐC cf. also ՀՆՋՅ and ՀԼ⁺ፕ. Arabic[1], Arabic[2] and Armenian all have lists of four seasons. They are described by name (summer, winter, etc.) in Arabic[1]; partly by name (winter, summer) and partly by agricultural activity (seed, harvest) in Arabic[2]. Armenian mentions agricultural activities in its glosses.

The three element list of Latin, Syriac and Ethiopic seems to be original. The order is the same in these three versions, except that Ethiopic, according to the translation

of Violet, I, reverses "summer" and "winter (spring)." Since
the words used in Ethiopic denote seasons which do not correspond to those of the Mediterranean lands, there is considerable confusion in the translation of the Greek names of the
seasons into Ethiopic and thus all the three words used in
this verse may translate Greek θέρος, see Dillmann, ibid.
Thus, in fact, the translations given by Violet are not conclusive. Since this whole passage deals with groups of three,
the four season lists of Arabic, Armenian are to be regarded
as secondary.

If Box' view expressed in Ezra Apocalypse, ad loc. is
accepted and the first two elements in this list are regarded
as translations of Hebrew קיץ וחורף then this third element
is probably קציר "harvest" or "harvest time" which is late
spring-early summer in Palestine for cereals, to which crop
this term is generally applied. This could then have been
translated into Greek (if קיץ was translated by θέρος) perhaps by ἀμητός which in the LXX generally translates Hebrew
קציר, but sometimes also קיץ (14 times: 3 times) or by
another Greek word, for example, θέρισμος which had the same
double sense. This would explain the aestum of Latin and the
"harvest time" of Ethiopic, Arabic[2] and the gloss on Armenian.
Syriac remains difficult.

[256]Thus Syriac, Ethiopic, Arabic[1]. Latin hiemem is
unique among the versions. The solution offered by Box ignores
the agricultural terminology used in the Oriental versions,
see n.255. It is better to see this as a secondary reading
of the Latin due to a haplography of aestum which precedes
and some similar word here, which would have disturbed the
strict metre of the list in Latin. The other terms of this
phrase might well have suggested hiemem to a scribe desiring
to supply the first element in the verse.
Read Ethiopic ⁱawelo "storm" with some MS support, rather
than 'awel as in Dillmann's text, cf. Arabic[1]. "Snow" in
Arabic[1] may represent "frost" of Latin, Syriac but both elements occur in Ethiopic. Arabic[2] omits the whole verse, but
the first part of it may occur in v.41 replacing "day and
night" of the other versions which Arabic had already read
in v.39. The order is best taken with Latin and Syriac. The
last three elements occur with some variation of order and
expansions in all versions except Arabic[2].

[257-257]The versions are not unanimous on this. For
Arabic[1] see Violet, II, ad loc. Arabic[2] and Armenian are
fragmentary, perhaps due to the fact that some of the elements
listed here are mentioned in their expansions on earlier
verses, see n.256.

[258]Or "light," "clarity" and "luminaries" see Violet,
II, Box, Ezra Apocalypse, ad loc.

[259] Thus Syriac, Ethiopic, Arabic[2]. Armenian is rather different, perhaps filling in a lacuna.

[260] Latin unde. The sense is clear in Syriac, Ethiopic. For this clause the best text is Latin, Syriac.

[261] Latin incipiant videre = μέλλουσι cf. Violet, II. See also 4:32, 7:47,75,88,122, 13:29,46 etc.

[262] Ethiopic "that day," Arabic[2] "judgement" are probably not original readings.

[263] Latin ebdomados, see Violet, I, ad loc. Thus too Syriac, Arabic[1]. Ethiopic "seven years" (some MSS 700), Arabic[2] 70, Armenian omits.

[264] Lacks in Syriac which reads hn' dyn "but this." This might well have been followed by dyny "my judgement" which could have been lost by haplography (homoioarkton).

[265] In spite of the arguments raised by Violet, II, גזר
רדיני does not seem to represent the Vorlage of this text. Rather should something like דדיני וחקתו (cf. Syriac wnmwsh) is desiderated by Latin, Syriac and Arabic[1]. Cf. Box, Ezra Apocalypse, ad loc. Compare 7:70.

[266] Ap. Bar. 72:2, Test. Our Lord I:2,3, Mk. 13:4, Bk. Zerub. ed. Even Shmuel, 1.59 et al.

[267] 8:50, 10:59, 13:16,19, 14:16f.

[268] 11:32-34 cf. 40-43, 12:32ff. On the anti-christ figure see above pp. 4f. and nn.17,19 there.

[269] See above pp. 86f.

[270] See also above pp. 79f.

[271] For example, Isa. 52:1, 54:11f., 60:10ff., Ezek. 40-48, Zech. 2:5-9, cf. Kaufmann, VIII, 236f.

[272] Tob. 13:16-18, 14:5, T. Dan. 5:12, II En. 55:2, Ap. Bar. 4:2-4, 32:2-4.

[273] Heb. 11:10-16, 12:22, Ap. Jn. 21:2,9f., Gal. 4:26 etc.

[274] Text called "Description of New Jerusalem," Barthélemy and Milik, Discoveries in the Judaean Desert, I (Oxford: Clarendon Press, 1955), 134 of which MSS have been found in at least three other caves, 4QpPs 37, iii:11, J. Allegro, Palestine Exploration Quarterly, 86 (1954), 71f.

[275]Ta^{c}an. 5a, Hag. 12b, J. Ber. IV, 8b-c, Mid. Teh. on
Ps. 90:3. In this last text it is one of the seven pre-
created things: Torah, Throne of Glory, paradise, Gehenna,
repentance, heavenly Temple and the name of the Messiah.

[276]For example, the Moses apocalypse called "Heavenly
Jerusalem," Even-Shmuel, 20-22 especially 11.25f.

[277]This may also be implied in 10:53f.

[278]85ff.

[279]Apokryphen, ad loc.

[280]Cf. Hagig. 12b, in the fourth heaven.

[281]Thus Keulers, 100-105 cf. 48, 78f., Vagany, 97. For
detailed discussion of the problems of this vision see
Kabisch, 80ff., Clemen, 241, Gunkel, Theologische Literaturzeitung, 7, Lagrange, Revue Biblique, 1905, 493f. Lagrange
unconvincingly interprets this of Jerusalem of the Restoration. 8:52 may be a reference to the city in heaven or in
the future age, see further discussion below. A similar
vision of a weeping woman who is Zion may be observed in
Pes. R. 131b-132a.

[282]Thus here, 8:52, 10:27,44,54.

[283]10:54, 13:36.

[284]See above pp. 57f.

[285]Apokryphen, ad loc.

[286]Ezra Apocalypse, ad loc., also Baldensperger, 162.

[287]Keulers, 79, Vagany, 97.

[288]IV Ezra 5:24, cf. I En. 27:1 "blessed land," 89:40,
Ap. Bar. 29:2.

[289]On this passage see n.194 and pp. 87f. above.

[290]Box, Ezra Apocalypse, commentary on 6:25. He also
cites Mek. 50a, 51b (ed. Friedmann).

[291]Thus, Gen. 45:7, Ju. 6:4, II Chr. 14:12, Am. 3:12,
5:3, Isa. 10:19, 11:11, 17:5f., 30:17, Zeph. 3:12-13.

[292]See Y. Yadin, מלחמת בני אור בבני חושך (2 ed.;
Jerusalem: Bialik Institute, 1957), commentary ad loc.

[293] See above, n.180.

[294] For example, I En. 83:8, Sib. V:384.

[295] See also Keulers, 86.

[296] Paul Volz, Die Eschatologie der jüdischen Gemeinde (Tübingen: Mohr, 1934), 340.

[297] Ezra Apocalypse on 6:25.

[298] For this verb in IV Ezra see Gunkel's emendation of 6:26, where all versions read incorrectly וַיִּרְאוּ for passive וַיֵּרָאוּ. A similar error may lie behind Arabic[2] and Georgian of 6:20.

[299] Thus, acts 4:26, 7:27, 9:6, 13:50,57: revelations 13:14, 13:56, 14:5.

[300] 6:48, cf. also Armenian 14:21 accepted as original by Violet, II.

[301] 13:44. Syriac expands in this place, evidently under the influence of Ex. 14:29, Jos. 3:17. The splitting of the Jordan in Jos. 3:5 is called נפלאות.

[302] 51:7, 54:9 cf. 54:11--creation.

[303] 87f.

[304] See further, above pp. 86ff.

[305] See Erik Sjöberg, Der Menschensohn im Äthiopischen Henochbuch (Lund: Gleerup, 1946), 134-139 for both a bibliography and an excellent critique of this view.

[306] On this title see above, pp. 71ff.

[307] Box, Ezra Apocalypse, xxiii-xxiv.

[308] Keulers, 47ff.

[309] See above, pp. 48ff.

[310] Box, Ezra Apocalypse, xxiii-xxiv, see discussion of this passage above pp. 65ff., 89f.

[311] See above, pp. 101f.

[312] Keulers admits the possibility that Visions V-VII are based on written traditions reworked by the author. Nonetheless he adduces further detailed considerations in favour of

the substantial common authorship of the supposedly different documents, including terminological consistencies, see 53-55.

[313]Only those relevant to the Messianic thought are discussed here.

[314]Box, Ezra Apocalypse, 247ff.

[315]Keulers, 115.

[316]Morfill and Charles, Secrets of Enoch, 91f. ch. 4 of text.

[317]See above pp. 83-97.

[318]On the uses of the term "end" in chapters 11-12 see above pp. 85ff.

[319]Box, Ezra Apocalypse, 260, n.i.

[320]Ibid., 247.

[321]Dan. 7:14,27.

[322]See above, pp. 86ff. for a full discussion of this passage. See also Kabisch, 68 who touches on the pre-figuring of judgement in the Messianic kingdom.

[323]Baldensperger, 98f., cf. 161.

[324]Dan. 7:9f., 26.

[325]I En. 62:2,3,5, 69:27 etc.

[326]I En. 62:2,3,5 etc.

[327]See also Sjöberg, Menschensohn, Ch. 3, 61-82. The Similitudes, which do not occur at Qumran, have been lately dated variously between the middle of the first century B.C.E. and the first or second centuries C.E. See the discussion of J. Starcky, "Les Quatre Etapes du Messianisme à Qumran," Revue Biblique, 70 (1963), 501f. Whatever the situation be, they are close enough to IV Ezra to serve as comparative material.

[328]Keulers, 115.

[329]See Keulers, 109ff., Baldensperger, 160, Box, Ezra Apocalypse, 283f. etc.

[330]See above, n.268.

[331]It is precisely the Son of Man's assuming the functions of universal judgement that makes the Similitudes so problematic in the eyes of many scholars.

[332]Thus vss. 3,4,12,25,51; "as the form of a man," v.3 cf. v.32.

[333]See above, pp.71ff.

[334]Apokryphen, 346f.

[335]Box, Ezra Apocalypse, 286.

[336]Box, ibid. Clemen, 244 claims that the tradition behind this vision must have been formed before the time of Pompey, for Rome does not figure as a world power. See, however, the considerations urged in the text here.

[337]The basic weakness of Box' arguments for redactoral adjustment is that they are based on the "original" eschatology of the vision which in turn can only be determined from the "original" vision without the adjustments, which of course is circular.

[338]Thus Box, Ezra Apocalypse, 282, Keulers, 123 and others. Keulers, for example, raises two problems. The man both rises from the sea and flies on the clouds, and if in v.4 everyone has melted, who makes up the innumerable host of v.5? The man rising from the sea is problematic. Generally, only evil forces rise from the sea, cf. Dan. 7:3. In Sib. III:72ff. a flaming power rises from the sea and destroys Beliar and in Ap. Bar. 56:3 a white cloud, symbolizing the length of the days of the world also comes up from the sea. Gunkel, quoted by Box, and Box himself think that this may come from a star-god myth, see Box, Ezra Apocalypse, 282. Gressmann, against this, is inclined to regard it as a secondary feature borrowed from Dan. 7, see Gressmann, Der Ursprung der israelitisch-jüdischen Eschatologie (Göttingen: Vandenhoeck und Ruprecht, 1905), 354. The Gunkel-Box explanation needs more support than is adduced. If Gressmann is not correct, and his explanation is likely, then it must be concluded that the origins and nature of the tradition of good forces rising from the sea are obscure. Keulers' second problem surely arises from an overly literalistic approach to what is clearly apocalyptic hyperbole.

[339]The verse has no main verb in Latin and Arabic[1]. This also seems to be the case in Ethiopic and Arabic[2] which combine it syntactically in differing ways with the preceding. Ethiopic adds, at the end of v.47 instead of "in peace," "were brought up and were found in my land"; Arabic[2] reads

"(47) and the multitude which you saw . . . (48) are those
who remain of my people on the holy mountain." One suspects
that v.48 serves to relate the ten tribes pericope, which
may preserve a block of old legendary material, to the
peacable multitude of v.12 in the vision, which in context
must include the survivors. This, if it is the case, is no
reason for the verse to be ungrammatical. Even if it were
redactional (as Box) the redactor was, presumably, capable
of writing complete sentences. The state of the versions
indicates that the verb was lost early in the history of
transmission and Syriac retains the best reading. "Your
people" alongside "my borders" worries Violet, II, ad loc.
In context, however, "your" could well refer to Ezra and
the remaining 2 1/2 tribes in contrast to the other 9 1/2,
he is in charge of "Israel" (5:16). For the reading "mountain" in the Arabic versions, cf. Arabic[1] in 9:8, perhaps a
confusion of ὄρος and ὄριον (Hilgenfeld).

[340]Since, however, Zion and Mt. Zion are to be regarded
as virtually identical, this point is not very strong.

[341]Thus vss. 25,51. For this formula compare 10:43,45,
47,48, 12:17,19,22,26,31 and many other places in apocalypses.

[342]Box, Ezra Apocalypse, 283, Volz (1 ed.), 214f., 216f.

[343]Sjöberg, Menschensohn, 190-198. On the relationship
of Adam to the Urmensch see A. Altmann, "The Gnostic Background of the Rabbinic Adam Legends," Jewish Quarterly Review
35 (1944-1945), 371-391.

[344]Cf. I Ki. 19:11-12, Job 40:6, Zech. 9:14 etc.

[345]Preceding epiphanies, Ezek. 1:4, I Ki. 8:10f., Ex.
19:9,16, 13:21, Nu. 12:5, 14:14; as the chariot of the Deity,
Ugaritic Ba'al as rkb ᶜrpt also Ps. 104:3, 68:5, Ex. 19:19,
Nah. 1:3, Isa. 14:14, 19:1 etc.

[346]Ps. 97:2-3 cf. I Ki. 19:12, II Sam. 22:9f.//Ps. 18:9f.,
Ezek. 10:2.

[347]Thus Ps. 97:5, Mic. 1:4, cf. Judith 16:15, I En. 1:6.

[348]See Box, Ezra Apocalypse, n.y on p. 295 and references
there.

[349]This verse may also be a reference to future judgement for "torture" is a technical term for eschatological
punishment, see above pp. 76f.

[350]See I En. 62:2, Wisd. Sol. 18:15f., Isa. 11:4, II

Thess. 2:8 cf. Isa. 49:2. Compare destruction by rebuke in chapters 11-12.

351 11:38ff., 12:32ff.

352 See, for example, woes p. 100, heavenly Jerusalem pp. 101f., survivors pp. 103f., wonders pp. 105f.

353 See above, p. 117.

354 See above, pp. 4f.

355 See above, p. 95.

356 All sources except 14:9 and the vision of chapter 13.

357 Lagrange, Revue Biblique, 1905, 499 regards this as interpolated, see also Revue Biblique, N.S.4 (1907), 615 in his review of Vagany.

358 See above, pp. 119, 130.

359 The view of the independent piece, the vision of chapter 13, is rather different. The title "man," the cosmic elements, the out and out military function, and the absence of any of the other common features except pre-existence distinguish this passage. See also pp. 128ff. above.

360 I En. 39:6b, cf. 70:4.

361 See 1QS ix:11, 4QTest. published by J. Allegro, "Further Messianic References in Qumran Literature," Journal of Biblical Literature, 75 (1956), 182-187. Re this figure see A.S. van der Woude, Die Messianischen Vorstellungen der Gemeinde von Qumran (Assen: Gorcum, 1957), 79-85, Cross, Ancient Library, 223f., Kuhn, "The Two Messiahs of Aaron and Israel," in The Scrolls and the New Testament, 54-64, especially para. 5, pp. 63f.

362 This probably stemmed from Deut. 18:15. See also I Macc. 4:46, 14:41, Jn. 6:14, 7:52, 9:17, cf. also T. Benj. 9:2, T. Lev. 8:15 (?).

363 See Mal. 3:23f., Ben Sira 48:10f. In New Testament, Mk. 9:4, 11f., cf. Mt. 17:1-8, Lk. 9:28-36. There Moses also appears at the Transfiguration, cf. perhaps Ap. Jn. 11:3ff. Elijah is specifically connected with the prophet in Jn.1:21. On this tradition in Rabbinic sources, see the materials collected by Klausner, 451ff.

364 Gunkel, Apokryphen, on 13:52. "Holy Ones" is a title

of angels, see Yadin, מלחמת בני אור, p.211. This may apply to I Thess. 3:12, cf. II Thess. 1:7 "angels of power in flaming fire."

[365]See, for example, I En. 89:52, Ap. Bar. 13:3, 25:1, 76:2, II En. 36:1 etc.

[366]This passage is followed by a reference to the changing of hearts. This is reminiscent of the turning of fathers to sons and sons to fathers in Mal. 3:24, cf. Ben Sira 48:10f. where Malachi is reflected. An older treatment of the forerunners of the Messiah is Drummond, Jewish Messiah, 222-225.

[367]See above, pp. 76f.

[368]See above, p. 108.

[369]See Ap. Bar. 74:2-3 and also above, pp. 48ff.

[370]See above, pp. 69f.

[371]Cf. 7:36, 7:84 and the discussion of the term, above pp. 76f.

[372]See above, pp. 65ff., 86f., 88f.

[373]The vision of chapter 13 says nothing about the length of that kingdom.

[374]See Dan. 7:14,27, I En. 10:16ff., Jub. 50:5 cf. 23:29ff., Sib. III:49f., 371ff., 767ff., I En. 49:1f., 62:14, 71:15ff., T. Lev. 18, T. Jos. 19:12 cf. T. Jud. 22. The majority of occurrences in I Enoch are in the Similitudes and those in T. Lev. deal with the Priestly Messiah and in T. Jos. with both the Priestly and Davidic Messiahs.

[375]See also 11:8.

[376]Thus Ap. Bar. 30:1, 40:3 and evidently 74:2-3. See also I En. 93:10, 91:12ff., Sib. III:751ff. Perhaps I Cor. 15:28. In general cf. Targ. Isa. 16:5.

[377]Klausner, 408ff., especially 413. On the confusions see 416f.

[378]Mid. Teh. to Ps. 90:15, Pes.R. 1 end (ed. Friedmann 4b), Sanh. 99a. On this see W. Bacher, Die Agada der Tannaiten (Strassburg: Truebner, 1884), I, 145f.

[379]Pes.R. 1 (ed. Friedmann 4b).

[380] Sanh. 99a.

[381] See, for example, Keulers, 39f. Baldensperger, 104ff. would attribute this to scholastic combination of prophetic and apocalyptic (Danielic) ideas.

[382] See Baldensperger, ibid.

[383] Thus Box, Ezra Apocalypse, liii ff., Keulers, 7-10, 36-41, Gunkel, Theologische Literaturzeitung, 1891, 11.

[384] 11 ff.

[385] It is not clear whether the reference in 10:16 is to final resurrection or to some miracle such as Elijah and the Shunamite woman. If Gunkel is correct and the story is part of some "novel" of the type of Tobit, then the latter is probably the case.

[386] The reference in 4:37 reads "he will not move, nor arouse until the predicted measures are full." The word translated "arouse" is Latin excitabit, Syriac n^{c}yr, Ethiopic yenaqeh (see Violet, I, ad loc.), Armenian զարթուցանէ. In context the only thing that this can refer to is resurrection.

[387] The meaning of v.33 is not clear in context. The best explanation is that it is to be connected with the tradition of the ten tribes.

[388] This element of silence is also mentioned in 6:39, the silence before the creation of man. In 7:30 the earth at the end returns to its primaeval silence for seven days "as at the time of creation." The same idea may also be observed in Ap. Bar. 3:7. The silence of the chambers of the souls of the righteous may best be connected with the elements of peace and quiet which are an integral part of paradise (7:36, cf. 7:38,75,85 etc.).

[389] The dwelling of the righteous souls may also be referred to as "habitations of health and safety" in 7:121, see also Ap. Bar. 21:23 "treasuries of souls."

[390] A detailed treatment of this same idea may be found in Mid. Tanh. Pequdê 3.

[391] Cf. also 5:48,50,54f. The image is further extended in its use in connection with the birth of men and is found, for example, of the treasuries of the souls bringing forth their contents in 4:41f.

[392] This may be observed in Jub. 23:25, Philo, De opif.,

49. Its roots may be seen, perhaps, in the traditions of the ancient or antedeluvian giants found in the Bible, e.g. Gen. 6:4, Num. 13:33. Rabbinic literature also knows traditions of loss of statute as a result of sin, thus Gen. R. 23:6-7. This is, interestingly, especially related of Adam who lost both stature and brightness of face (see below) when he transgressed, cf. Tanḥ., ed. Buber, I, 7a, Gen. R. 12:6. Man will again receive these gifts in Messianic times. Abraham in his pursuit of the four kings had great height and he lost this extraordinary strength, Rabbinic tradition says, when he reached Dan, where Jereboam was to erect his idols. Wickedness again reduces stature. See also Tanḥ., ed. Buber, I, 37a-b.

[393]Latin _sensus_ etc.

[394]Two additional cases, 5:8 and 13:45 were not considered as they present special difficulties.

[395]See below, Section D.

[396]The cases of _terra_ = ^{c}lm' will be discussed below.

[397]Jenni, "Das Wort ^{c}ōlām im Alten Testament," _Zeitschrift für die alttestamentliche Wissenschaft_, 64 (1952) 197-246 idem, 65 (1953), 1-35. Part I, 217ff. especially 219. Cf. Brockelmann, _Lexicon Syriacum_, s.v. ܥܠܡ. Compare the opinion of Nöldeke in a private communication quoted by Franz Cumont, _The Oriental Religions in Roman Paganism_ (reprint; New York: Dover Publications, 1956), 258, n.80. Nöldeke foreshadowed nearly all the conclusions drawn by Jenni.

[398]Gen. 4:2, 4:12[1], 6:11[2] in all of which the Vulgate omits _terra_.

[399]Gen. 1:12[2], 1:14, 1:28[2] in all of which Vulgate and Syriac omit.

[400]Gen. 1:30[1], 3:14.

[401]Gen. 2:7.

[402]See above, n.399.

[403]Gen. 2:20.

[404]Gen. 2:20, 3:1,14.

[405]Thus 2:5 (twice), 2:19, 2:20, 3:18.

[406]It also omits the occurrence in 2:19 and has an unique reading of ܒܪܟܪ in 1:12.

[407] This excludes from consideration passages and books not extant in the Hebrew Bible, such as the additions to Daniel. Numbering for the Vulgate, Armenian and LXX is as in those versions.

[408] This count treats repetitive uses as one unit.

[409] Syriac omits Ps. 118:44 and one of two occurrences in each of Ps. 144:1, 2, 21.

[410] It omits Isa. 34:10 and reads as M.T. qdmyk in Ps. 102:28.

[411] deserta saeculorum Isa. 58:12, superbiam saeculorum Isa. 60:15, mortuos saeculi Ps. 142:3 (143:3), generationibus saeculorum Isa. 51:9.

[412] Isa. 9:6 which posed a problem and a temptation to all versions and will be omitted from further discussion, Isa. 46:9 (prioris saeculi), Qoh. 9:6 (in hoc saeculo).

[413] See Swete, Introduction to the Old Testament in Greek (Cambridge: Cambridge University Press, 1902), I, 98-103. The question of the interdependence of Jerome's three versions of Psalms is discussed by D. Gutschmidt, "הערות לשלשת תרגומיו של הירונימוס לס' תהילים," in Commentationes Iudaico-Hellenicae, 40f.

[414] Job 22:15, Ps. 73:11 (72:12), Isa. 9:6 (see n.412 above), Isa. 63:9.

[415] See above, 151f.

[416] See also n.412 above.

[417] Job 22:15, Jer. 18:15, Isa. 63:11, 58:12, 60:15. Cf. items 2), 3), and 4) above on p. 171.

[418] The only other occurrence of this word is Mal. 3:4 where Latin has a genitive with adjectival force.

[419] As noted above, the LXX to Hab. 3:6 is problematic. LXX Ps. 40:14 (M.T. 41:14)--Latin, Syriac, Armenian read ἀπὸ τοῦ αἰῶνος καὶ εἰς τὸν αἰῶνα, M.T. has merely לעולם. Perhaps LXX reflects a Hebrew reading מן עולם ועד עולם, cf. Jer. 7:7, 25:25. M.T. does not read לעולמים presupposed by LXX + versions in Ps. 47:15b (M.T. 48:15).

[420] Thus II Sam. 22:16, Ps. 9:9, 33:8, 89:12, 97:4, Isa. 13:11, Jer. 10:12, Lam. 4:12, Nah. 1:15.

[421] ալ ե զ ե ր ք in II Sam. 22:16, Ps. 97:4, Isa. 13:11, Jer. 10:12, Lam. 4:12. The rest have ա շ խ ա ր հ ՝.

[422] An exception is Isa. 26:18.

[423] Nah. 1:5, Prov. 8:26.

[424] Thus perhaps Job 1:5, certainly Esth. 9:28 et al.

[425] Part II, 246.

[426] Part I, 221.

[427] The uses of αἰών in the New Testament show, in part, the normal range of meaning of the word in Greek. Other uses, however, are identical with those of translation Greek such as the LXX. Thus while in classical Greek ὁ μέλλων αἰών (Dem. 18:199) means "the coming generation," this can be well contrasted with uses such as Mt. 12:32 where it means "the world/age to come," cf. also Heb. 6:5 etc. Similarly the phrase ὁ αἰών οὗτος meaning "this age/world" is found, for example in Mt. 12:32 etc. These latter show the imprint of Jewish Greek usage. They cannot help us, however, in the isolation of exact periods of development in Hebrew, although they show the influence of the Jewish koine, for they are not translations from Hebrew. The range of special meanings shows, nevertheless, that Hebrew had, by this time moved from the classical situation in the Hebrew Bible.

[428] See Jacob Levy, Neuhebräisches und Chaldäisches Wörterbuch über die Talmudim und Midraschim (Leipzig: Brockhaus, 1883), III, 665f. and the excellent examples there. Similarly G. Dalman in his Aramäisches und Neuhebräisches Handwörterbuch, sub עולם lists as possible meanings 1) Aeon, Periode 2) Weltzeit 3) Welt 4) Ewigkeit. Levy adds lifetime to these meanings. Uses in Rabbinic sources, even where they may preserve early traditions, such as Avot 1:2,18, cannot be used except as evidence for the meaning at the time of the editing of the text. They cannot, in a lexicographical study, serve as witness to the usage in the time of the author of the statement quoted.

[429] The problem of saeculum and equivalents was discussed by Keulers, 144f. He assumes, but does not demonstrate the equivalence with αἰών and עולם. He then isolates, also without demonstration, the following meanings:

1. Old Testament "eternity"   4 times   8:23, 9:8, 31, 14:50,
2. "Heaven"   3 times   3:18, 6:1, 8:20,

3. "Material world"   22 times   3:9,24, 5:44,49,55,
6:59, 7:11,30,70,74,137, 8:50, 9:2,3,5,18,20, 11:40, 14:10,
16,20,22,
4. "This age"   5 times   4:26,36, 6:9, 11:44,
14:11.
5. The others show a combination of temporal and
spatial meaning.

This division of uses is not based on any historically
grounded study of the meanings of עולם. Differences between
Keulers' analysis and that offered here may be found at many
points. Since no supporting arguments are offered by
Keulers and since he sets forth no basis for the drawing of
distinctions between these various uses, it is difficult to
write any critique of his statements. The support for our
own views may be found in the text of this section.

The use as "heaven," however, unknown as it is for
on its own, should be further examined in some detail. The
suggestion of the existence of this meaning was made by
Gunkel, Apokryphen, 353, n.v. He notes that αἰών--again
assumed without demonstration to be the equivalent of
saeculum--in 3:18 as in 6:1 and 8:20 means "heaven." At
this point then, Keulers is simply echoing the unsupported
view of Gunkel. 8:20 was discussed on p. 117 above and
saeculum (the Latin reading is the relevant one) probably
should be emended to in saeculo to conform to Syriac etc.
and probably means "eternity." This view is strengthened
by the fact that "heaven" appears in the next hemistych.
6:1 should be compared, as Box notes, Ezra Apocalypse, 64
n.d, to I En. 34 which describes the doors between heaven
and earth through which the winds pass. These doors could
equally well be described as exits or ways from heaven to
earth, or from earth to heaven. The parallelism of 6:1 and
the cosmic nature of the discussion make the meaning "world"
most likely, see n. 432 below. To posit an otherwise
unknown meaning for עולם in a case like this is clearly
unconvincing. In 3:18 there is a discussion of the events
surrounding the theophany at Sinai. Latin, Ethiopic and
Georgian read singular saeculum, beḥēr ("land" emended from
bāher "sea" as Hilgenfeld, MJ). Syriac and Arabic[1] have the
plural, Arabic[2] omits. The verse describes the awesome
effects of God's descent from heaven to Mt. Sinai. Thus,
in this order, the earth tells of the shaking of caelos,
terram, orbem, abyssos and saeculum (saecula ?). It is
clear that a meaning "heaven" for saeculum does not suit
here at all. Not only has heaven already been mentioned in
this verse, but the order of descent makes it most awkward
following abyssos. Two possibilities suggest themselves,
either to accept the reading of Latin, Ethiopic and Georgian
and read singular עולם in the sense of "world," or to accept
the plural עולמים and suppose an original word, perhaps
"foundations" (אושי cf. 1QH vii:8-9) to have been lost. In

this case the meaning could well have been "eternal."

Be this as it may, none of the cases quoted by Gunkel and Keulers seems to indicate a clear, unequivocal meaning "heaven." Thus in this, the most notable case, the results of Keulers' analysis must be rejected. In general, they must be rejected unless they can be confirmed by a study based on the historical development of the meaning of the word and on a properly supported analysis of particular examples of the various meanings revealed by such a historical study. This section is an attempt to carry out an analysis of this type and the results obtained vary at many points with those of Keulers.

[430] 11:44 "And the Most High looked at his times, and behold they were finished, and his ages were filled." "Ages" is Latin saecula, Syriac ᶜlmwhy. This is parallel to "times" and there is no doubt about the meaning. This is, incidentally, the only case of a plural. In 14:10f. we find: "Since the age has lost its youth and the times begin to be old. (11) For the age is divided into 12 (10) parts . . . ." The text is difficult, vss. 10-12 are not found in Armenian and vss. 11f. lack in Syriac. Nevertheless the word definitely means "age" in 14:11 and most probably in 14:10.

[431] 4:36, 7:12f., 14:16.

[432] 5:49 uses the mother, birth image and applied it to saeculum-ᶜlmʼ-երկիր. As was noted above this image is typical in IV Ezra of the description of the relationship of man to the earth and it is most likely that here saeculum etc. has spatial connotation, enabling it to fill the role usually played by terra etc. in these expressions. 6:1b reads terrena orbis, ʼryh dtbyl, բնութեան երկրի parallel to exitus saeculi, mpqnwhy dᶜlmʼ, զելս աշխարհին and to various expressions denoting the directions of the winds. This occurs in a list of natural elements, before whose creation God existed. Here too saeculum etc. clearly has a material, spatial meaning, that is it means "world." In 6:59, after a statement of the chosenness of Israel, Ezra remarks that if the world (saeculum, ᶜlmʼ) is created for Israel, why does Israel not possess its world (saeculum nostrum, ᶜlmn)? This statement draws on the widespread tradition that creation was for the sake of Israel, cf. Ap. Bar. 14:19, 15:7 and many other places. The context will only permit the reading "world."

7:30 reads: "And the world will return to its primaeval silence for seven days as in the beginning. . . ." This instance too refers clearly to the created world, and can only be understood in these terms.

In 9:20 saeculum meum, ᶜlmy is, as in 6:1b, parallel to orbis etc. Likewise in 11:40 the rule of the eagle over

the world is described in terms of the same parallelism. In
13:20 the text is: "Yet it is easier to come into these
things in danger than to pass like a cloud from the world
and not to see that which will happen in the end of times."
Again the context makes the rendering "world" given here,
the most probable.

[433]4:24,26f., 5:44, 3:34, 7:74?, 8:41, 9:5,18^2, 11:39.

[434]4:11, 7:11,31,132, 9:2, 14:22, 7:112f.

[435]4:2, 6:20,25, 7:47,50,137, 8:1,2, 9:13 (twice),
10:45, 14:20. In addition 9:8,31 are definitely in neither
category as is most probably 9:18^1. 8:20 is difficult to
interpret and perhaps belongs, like the latter examples
quoted, to the group with the sense "most distant time."
Expressions like Rabbinic הזה עולם may perhaps be discerned,
for example, in 4:2,24, 6:20, 7:13,112, 8:1 cf. 7:47 which
perhaps reflects הבא עולם: See discussion of these expressions above.

[436]These latter types of meaning may be observed, for
example, in 4:19,21^1, 5:24, 13:40 (twice), 14:31^2.

[437]3:12,35, 4:21^2,39, 5:1,6, 6:18, 7:72, 10:59, 14:16.

[438]13:29,52.

[439]9:19 cf. 11:6.

[440]Earth is also that ruled over by the eagle and its
wings and heads. Thus 11:2,5,40^2, 11:12,16, 11:32,34, 12:23,
11:41, 12:3.

[441]4:27, 5:50,55, 9:20 (?), 14:10,16.

[442]Thus 4:36f., 5:49, 6:5, 7:74, 11:44, 13:57, 14:9.

[443]3:14, 12:9, 14:5.

[444]4:36, 5:49 cf. 11:44, 13:57f., 14:9-12.

[445]145.

[446]17:3, 19:8, 23:4 cf. I En. 69:11, Wisd. Sol. 1:13f.,
2:23f., II En. 30:16f. and Charles n. there.

[447]Adam is evidently said to be the source of sinfulness
in 48:42 but the verse is not very clear.

[448]Compare also 70:2.

[449] 56:2, cf. 5:2. The fixed times of the Messianic kingdom feature in 40:3 and see also 30:1.

[450] The idea that human sinfulness causes a deterioration of the elements of the world may be observed in Rabbinic literature, for example of the marvelousness of the light of the time of creation, Gen. R. 12:6.

[451] Thus most versions, perhaps "the thoughts of death" cf. Syriac.

[452] Armenian omits.

[453] Latin temporibus his and thus Syriac and Arabic, Ethiopic zentu ᶜalam, Armenian յայս երկրէ "from this earth."

[454] Compare the versions of 8:31 where "mortal" and "corruptible" appear to be interchangeable. See further Ap. Bar. 42:7 where "corruption" is parallel and opposite to "life."

[455] 160-171.

[456] 104ff.

[457] 7:19.

[458] 5:34,40, 7:11, cf. 3:7, see Keulers, 160.

[459] Above, n.151.

[460] See, for example, 7:66 and above pp. 76f.

[461] In general, see Keulers, 163 and references there.

[462] See Violet, II, n. ad loc. Compare also 3:21, 7:128. In 7:104 the word רשו, a technical term for delegation of legal authority in Mishnaic and Talmudic language occurs, cf., for example, Gitt. 4:1.

[463] Ps. 122:5, Isa. 16:5 speak of the judgement seat of the Davidic king. In I Ki. 7:7 Solomon's construction of the hall in which the throne of judgement stands is mentioned. The king's judgement seat also features in Prov. 20:8. Ps. 9:5 speaks of God's judgement seat.

[463a] Cf. Lk. 22:30, Ap. Jn. 20:11.

[464] Pesah. 54a, Ned. 39b. See also in general Ab. Zar. 3b.

[465]I En. 25:3, 90:20 cf. 45:3, 55:4, 62:3,5 of the son of man. He is also said to be on the throne of glory, perhaps reflecting a combination of two traditions, see Sjöberg, Menschensohn, 62ff.

[466]6:1, cf. 6:6, 7:70. In general compare 9:4, of the Messiah 12:32, 13:26 etc.

[467]Thus following Syriac gzyr'. Ethiopic and Latin may reflect inner-Greek corruption, see Violet, II, Box, Ezra Apocalypse, ad loc. Violet, II suggests a theoretical Hebrew form, unknown in either Biblical or post-Biblical Hebrew גְּזִיר* or גְּזִיר*.

[468]Ethiopic adds a phrase here. The suggestions of Violet, II do not seem acceptable.

[469]154. He quotes Eccl, R. to Qoh. 4:1. On strict judgement see further Ben Sira 2:13, 5:8-9, 6:12-15.

[470]S. Schechter, Some Aspects of Rabbinic Theology (London: Black, 1909), 170-198, especially 179.

[471]See Ag. Ber. Ch. 10, cf. Avot 1:14, Av. de R.N., p.69 (tr. Judah Goldin (New Haven: Yale, 1955)).

[472]Der Prophet, xiv.

[473]See also Avot 3:15, Schechter, Aspects, 304-306.

[474]See above, pp. 36f.

[475]Apokryphen, 376, n. n.

[476]חותמו של הקב"ה אמת. The supposed reading with the same meaning in Gen. R. 8:5 is far from clear. Although it has been explained as meaning "seal of truth" the text is probably corrupt, see J. Levy, Worterbuch, s.v. אלטיכסייה Even Levy's view is considered unlikely on a textual basis, see Theodor and Albek, Bereschit Rabba (Berlin: Akademie Verlag, 1929), n. ad loc. For the words see also S. Krauss, Additamenta ad Librum Aruch Completum (Vienna; Kohut Memorial Foundation, 1937), s.v. אלטיכסייה.

[477]Truth, 6:28, 7:34,114, 14:17; deceit, 6:27; falsehood, 14:17.

[478]6:28, 7:114, 8:53. Also infirmity, death, Sheol, distresses, and the root, 8:53. With this latter compare the roots of unrighteousness, I En. 91:8.

[479]6:28, 7:34,114.

[480]6:27, 8:52.

[481]7:35,114.

[482]7:33,114, 8:52.

[483]6:27, 8:53.

[484]6:28, 7:114, cf. 7:34.

[485]6:27, 7:34, 8:52.

[486]One need only consider the Similitudes of Enoch or Ap. Bar. 66:2 etc.

[487]Similar materials, although lacking the full-blown poetic form may be observed in what seems to be an eschatological prophecy in "The Book of Mysteries," Discoveries in the Judaean Desert, I, 103 Col. 1, 11. 4-8.

[488]For instance, Col. 3:8-4:12, Eph. 4:22-6:18.

[489]D. Daube, The New Testament and Rabbinic Judaism (London: Univ. of London, 1956), 90-105, cf. W.D. Davies, Paul and Rabbinic Judaism (London: S.P.C.K., 1948), 119-146.

[490]See W.D. Davies, "Paul and the Dead Sea Scrolls: Flesh and Spirit," in The Scrolls and the New Testament, 157-182, especially 169-173 and the literature cited there.

[490a]Benadikt Otzen, "Some Text Problems in 1QS," Studia Theologica, 11 (1957), 96-98. The only terms showing any similarity are "health" and "eternal life." Literary form and function are quite different.

[491]Thus, for example, I En. 25:3-7, 91:14.

[492]Concerning 6:27f. see above, pp. 69ff.

[493]See Vagany, 110ff.

[494]See Vagany, ibid., L. Atzberger, Die christliche Eschatologie in den Stadien ihrer Offenbarung im Alten und Neuen Testamente (Frieburg: Herder, 1890), 186ff., E. Schiefer, Die Religiosen und Ethischen Anschauungen des IV Ezrabuches (Leipzig: Dörffling und Franke, 1901), 31-33, Keulers, 188-193.

[495]189f.

[496] Job 26:6, 28:22, 31:12, Prov. 15:11 cf. 27:20, Ps. 88:12.

[497] Job 26:6, 28:22, Prov. 15:11, cf. 27:20 and Ps. 88:12. This is also the original meaning of "Belial."

[498] See, for instance, Ap. Jn. 9:11 etc., 1QH iii:16,19.

[499] See above, pp. 184ff.

[500] Sheol and the knowledge of it are part of the catalogue of things said to be beyond the realm of human knowledge in 4:7-8. Although Ezra does evince some knowledge of these things, the book as a whole is characterized by the absence of any details of heavenly geography and the like, cf. also 5:36f. The secret knowledge given to Moses according to Ap. Bar. 59:5 ff. consisted precisely of those elements which Ezra proclaims beyond the realm of human knowledge. In 59:10 Gehenna is listed as one of these elements.

[501] See Charles' note on I En. 63:10.

[502] In 5:19 it is called the "pit of destruction," cf. IV Ezra 7:33 "the pit of torment."

[503] Thus Pesah.54a, Ned. 39b. Targ. O. and Ps.-J. to Gen. 2:8.

[504] "Future world" permits of no other interpretation.

[505] Read in 4:8 "I have not entered (seen ?) paradise." Thus Armenian, 2 Ethiopic MSS, Georgian, Arabic[2].

[506] Major Trends, 52ff., Jewish Gnosticism, 14-19.

[507] See n.162 above.

[508] In view of the considerations adduced above, one might be tempted to suggest an original פרדס in 4:7-8. 6:2, however, must be connected with the tradition of 3:6 and it exhibits the same text as 4:7-8.

[509] The problem whether 6:44 contains a description of the Garden of Eden, is difficult to solve. Gunkel thinks so, but this seems unlikely in view of the considerations urged against this, see Box, Ezra Apocalypse, Violet, II, ad loc. In any case vegetation was created on the third day according to Gen. 1:9-13. Eden was created on the third day according to some traditions, such as Gen. R. 15:3, Jub. 2:7, II En. 30:1, see also R.H. Charles, The Book of Jubilees (London:

Black, 1902), n. on 2:7. Eden is not mentioned here, however, and there seems to be no doubt that the text in its
present form, must refer to the creation of vegetation in
general.

[510] Thus Box, Ezra Apocalypse, 195ff., Schiefer, 31,
Keulers, 186ff.

[511] See Scholem, Jewish Gnosticism, 18. Compare the
expression "entered" in 4:8 here, see n. 505 above.

[512] 183f.

[513] 186, cf. 187.

[514] 196.

[515] The city present here is to be seen as a function of
the mixing of elements drawn from different cycles of ideas.
The theme of the preparedness of reward is frequent, thus
7:14, Armenian, Arabic^2, 7:38, 95, 121, etc.

[516] See Keulers, 186f., Schiefer, 30f. etc.

[517] 196f.

[518] For detailed treatments of and parallels to most of
the elements involved, see Vagany, 110-119, Keulers, 172-181
cf. 181-185, 189-193.

[519] See pp. 76f., cf. also Ap. Bar. 15:6, 30:5, 44:12,15,
54:15,21, 55:2, 59:11, 87:9,13, cf. 54:14 all of torment.
The term "joy" is very rare in Ap. Bar. In contrasting
phrases in IV Ezra this is the most frequent pair. Other
such are salvation and punishment, 9:13, perdition, 7:131,
cf. 7:60f.

[520] Compare also, Ps. 18:20, 118:5.

[521] See also above, pp. 60f., 189f.

[522] Cf. Isa. 60:19, Ap. Jn. 21:23.

[523] 1QH xi:27, vi:12.

[524] Apokryphen, n. ad loc.

[525] See also W. Bousset, Die Religion des Judentums im
Späthellenistischen Zeitalter (rev. H. Gressmann; Tübingen:
Mohr, 1926), Ch. XVI.

[526] See below, pp. 209f.

[527] A. Jellinek, Bet Ha-Midrasch (Leipzig: Nies, 1853), I, 25-34, especially p. 26.

[528] Compare Ps. 13:4, 19:9, also Nu. 6:25, Ps. 31:17, 67:2.

[529] Thus Tanḥ. ed. Buber, I, 7a,b, cf. Gen. R. 12:6, Pes. R. 118a.

[530] Gen. R. 23:6.

[531] Legends of the Jews (Philadelphia: Jewish Publication Society, 1928), V, 112f.

[532] Gen. R. 12:6 cf. Pes. R. 118a, 186b-187a, Mid. Teh. on 92:1. See also the tradition in which God gives man קלסתר פנים, Nid. 31a, Kid. 30b.

[533] In Mid. Teh. on Ps. 72:7 the righteous are found as a source of light. The curious reference in Jub. 19:25 is otherwise unparalleled. Other materials are preserved in Philo, Vit. Mos., II, 288, Atrapanus in Eusebius, Praep. Ev., 436c (9:27), Wisd. Sol. 3:7. The shining light of the righteous may be noted in I En. 108:11ff.

[534] See Jer. 19:13, 33:22, Jud. 5:20, Ps. 148:2f., Neh. 9:6, II Ki. 23:5 cf. 21:5, Deut. 4:19, cf. also Joseph's dream, Gen. 37:9.

[534a] See above, pp. 54f.

[535] Thus Syriac, Ethiopic.

[536] See also above, pp. 57, 185f., 196.

[537] 181f.

[538] Above, pp. 56ff.

[539] xlvii ff.

[540] P. 92.

Chapter III

[1] See pp. 56ff.

[2] See pp. 57, 185f etc.

[3] See pp. 147, 186.

[4] See p. 183.

[5] See p. 142, cf. 4:35,37.

[6] See also pp. 212, 213ff.

[7] See also the Rabbinic parallels quoted above, Ch. 2, n.378 where this is made explicit.

[8] 13:44, see above, Ch. 2, n.301.

[9] See above, pp. 78ff.

[10] See pp. 209f.

[11] See pp. 138f., 212f.

[12] See pp. 26f.

[13] See pp. 133, 135f., 137.

[14] See pp. 120-130, in particular pp. 128-130.

[15] See especially pp. 114f.

[16] See above, p. 188.

[17] See above, pp. 133ff.

[18] See above, p. 117.

[19] See above, pp. 191-195.

BIBLIOGRAPHY

Books

Albright, William F. History, Archaeology and Christian
    Humanism. New York: McGraw-Hill, 1964.

Atzberger, L. Die christliche Eschatologie in den Stadien
    ihrer Offenbarung im Alten und Neuen Testaments.
    Freiburg: Herder, 1890.

Bacher, W. Die Agada der Tannaiten. Strassburg: Truebner,
    1884.

Baldensperger, Wilhelm. Das Selbstbewusstein Jesu im
    Licht der messianischen Hoffnungen seiner Zeit,
    I. "Die messianisch-apokalyptischen Hoffnungen
    des Judentums." 3d ed. revised. Strassburg:
    Heitz und Mündel, 1903.

Barthélemy, D., and Milik, J. Discoveries in the Judaean
    Desert, I. Oxford: Oxford University Press, 1955.

Bensly, R. L. The Fourth Book of Ezra, "Introduction"
    by M. R. James. Cambridge: Cambridge University
    Press, 1895.

_____. The Missing Fragment of the Fourth Book of Ezra.
    Cambridge: Cambridge University Press, 1875.

Bietenhard, H. Die himmlische Welt im Urchristentum und
    Spätjudentum. Tübingen: Mohr, 1951.

Bousset, Wilhelm. The Antichrist Legend. Translated by
    A. H. Keane. London: Hutchinson, 1896.

_____. Die Religion des Judentums im späthellenistischen
    Zeitalter. 3d ed. revised by H. Gressmann. Tübingen:
    Mohr, 1926.

Box, G. H. The Apocalypse of Ezra. London: S.P.C.K., 1917.

_____. The Ezra-Apocalypse. London: Pitman, 1912.

Braude, W. G. (ed. and translator). The Midrash on Psalms. New Haven: Yale University Press, 1959.

Brockelmann, C. Lexicon Syriacum. 2d ed. revised. Göttingen: Niemeyer, 1923.

Buber, S. (ed.). Agadath Bereschith. Krakau: Fischer, 1902.

_____ (ed.). Midrasch Tanchuma. Wilna: Romm, 1885.

_____ (ed.). Pesikta von Rab Kahana. Lyck: Silbermann, 1868.

Ceriani, A. M. Monumenta Sacra et Profana. Mediolani: Ambrosian Library, 1864.

Charles, R. H. The Apocalypse of Baruch. London: Black, 1896.

_____. The Book of Jubilees. London: Black, 1902.

_____. "Introduction to II Baruch" in The Apocrypha and Pseudepigrapha of the Old Testament, II, 474-476. Oxford: Oxford University Press, 1913.

Cohn, L., and Wendland, P. Philonis Alexandri Opera quae Supersunt. Berlin: Reimer, 1896-1930.

Cooper, J. (ed. and translator). The Testament of Our Lord. Edinburgh: T. & T. Clark, 1902.

Cross, Frank Moore, Jr. The Ancient Library of Qumran and Modern Biblical Studies. Revised ed. New York: Anchor Books, 1961.

Cumont, Franz. The Oriental Religions in Roman Paganism. Reprint. New York: Dover Publications, 1956.

Dalman, G. Aramäisch-Neuhebräisches Handwörterbuch zu Targum, Talmud und Midrasch. Frankfort: Kauffman, 1922.

Daube, David. The New Testament and Rabbinic Judaism. London: University of London, 1956.

Davies, W. D. Paul and Rabbinic Judaism. London: S.P.C.K., 1948.

de Faye, E. Les apocalypses juives. Paris: Fischbacher, 1892.

Dillmann, A. Biblia Veteris Testamenti Aethiopica, V. ("Libri Apocryphi") Berlin: Asher, 1894.

_____ . Lexicon Linguae Aethiopicae. Reprint. New York: Ungar, 1955.

Drummond, J. The Jewish Messiah. London: Longmans, Green & Co., 1877.

Evelyn-White, E. (ed. and translator). Hesiod, the Homeric Hymns and Homerica. London: Heinemann, 1915.

Even-Shmu'el, Y. ____ מדרשי גאולה . Tel-Aviv, Bialik Institute, 1943.

Ewald, H. Das vierte Ezrabuch nach seinem Zeitalter, seinen Arabischen Übersetzungen und einer neuen Widerherstellung. Göttingen: Dieterichs, 1863.

Fabricius, J. A. Codicis Pseudepigraphi Veteris Testamentis. Hamburg: Felginer, 1722.

Frankfort, H. A., and others. Before Philosophy: The Intellectual Adventure of Ancient Man. Harmondsworth: Penguin, 1963.

Friedlander, G. (ed. and translator). Pirqe de Rabbi Eliezer. London: Kegan Paul, 1916.

Friedmann, M. (ed.). Pesikta Rabbati. Wien: The Author, 1880.

_____ (ed.). Sifra, der älteste Midrasch zu Leviticus. Breslau: Marcus, 1915.

_____ (ed.). Sifré debé Rab. Wien: The Author, 1864.

Gfrörer, A. Geschichte des Urchristentums, I, "Das Jahrhundert des Heils." Stuttgart: Schweitzer- bart, 1838.

Gildermeister, J. Esdrae Liber Quartus Arabice. Bonn: 1877.

Ginzberg, L. Legends of the Jews. Philadelphia: Jewish Publication Society, 1928.

Goldin, Judah (ed. and translator). The Fathers according to Rabbi Nathan. New Haven: Yale University Press, 1955.

Gressmann, Hugo. Der Ursprung der Israelitisch-jüdischen Eschatologie. Göttingen: Vandenhoeck und Ruprecht, 1905.

Gry, L. Les Dires prophétiques d'Esdras. Paris: Geuthner, 1938.

Gunkel, H. Der Prophet Esra. Tübingen: Mohr, 1900.

_____. "Das vierte Buch Esra" in Die Apokryphen und Pseudepigraphen des alten Testaments, II. Edited by E. Kautzsch. Tübingen: Mohr, 1900.

_____. Schöpfung und Chaos in Urzeit und Endzeit. Göttingen: Vandenhoeck und Ruprecht, 1895.

Hatch, E., and Redpath, H. A Concordance to the Septuagint. Oxford: Clarendon Press, 1897.

Heinemann, I. דרכי האגדה. Jerusalem: Magnes Press, 1954.

Hilgenfeld, A. Die jüdische Apokalyptik in ihrer geschichtlichen Entwickelung. Jenna: Mauke, 1857.

_____. Messias Judaeorum. Lipsiae: Reisland, 1869.

_____. Die Propheten Esra und Daniel und ihrer neusten Bearbeitungen. Halle: Pfeffer, 1863.

Holm-Nielsen. Hodayot---Psalms from Qumran. Universitetsforlaget I Aarhus: 1960.

Hovsēpʰeanç, S. ԱՆԿԱՆՈՆ ԳԻՐՔ ՀԻՆ ԿՏԱԿԱՐԱՆԱՑ . Venice: Monastery of St. Lazarus, 1896.

Issaverdens, J. (ed. and translator). The Uncanonical Writings of the Old Testament. Venice: Monastery of St. Lazarus, 1900.

Jellinek, A. Bet Ha-Midrasch. Leipzig: Nies, 1853.

Kabisch, Richard. Das vierte Buch Esra auf seine Quellen untersucht. Göttingen: Vandenhoeck und Ruprecht, 1889.

Kadushin, Max. Organic Thinking. New York: Jewish Theological Seminary, 1938.

_____. The Rabbinic Mind. New York: Jewish Theological Seminary, 1952.

Kadushin, Max. The Theology of Seder Eliahu. New York:
    Bloch, 1932.

Kahana, A. הספרים החיצונים. Tel-Aviv: Masada, 1956.

Kaminka, A. Beiträge zur Erklärung der Esra-Apokalypse und
    zur Rekonstruction ihres hebräisches Urtextes.
    Breslau: Marcus, 1934.

Kaufmann, E. תולדות האמונה הישראלית מימי קדם עד סוף בית שני.
    Jerusalem: Bialik Institute, 1956.

Kraus, S. Additamenta ad Librum Aruch Completum. Vienna:
    Kohut Memorial Foundation, 1937.

Lake, Kirsopp (ed. and translator). The Apostolic Fathers.
    London: Heinemann, 1912-1913.

Laurence, Richard. Primi Ezrae Libri Versic Aethiopica.
    Oxford: Oxford University Press, 1820.

Le Hir, A. M. Etudes bibliques par M. l'abbé Le Hir.
    Paris: Albanel, 1869.

Levy, Jacob. Neuhebräisches und Chaldäisches Wörterbuch
    über die Talmudim und Midraschim. Leipzig: Brockhaus,
    1883.

Lücke, F. Versuch einer vollständingen Einleitung in die
    Offenbarung des Johannes und in die apokalyptische
    Literatur überhaupt. 2d ed. Bonn: Weber, 1848.

Maier, Johann. Die Texte vom Toten Meer. München:
    Reinhardt, 1960.

Marchant, E. C. (ed. and translator). Xenophon's Memorabilia
    and Oeconomicus. London: Heinemann, 1953.

Morfill, W. R., and Charles, R. H. The Book of the Secrets
    of Enoch. Oxford: Oxford University Press, 1896.

Porter, F. C. The Messages of the Apocalyptical Writers.
    New York: Scribners, 1905.

Preuschen, E. Review of Violet in Berliner Philologischer
    Wochenschrift, 18 (1913), 547-551.

Rigaux, P. B. L'antéchrist et l'opposition au royaume messi-
    anique dans l'ancient et le nouveau Testament.
    Paris: Gabalda, 1932.

Rosenthal, F. Vier Apokryphischer Bücher aus der Zeit und Schule R. Akiba's. Leipzig: Schulze, 1885.

Rowley, H. H. The Relevance of Apocalyptic. New York: Association Press, 1964.

Schechter, S. (ed.). Midrash Haggadol. Cambridge: Cambridge University Press, 1902.

_____. Some Aspects of Rabbinic Theology. London: Black, 1909.

Scheifer, E. Die religiösen und ethischen Anschauungen des IV Ezrabuches. Leipzig: Dörffling und Franke, 1901.

Scholem, Gershom G. Jewish Gnosticism, Merkabah Mysticism and Talmudic Tradition. New York: Jewish Theological Seminary, 5720-1960.

_____. Major Trends in Jewish Mysticism. 3d ed. revised. New York: Schocken, 1954.

Schürer, E. Geschichte des jüdischen Volkes im Zeitalter Jesu Christi. 3d ed. Leipzig: Hinrichs, 1898.

Schwabe, M., and Gutman, I. (eds.). Commentationes Iudaico-Hellenisticae in Memoriam Iohannis Lewy. Jerusalem: Magnes Press, 1949.

Sigwalt, C. "Die Chronologie des 4 Buches Esdras." Biblische Zeitschrift, 9 (1911), 146-148.

Sjöberg, Erik. Der Menschensohn im Äthiopischen Henochbuch. Lund: Gleerup, 1949.

Stendahl, Krister. The School of St. Matthew. Uppsala: 1954.

_____. (ed.). The Scrolls and the New Testament. New York: Harper & Bros., 1957.

Strählin, O. (ed.). Clemens Alexandrinus. 3d ed. revised by L. Fruechtel. Berlin: Akademie Verlag, 1960.

Swete, H. B. Introduction to the Old Testament in Greek. Cambridge: Cambridge University Press, 1902.

Theodor, J., and Albek, Ch. Bereschit Rabba. Berlin: Akademie Verlag, 1929.

Vagany, L. Le Problème eschatologique dans IVme livre d'Esdras. Paris: Picard et Fils, 1906.

van der Vlis, C. J. Disputatio Critica de Ezrae Libro Apocrypho Vulgo Quarto Dicto. Amsterdam: Müller, 1839.

van der Woude, A. S. Die Messianischen Vorstellungen der Gemeinde von Qumran. Assen: Gorcum, 1957.

Violet, Bruno. Die Apokalypsen des Esra und des Baruch in deutscher Gestalt. Leipzig: Hinrichs, 1924.

_____. Die Ezra-Apokalypse, I "Die Überlieferungen." Leipzig: Hinrichs, 1910.

Volkmar, G. Handbuch der Einleitung in die Apokryphen, Part II "Das vierte Buch Esrae." Tübingen: Fues, 1863.

Volz, Paul. Die Eschatologie der jüdischen Gemeinde. Tübingen: Mohr, 1934.

Wellhausen, J. Skizzen und Vorarbeiten, VI. Berlin: Reimer, 1899.

Yadin, Yigal. מלחמת בני אור בבני חושך. 2d ed. Jerusalem: Bialik Institute, 1957.

Yalqut Shimoni. Frankfort: 1687.

Articles

Allegro, J. "Further Messianic References in Qumran Literature," Journal of Biblical Literature, 75 (1956), 174-187.

_____. "A Newly Discovered Fragment of a Commentary on Psalm XXXVII from Qumran," Palestine Exploration Quarterly, 86 (1954), 69-75.

Altmann, Alexander. "The Gnostic Background of the Rabbinic Adam Legends," Jewish Quarterly Review, 35 (1944-1945), 371-391.

Audet, J.-P. "Affinités littéraires et doctrinales du 'Manuel de Discipline'," Revue Biblique, 59 (1952), 219-238, idem, 60 (1953), 41-82.

Blake, Robert P. "The Georgian Version of Fourth Esras from the Jerusalem Manuscript," Harvard Theological Review, 19 (1926), 299-320.

_____. "The Georgian Text of Fourth Esras from the Athos Manuscript," Harvard Theological Review, 22 (1929), 57-105.

Bloch, Joshua. "Was there a Greek Version of the Apocalypse of Ezra?," Jewish Quarterly Review, N.S. 46 (1956), 309-320.

Boehmer, E. "Zur Lehre von Antichrist, nach Schneckenburger," Jahrbücher für deutsche Theologie, 4 (1859), 405-467.

Braun, F. M. "L'arrière-fond judaïque du quartrième évangile et la Communauté de l'Alliance," Revue Biblique, 62 (1955), 5-44.

Clemen, C. "Die Zusammensetzung des Buch Henoch, Ap. Baruch und IV Ezra," Theologische Studien und Kritiken, 71 (1898), 237-246.

Cross, Frank Moore, Jr. "Qumran Cave I," Journal of Biblical Literature, 75 (1956), 121-125.

Davies, W. D. "Paul and the Dead Sea Scrolls: Flesh and Spirit," in The Scrolls and the New Testament, edited by K. Stendahl, 157-182.

Dillmann, A. "Pseudepigrapha" in Herzog's Real-Encyklopädie für protestantische Theologie und Kirche (1st ed.; Gotha: Bessar, 1860).

_____. "Über das Adlergesicht in der Apokalypse des Esra," Sitzungberichte der Berliner Akademie (1888), 215-237.

Gudschmit, D. " הערות לשלשת תרגומיו של הירונימוס לספר תהילים," in Commentationes Iudaico-Hellenisticae in Memoriam Iohannis Lewy, edited by M. Schwabe and I. Gutman.

Gunkel, H. Review of Kabisch in Theologische Literaturzeitung, 16, No. 1 (1891), 5-11.

Gutschmid, A. von. "Die Apokalypse des Esra und ihrer spätern Bearbeitungen," Zeitschrift für wissenschaftliche Theologie, 3 (1860), 1-81.

Heinemann, I.   " לפילון פרט ההלניסטים היהודים של האלגוריסטיקה ,"
    in Commentationes Judaico-Hellenisticae in Memoriam
    Iohannis Lewy, edited by M. Schwabe and I. Gutman.

Hilgenfeld, A.   "Die jüdische Apokalyptik und die neuster
    Forschungen," Zeitschrift für wissenschaftliche
    Theologie, 3 (1860), 300-362.

Jenni, E.   "Das Wort ^{c}ôlām im Alten Testament," Zeitschrift
    für die alttestamentliche Wissenschaft, 64 (1952),
    177-246, idem, 65 (1953), 1-35.

Keulers, J.   "Die eschatologische Lehre des vierten Esrabuches,"
    Biblische Studien, 20, Nos. 2-3 (1922), 1-204.

Kuhn, K. G.   "The Two Messiahs of Aaron and Israel," in
    The Scrolls and the New Testament, edited by K.
    Stendahl, 54-64.

Lagrange, M. J.   "Notes sur le Messianisme au temps de
    Jesus," Revue Biblique, N.S. 2 (1905), 486-501.

_____ .   Review of Vagany, Revue Biblique, N.S. 4 (1907),
    614-616.

Milik, J.   "Hénoch au Pays des Aromates," Revue Biblique,
    65 (1958), 70-77.

Otzen, Benedikt.   "Some Text Problems in 1QS," Studia
    Theologica, 11 (1957), 89-99.

Starcky, J.   "Les Quatre Etapes du Messianisme à Qumran,"
    Revue Biblique, 70 (1963), 481-505.

_____ .   "Un texte messianique araméen de la grotte 4 de
    Qumran," in Memorial du Cinquantenaire de l'Ecole
    des langues orientales anciens de l'Institut
    Catholique à Paris (Paris: Blond et Gay, 1964), 51-66.

Wieseler, K.   "Das vierte Buch Esra nach Inhalt und Alter
    untersucht," Theologische Studien und Kritiken, 43
    (1870), 263-304.

Yadin, Yigal.   "A Crucial Emendation in the Dead Sea Scrolls,"
    Journal of Biblical Literature, 78 (1959), 238-241.

Unpublished

Stone, M.   "Contradictions of Translation as Revealed in
the Apocrypha," to appear shortly in Proceedings of
the International Conference on the Armenian
Language.

INDEX

This index includes references to ancient writings, including 4 Ezra itself. **Bold script** indicates major discussion of the text.